MW00935830

The Secret Place

The True Tabernacle Yeshua

"He that dwelleth in the secret place of the most High shall abide under the shadow of the Almighty" Psalm 91:1 KJV

LYNN LIEBENGOOD

WESTBOW PRESS®
A DIVISION OF THOMAS NELSON & ZONDERVAN

Cover and interior images on pages 17, 114, 168, 177, 180, and 224 by Christa L. Shore. All other images by the author.

All Scripture is taken from the King James Version of the Bible, unless otherwise noted.

WestBow Press books may be ordered through booksellers or by contacting:

WestBow Press
A Division of Thomas Nelson & Zondervan
1663 Liberty Drive
Bloomington, IN 47403
www.westbowpress.com
1 (866) 928-1240

ISBN: 978-1-5127-2769-2 (sc)
ISBN: 978-1-5127-2770-8 (hc)
ISBN: 978-1-5127-2768-5 (e)

Library of Congress Control Number: 2016901144

Print information available on the last page.

WestBow Press rev. date: 3/18/2016

Contents

Preface

The revelation of the Messiah, whose Hebrew name is Yeshua, is the fulfillment of the Tabernacle that God instructed the children of Israel to build. Every aspect of the Tabernacle, down to the smallest detail, contains a revelation of Yeshua.

The offerings and the sacrificial system of the Tabernacle reveal the immensity of God's love. In them the very heart of God's plan for salvation is revealed.

You will see the complete gospel message unfold through the names of the Sons of Israel. Each of their Hebrew names declares a portion of the good news of the gospel. When you see the importance of the names found throughout the scriptures, you will no longer want to skip over them because they are hard to pronounce. The words of Yeshua found in John chapter 10 reveal the importance of names; "and he calleth his own sheep by name" (Jn. 10:3; my emphasis). The duties appointed to the priesthood teach that every believer's actions affect the lives of others. The numbers and measurements used to describe the Tabernacle and its furnishings make known the depth, breadth, and height of God's love (Eph. 3:14-21).

The God of the Old Testament will become as real to you as the Lord of the New Testament; because God never changes (Heb. 13:8).

The Tabernacle points to God's master plan for the redemption of the human race. The death and resurrection of Yeshua was not meant to establish a new religion. On the contrary, it was to reunite all humankind as one family, the family of God, where there is neither Jew nor Gentile, bond or free, male or female (Gal. 3:28).

Through faith in Yeshua, individuals are changed into a new creation that is designed to worship and glorify God (2 Cor. 5:17-19). This plan was in God's heart before the foundation of the world (Eph. 1:4-7, 1 Pet. 1:18-20). God desires a relationship of intimacy, one in which He lays open His heart. According to Bishop T.D. Jakes, the word intimacy implies *in...to...me...see*.

As I prepared *The Secret Place*, I realized that it is impossible to fully appreciate the "shadows" of Yeshua found in the Tabernacle without first understanding blood covenant. God established a blood covenant in the book of Genesis and it continues through the book of Revelation.

I believe when people understand that God's Blood Covenant seals their relationship with Him for all eternity; intimacy will be the result. How can we expect to receive God's promises without knowing the One who promised?

Most believers understand that Yeshua shed His blood on the Cross of Calvary for their sin, but few understand the far reaching power of that blood. The blood covenant between God the Father and God the Son goes beyond the Cross. It has terms and conditions, promises and exchanges, but most importantly, it is forever.

My prayer for all who read this book is found in the book of Ephesians. My husband prayed this prayer over me and others in our Sunday School Class every week for many years. I had no idea how the words of his prayer would affect my life. May God grant you revelation knowledge of his love.

> "For this cause I bow my knees unto the Father of our Lord Jesus Christ, Of whom the whole family in heaven and earth is named, That he would grant you, according to the riches of his glory, to be strengthened with might by his Spirit in the inner man; That Christ may dwell in your hearts by faith; that ye, being rooted and grounded in love, May be able to comprehend with all saints

what is the breadth, and length, and depth, and height; And to know the love of Christ, which passeth knowledge, that ye might be filled with all the fullness of God" (Eph. 3:14-19)

All Biblical quotes are from the King James Translation unless otherwise noted.

Introduction

God had a plan to reveal his heart to man before the foundation of the world (Eph. 1:4-7, 1 Pet. 1:18-20). God desires a relationship of intimacy. One in which He allows man to know Him through His Son, Yeshua the Messiah. As I said earlier, the word intimacy implies *in..to..me..see.*

While teaching a Sunday school class, my husband used an analogy to explain why God chose to be born a man. His simple analogy opened my eyes to the compassion of God. Following is that analogy.

Men are like the ants that have an anthill in the middle of a farmer's field. The ants were busy at work taking care of everyday tasks. One day, the farmer began tilling the soil, preparing it for planting. The farmer was a compassionate man. And when he noticed the ant hill, he wanted to warn the ants of the danger that was imminent. The farmer stopped his tilling and contemplated how to help the ants. How could he, a human being, communicate the impending danger to the ants? Suddenly, he realized the only way to help the ants was for him to become an ant. As an ant, the farmer was able to show the ants the way of escape from the approaching death and destruction.

That is what God did for the human race. God put on human flesh and became the man, Yeshua. Yeshua came to show humanity the love of God the Father, and teach them how to escape God's wrath. God the Father sent His Son to be the only means of escape from the inevitable death sentence that comes to all men through Adam.

Adam was disobedient and his sin had to be reckoned with. In order for Adam to live, something had to die. God began teaching the human race of His great love by killing an innocent animal to cover the sin of Adam. Beginning with Adam, God taught His people how to recognize Yeshua, who is the ultimate gift of God's love. The Bible teaches of the rapidly approaching judgment that is coming to all mankind. Accepting the sacrifice of Yeshua's innocent blood is the only means of escape from the wrath of God.

God chose the children of Israel, out of millions of other peoples, to be the instrument through which He would show Himself to the world (Deut. 6:7-9). He gave Israel two significant keys revealing the kind of relationship that would come through Messiah Yeshua.

(1.) <u>The Tablets of Stone</u> - - *God's handwritten (Ketuba) marriage covenant.* God declared Himself the husband of Israel. He chose the monogamous, intimate, dependent, loving relationship between a husband and wife as the example of how He wants to relate to man (Isa. 54:5). Marriage is a blood covenant.

(2.) <u>The Tabernacle and its sacrificial system</u> - -*the shadow of redemption and God's relationship with ALL men through Yeshua.* Through Israel came the birth of God's only begotten Son. The Tabernacle and its sacrificial system were designed to demonstrate how God would become the substitute for all of humanity and pay the penalty for ALL sin (Lev. 6:25; Rom. 6:23). It is the perfect illustration of the life, death and resurrecting power of God that comes through Yeshua. Yeshua is the True and Living Tabernacle that is not made with hands (Heb. 8:2, 9:11; Rev. 21:3). He is the dwelling place of God (Jn. 1:14). He is "God with us" – Immanuel (Isa.

7:14; Mat.1:23; Lk. 1:26, 31, 34, and 35). His Hebrew name, "Yeshua" means *YAHveh is salvation* (Lk. 2:21).

God established the ministry of the priesthood to demonstrate that His relationship with them is eternal. Yeshua's death and resurrection reestablished the eternal relationship between God and humanity. Yeshua is the Eternal High Priest and the mediator between God and men. Because His position is never-ending, it ensures the believer's relationship with the Father (Heb. 5:4-5; 7:14-17, 22-25; 1 Tim. 2:5). Through Yeshua, all believers are members of a royal priesthood, a kingdom of priest. And like the priest of the Tabernacle, the believers are workers together with God, revealing his endless love to the world (1 Pet. 2:9-10; 1 Cor. 12:4-7, 11-14; 2 Cor. 6:1).

I believe that there are many like myself who have overlooked the infinite treasures found within the Old Testament Scriptures simply because we have not understood the roots of our faith. Paul teaches, in the eleventh chapter of the book of Romans, about two types of branches, the Gentiles (the wild branches) and the Hebrews (the natural branches). He describes how the Gentiles are grafted into the root of the olive tree, which is synonymous with Yeshua. Paul issues a warning, to those who are grafted in, about boasting against the natural branches (Rom. 11:18-21).

Paul says in verse 18, the branches do not support the root, but the root supports the branches. Yeshua came to unite all men into one family, (the family of God). It is through Yeshua that all men become new creations. Therefore, whether you are Jew or Gentile, in Yeshua we become *one new man* (Eph. 2:15-17). Scripture says that Yeshua came to fulfill the law and the prophets; what does that mean? The word fulfill by definition is to expound on, reveal, give life to, bring to realization. Yeshua came to reveal the heart of the Father to all people; to the Jew first and then the Gentile. God's people had the letter of the law (the Torah). Yeshua came to demonstrate the Spirit of the law.

Therefore, it is my heart's desire that through the revelation of Messiah found in the Tabernacle, many will come to love the God of the Old Testament. Individuals who know only the love of Yeshua found in the New Testament are like people who try to build a two story house without the first floor. It is impossible to live and appreciate the new life provided by the Lord of the New Testament without first getting to know and understand the heart of the God of Abraham, Isaac, and Jacob in the Old Testament, because God never changes. He is the same yesterday, today, and forever (Heb. 13:8). We see His redemptive plan for humankind revealed in the Garden of Eden when He shed the first blood. His plan has never changed. St. Augustine once said, "*The New is in the Old contained; the Old is by the New explained.*" May this truth become alive in your spirit as we continue our journey through God's "Tabernacle in the Wilderness".

CHAPTER 1

Blood Covenant

God established a relationship with humankind through a blood covenant; therefore, it is imperative for us to understand God's covenant to understand His heart. He never changes. He said, "Verily, verily, I say unto you, before Abraham was, I am" (Jn. 8:58). It is said of Yeshua that He is the same yesterday, today, and forever (Heb. 13:8). This statement alone requires us to know the God of the Old Testament as well as His Son, because they are one. God is ONE (Deut. 6:4).

A blood covenant goes further than merely shedding blood. There are terms, conditions, promises, and exchanges, but most importantly, a blood covenant is forever and it absolutely cannot be broken.

I recommend *The Miracle of the Scarlet Thread* by Richard Booker, published by Destiny Image Publisher. His book is easy to understand and inspires readers to reread the Bible looking for God's covenant terms and promises.

According to Richard Booker,

> "The Hebrew word for covenant is *Berith.* The Greek word is *Diatheke*. It actually means to "cut covenant". By definition, it is an agreement to "Cut a covenant by the shedding of blood and walking between pieces of flesh." So the two divisions in the Bible are about an Old Blood Covenant and a New Blood Covenant. *A blood*

covenant between two parties is the closest, the most enduring, the most solemn and sacred of all contracts. It absolutely cannot be broken."[1] The Old Testament is more than just meaningless rituals, customs, places, names and unrelated events. On the contrary, it is an orderly, progressive, unfolding revelation from God, of the blood covenant He has entered into with man through the Lord Jesus Christ".[2]

The Following are two examples of blood covenants:

1. **The American Indian:** When America's government officials entered into a covenant with the Native Americans, the idea of a blood covenant was foreign to these officials. They did not understand the consequences of breaking a covenant. The Native Americans, on the other hand, were very familiar with covenant making. When the American settlers dishonored the covenant, the Native Americans were obligated to kill the covenant breaker and anyone who was related to him. As a result, there was much blood-shed, which caused the Native Americans to be unjustly labeled as savages.
2. **A Marriage:** Couples enter into a blood covenant when they stand before a minister or a justice of the peace. They declare the terms and conditions of the beginning relationship. Promises are made before God and the people of the congregation. At the consummation of a marriage, blood is shed when the vaginal hymen is broken, if the bride is a virgin. The Bible tells us that God required proof of the bride's virginity. The parents of the bride kept the blood stained cloth as proof of her purity (Deut. 22:13-21).

Why do we need to understand blood covenants today? Without this understanding, it is impossible to live a victorious life in Yeshua because God is a covenant- making, covenant-keeping God. He established a relationship with His people through a blood covenant. Therefore, in order to understand our relationship with Him, we *must* learn about covenant relationships.

Blood covenants are practiced today in many countries. In the making of a blood covenant, the participants exchange items of importance i.e. clothing and weapons. They declare terms and conditions, and promise allegiance to one another; they make a memorial scar and walk through the blood of the animals. The animals, who give their lives, are representatives of the covenant partners. Those entering into a covenant share a memorial meal and establish some form of a memorial as a reminder of their covenant. Each of these ritual practices is found throughout the Bible. Although not all are found together, it is understood that a blood covenant was made.

Why do individuals need this type of covenant? The blood covenant is the exchange of strengths and weaknesses of the two covenant partners. Each of the covenant partners benefits through the covenant.

Here is an example of the covenant partners exchanging items of clothing that is representative of their identity. A doctor and a policeman enter into a covenant. The doctor's coat identifies him as a man of compassion, and it reflects his desire to heal the sick. The police man's coat carries his badge, which identifies him as a protector, and as a person of authority. When the doctor and the policeman exchange coats, each has taken the identity of the other; it is difficult to distinguish between the two. They have exchanged places.

The best Biblical example of two men cutting covenant is the covenant between Jonathan and David (1 Sam. 18:1-4. "Then Jonathan and David made a covenant, because he loved him as his own soul. And Jonathan stripped himself of the robe that was upon him, and gave it to David, and his garments, even to his sword, and to his bow, and to his girdle" (vv. 3- 4).

Jonathan was the son of a king and David was a shepherd. When Jonathan gave David his robe, he was prophetically declaring God's promise that David would reign as king. Although all of the rituals that are associated with a blood covenant were not present, the exchange of robes and weapons between Jonathan and David are evidence that a blood covenant was made.

The first blood covenant recorded in the Bible is between God and Adam. Adam's sin removed the covering of God's glorious presence. Without the covering, Adam stood naked. Adam made an attempt to cover himself with fig leaves, but God alone is able to cover sin. Forgiveness of sin requires innocent blood. So, God killed an innocent animal to cover Adam and his wife; afterward God cast them out of the garden paradise.

God's covenant continues through His Son. Isaiah, speaking of the coming Messiah, describes His apparel as garments of salvation, and His robe as righteousness (Isa. 61:10). Yeshua, God's only begotten Son, left His place in heaven to become the perfect man who would exchange robes with everyone who will believe. Yeshua exchanges His robe of righteousness for man's robe of sin. Paul writes, "For he hath made him to be sin for us who knew no sin; that we might be made the righteousness of God in him" (2 Cor. 5:21).

The day is coming when Yeshua will come back for His church. Paul describes it as "a glorious church, not having spot, or wrinkle, or any such thing; but that it should be holy and without blemish" (Eph. 5:27). Yeshua said, speaking of believers (His church), that all who overcome shall be clothed in white raiment (Rev. 3-5). One day, every believer will receive a new white robe.

The exchange of weapons is another part of making a blood covenant. A man's belt held his weapons - and it held his armor together. Exchanging belts and weapons symbolizes the exchange of one's strength and ability to fight. The covenant partners are saying to one another, "Your battles are my battles,

I will defend and protect you, and your enemies are now my enemies".

In the covenant between Jonathan and David found in 1 Samuel 18:1- 4, this step was done when Jonathan gave David his sword, bow and girdle. The word translated as *girdle* in this passage is the Hebrew word *hagor,* which is a belt used to hold weapons. Scripture does not say what David exchanged with Jonathan, but it does say many times that David depended on the Lord to fight his battles. He said, "The Lord is on my side; I will not fear: what can man do unto me?" (Ps. 118:6). "Thou hast also given me the *shield* of thy salvation" (Ps. 19:35; my emphasis). "For thou hast *girded me with strength* unto the battle: thou hast subdued under me those that rose up against me" (Ps. 19:39; my emphasis). The strength of God was David's weapon, and because of their covenant, it became Jonathan's as well.

Yeshua fulfilled this part of the covenant when he exchanged his armor for our weakness. His armor is accessible to every believer (Eph. 6:10-18). His *belt* is TRUTH, and on it hangs His *breastplate*, which is RIGHTEOUSNESS, his *feet carry* the GOSPEL OF PEACE, His *shield* is FAITH, His *helmet* is SALVATION, and His *sword* is the SPIRIT REVEALED WORD OF GOD. His provision is complete. Yeshua's armor covers the believer from head to toe. His armor was designed to teach the believer to face the enemy. Yeshua's armor covers your front side but even if the enemy tries to attack from behind, God the Father has your back. Believers are protected so that nothing is exposed to the enemy's attacks. "For ye shall not go out in haste, nor go by flight: for the Lord will go before you; and the God of Israel will be your rearward" (Isa. 52:12).

Animals are used as substitutes for the parties making a blood covenant. Each animal is cut in half from head to tail. The two halves fall opposite each other. The blood from the animals fills the space between the two halves. The covenant partners stand back to back between the bloody halves and each one walks forward through his own animals' blood and then turns and walks toward the covenant partner; The partners pass each other and continue to walk through the blood of each partner's animals. When they come to the end, they turn and walk back toward each other, stopping in the center of the animals face to face. In doing so, they have formed a figure eight pattern. Each man is acknowledging that he is relinquishing all rights to his own life and placing his covenant partner's life first even unto death. They proclaim to each other, "God, do to me what was done to these animals, if I ever try to break our covenant." David and Jonathan made this declaration to one another in 1 Samuel 20:42.

Cutting the animals in half and walking through the blood of the animals is found in the covenant God made in Genesis chapter 15. God asked Abram to provide five animals for the cutting of the covenant. Abram provided God with a heifer, a she-goat, a ram, a turtledove, and a young pigeon. A close look at Genesis chapter 15 reveals that Abram did not participate in walking through the blood of the animals. God caused a deep sleep to come over Abram. If Abram had taken part in the covenant at this point, the covenant would be imperfect. No man was worthy to make such a covenant. God the Father and God the Son are the covenant partners. "And it came to pass, that, when the sun went down, and it was dark, behold a smoking furnace, and a burning lamp that passed between those pieces" (Gen.15:17). God the Father's presence is characterized as a Smoking Furnace and Yeshua is symbolized by the Burning Lamp (Gen. 15:17).

There was no man worthy to swear the terms of the covenant with the God of all creation, so God swore by himself. "For when God made promise to Abraham, because he could swear by no greater, he swear by himself" (Heb. 6:13). Abram's only part in the covenant was to believe the promise of God and accept what God had done on his behalf (Gen. 15:18-21). Later, Abram circumcised himself and every male member of his household as a sign that he had accepted God's covenant.

Yeshua's blood is the fulfillment of the covenant that began with Abram. Since Yeshua is both God and man, at last God was able to put His own blood into the covenant. Yeshua is the only man who never sinned; His blood is the only blood worthy to fulfill God's covenant. "In the beginning was the Word, and the Word was with God, and the Word was God. And the Word was made flesh, and dwelt among us, (and we beheld his glory, the glory as of the only begotten of the Father,) full of grace and truth" (Jn. 1:1, 14).

Each of the covenant partners makes a cut in the hand or possibly the finger. As the blood runs out, the covenant partners bring their hands together and raise their right arm. This action represents the union of the two partners; they are symbolically becoming one life. God says the life is in the blood (Lev. 17:11). Therefore, each man is taking on the nature of his covenant partner. As the blood intermingles, the covenant partners declare, "We are now one new life."

We can see this in the covenant between Jonathan and David. "The soul of Jonathan was knit with the soul of David, and Jonathan loved him as his own soul." Then Jonathan and David made a covenant, because he loved him as his own soul" (1 Sam. 18:1b, 3). The love of Yeshua is greater than that of Jonathan and David. Yeshua prayed for all believers saying, "That they all may be one; as thou, Father, art in me, and I in thee, that they also may be one in us: that the world may believe that thou hast sent me" (Jn. 17:21).

Paul explains it this way, "Therefore if any man be in Christ, he is a new creature: old things are passed away; behold all things are become new" (2 Cor. 5:17). "Know ye not that ye are the temple of God, and that the Spirit of God dwelleth in you?" (1 Cor. 3:16).

Like Abram, the believer's only requirement is to accept and believe what God did through Yeshua. When we raise our hands to the Lord, we are showing Him that we accept and believe that His blood makes us holy before the Father. Therefore, we have the assurance that whatever He has promised will come to pass.

As the reality of this wonderful truth becomes alive to you, you will understand the significance of what Paul was saying to Timothy when he said, "Pray every where, lifting up holy hands, without wrath and doubting" (1 Tim. 2:8). The writer of Psalms said, "Thus will I bless thee while I live: I will lift up my hands in thy name" (Ps. 63:4). and "Hear the voice of my supplications, when I cry unto thee, when I lift up my hands toward thy holy oracle" (Ps. 28:2).

The exchange of names is part of the blood covenant. The last name of the covenant partners is added to the last name of the other. This practice is accepted today and found most frequently in the marriage ceremony when the bride takes the last name of her husband.

Example: When I married, I became Lynn Barber Liebengood. Taking the last name of my husband entitles me to the same benefits as one who was blood born into the Liebengood family; the same applies to my husband and the Barber family.

We can see this in the covenant with Abram. God changed Abram's name to

Abra– *H* – am. "Neither shall thy name any more be called Abram, but thy name shall be Abraham" (Gen. 17:5). "Thou art the LORD the God, who didst choose Abram, and broughtest him forth out of Ur of the Chaldees, and gavest him the name of Abraham" (Neh. 9:7; my ehasis).

God added the Hebrew letter ה (*Hey*) to Abram's name. This letter is also found in the name ascribed to God, יְהוָה (*Yod Hey Vav Hey*). The more familiar name for God (*Jehovah*) comes from these four letters of the Hebrew alphabet. Therefore, we see God adding a part of His name to Abraham, and from that time forward, God referred to Himself as the God of Abraham. "And the Lord appeared unto him that night, and said, I am the God of Abraham thy father" (Gen. 26:24; Ex. 3:6).

As God's covenant grew, He appeared to Isaac and then to Jacob. God offered each man the same opportunity to enter covenant as He did Abraham. Then God referred to himself as the God of Abraham, Isaac and Jacob.

Yeshua, quoting the words of His Father, said, "I am the God of Abraham, and the God of Isaac, and the God of Jacob (Mt. 22:32). God is not the God of the dead, but of the living" (Mk. 12:26). God also referred to Himself as the God of Israel (Ex. 5:1). God's covenant has grown from one man, Abraham, to include the entire nation of Israel, and through Yeshua the whole world.

Every man must make the choice for himself. Accepting Yeshua as your Savior is the way into God's blood covenant. God wants to give you His new name.

Isaiah said, "Even unto them will I give in mine house and within my walls a place and a *name* better than of sons and of daughters: I will give them an *everlasting name* that shall not be cut off" (Isa. 56:5; my emphasis). "The Gentiles shall see thy righteousness, and all kings thy glory: and thou shalt be called by a *new name*, which the mouth of the Lord shall name (Isa. 62:2; my emphasis)

Yeshua said, "He that overcometh, the same shall be clothed in white raiment; and I will not blot out his *name* out of the book of life, but I will confess his *name* before my Father, and before his angels. Him that overcometh will I make a pillar in the temple of my God, and he shall go no more out: and I will write upon him the *name* of my God, and the *name* of the city of my God, which is new Jerusalem, which cometh down out of heaven from my God: and I will write upon him *my new name*" (Rev. 3:5, 12; my emphasis).

Believers are members of the household of God and joint heirs with Yeshua (Eph. 2:19; Heb.3:6; Rom. 8:17). The day is coming when we will have the name of the Lord written on us. The exchange has been made. You can now add your own name to the list of the living. God is now the God of

Abraham, the God of Isaac, the God of Jacob, and the God of ____________________, put your name in the blank space.

The covenant partners rub their bloody wounds together to make a scar. The scar is a permanent testimony of the covenant between them. It serves as a reminder of their responsibilities to one another. It is also a sign that they no longer have to stand alone. The power and authority of each man is at the disposal of his partner. The scar serves as the *guarantee of the covenant.* In time of trouble, revealing the scar assures full participation from the covenant partner.

We see this practiced in the covenant between God and Abraham. "This is my covenant, which ye shall keep, between me and you and thy seed after thee; every man child among you shall be circumcised. And ye shall circumcise the flesh of your foreskin; and it shall be a token of the covenant betwixt me and you" (Gen. 17:10, 11). Paul explains in Romans 4:11 that Abraham's circumcision was a sign, a seal of his faith. It is interesting that God chose circumcision of the male foreskin as the scar of the covenant. The location of the circumcision meant that several times a day, as Abraham relieved himself, the scar served as a reminder of the covenant, and his responsibility to teach his children of God's promises. It also meant that Abraham was not likely to be boastful about his scar and readily show it off.

When God made a covenant with the nation of Israel, He promised that one day He would circumcise their hearts. "And the Lord thy God will circumcise thine heart, and the heart of thy seed, to love the Lord thy God with all thine heart, and with all thy soul, that thou mayest live" (Deut. 30:6).

The Covenant grew and so did the promise of God. He said, "*A new heart* also will I give you, and *a new spirit* will I put within you: and I will take away the stony heart out of your flesh, and I will give you a heart of flesh. And *I will put my Spirit* within you and cause you to walk in my statues, and you shall keep my judgments, and do them" (Ezek. 36:26, 27; my emphasis).

Paul teaches that God has fulfilled His promise. Every believer is sealed with the *Holy Spirit*, who is the *guarantee* of our inheritance until Yeshua returns. Paul said, "Now he which stablisheth us with you in Christ, and hath anointed us, is God; Who hath also *sealed* us, and given the *earnest* of the *Spirit* in our hearts" (2 Cor. 1:22; my emphasis). "In whom ye also trusted, after that ye heard the word of truth, the gospel of your salvation: in whom also after that ye believed, ye were *sealed* with that *Holy Spirit* of promise, Which is the *earnest* of our inheritance until the redemption of the purchased possession, unto the praise of his glory" (Eph. 1:13, 14; my emphasis).

We, unlike Abraham, do not make a scar when we enter God's covenant. God, himself, performs this surgery for every believer. Part of the ministry of the Holy Spirit is to remind us of God's covenant promises. *The scar is visible only to God*, therefore we cannot boast. Like Abraham who slept while God the Father and God the Son walked through the blood of the covenant, we have the promise of eternal life through Grace not by any works of the flesh.

Anytime a blood covenant is made there must be witnesses. The witnesses are present to hear the swearing of the terms of the covenant. The covenant partners proclaim their assets and liabilities. By doing so, they are promising God and each other that everything they posses; money, property, and possessions now belong to their covenant partner. The witnesses are accountable to God to make certain that the covenant partners adhere to the covenant terms.

Did you know that when you attend a wedding ceremony you are a witness to the covenant entered into by the bride and groom? What an awesome responsibility. As a witness, you are responsible for helping the bride and groom keep the promises they made before God and the congregation.

An example of swearing an oath is a witness called to testify at a trial. The witness is asked to put his/her hand on the Bible and swear to tell the truth. They are swearing by something greater than themselves. The Bible is the infallible word of God. It is unchangeable. When God made covenant with Abraham He could swear by nothing greater than Himself, so He swore by two unchangeable things. "For when God made his promise to Abraham, he swore an oath to do what he had promised; and since there was no one greater than himself for him to sware by, *He swore by Himself*" (Heb. 6:13; Gen. 22:16; my emphasis). "Therefore, when God wanted to demonstrate still more convincingly the unchangeable character of his intentions to those who were to receive what he had promised, he added an oath to the promise; so that through two unchangeable things, in neither of which God could lie, we, who have fled to take a firm hold on the hope set before us, would be strongly encouraged" (Heb. 6:17, 18). What are these two unchangeable things that God swore by?

They are the two who walked together through the blood of the animals while Abraham slept. They are God the Father and God the Son. God the Father's appearance was that of a *smoking furnace*, and God the Son appeared as the *burning lamp* (Gen. 15:17).

Moses and the writer of the book of Hebrews refer to God as a consuming fire (Deut. 4:24; Heb. 12:29). God told the nation of Israel that he would appear to them in a Pillar of Fire by night and a Pillar of a Cloud by day (Ex. 13:21, 22). The burning lamp in Revelation and in many other passages of scripture is descriptive of Yeshua (Rev. 1:12, 13; 21:23; Ps. 119:105; Jn. 1:7-9).

How do we know they are unchangeable? Speaking of Yeshua, the writer of the book of Hebrews said, "Jesus Christ the same yesterday, today, and for ever" (Heb. 13:8). James said the same of God the Father, "Every good gift and every perfect gift is from above, and cometh down from the Father of lights, with whom is *no variableness*, neither shadow of turning" (James 1:17; my emphasis).

Both parties in God's blood covenant are *unchangeable.* Therefore, this covenant can never be broken. Remember, a blood covenant can only be broken by the death of one of the covenant partners, and in God's covenant the two covenant partners are sovereign and eternal!

God offered the Nation of Israel the opportunity to enter into His covenant. Moses declared all of the terms of God's covenant to Israel and then he called for two witnesses. On three different occasions, Moses said, "I call *heaven* and *earth* to witness against you this day" (Deut. 4:26a; my emphasis). "I call *heaven* and *earth* to record this day against you, that I have set before you life and death, blessing and cursing: therefore choose life, that both thou and thy seed may live" (Deut. 30:19; my emphasis). "Gather unto me all the elders of your tribes, and your officers, that I may speak these words in their ears, and call *heaven* and *earth* to record against them" (Deut. 31:28; my emphasis).

Abraham was asleep during this part of the covenant process, so who were the witnesses? They are the same two that Moses called on. *Heaven* and *earth* witnessed God the Father and His Son entering into a covenant together for the benefit of humanity (Gen. 1:26; Ps. 8:4-8; Heb.2:6-8).

The same two witnesses are watching each of us to see if we observe the terms of God's covenant. Heaven: Yeshua said, "Take heed that ye despise not one of these little ones; for I say unto you, that in *heaven* their angels do always behold the face of my Father which is in heaven" (Mt. 18:10; my emphasis). "Likewise, I say unto you, there is joy in the presence of the angels of God over one sinner that repenteth" (Lk. 15:10). The Earth: Paul said, "You yourselves are our letter of recommendation, written on our hearts, *known* and *read* by *everyone* (2 Cor. 3:2; my emphasis). How awe-inspiring to know that the angels of God rejoice in Heaven when a human being repents. The whole world, (the lost and the saved) are watching our lives trying to see God in us. What are they witnessing in your life?

What exchange was made between God and man at this stage of making the covenant? What are the *assets* and the *liabilities* in God's covenant?

Assets: All of the assets come from God.

Yeshua gives us *all Power* (Mt. 28:18-20).

Yeshua gives us the use of *His name* (Mk. 16:15-18).

Yeshua gives us *power over the enemy* and *protection* (Lk.10:19, 20).

The Father gave us *His only begotten Son* who gives us *eternal life* (Jn. 3:16).

The Father gave us *His Holy Spirit* (Lk. 11:13).

God has no liabilities. All of the liabilities in the covenant come from man.

In exchange for man's liabilities God gives His assets.

Liabilities: Yeshua took His flesh from man.

Flesh is representative of His only weakness (Jn. 1:14).

Yeshua became sin so that we could become righteous (Rom. 5:12; 1 Cor. 15:21; 2 Cor. 5:21).

Yeshua took our diseases and gave us health (Isa. 53:5; 1 Pet. 2:24).

Yeshua took our pain and gave us his peace (Isa. 53:4).

Yeshua paid our death sentence and gave us eternal life (Rom. 5:8; 6:23).

Looking at the list of assets and liabilities, it is easy to see why God entered into a covenant with man through Yeshua, because man has nothing good to offer God. After accepting the terms of God's covenant and receiving His great mercy, we, as a member of His royal priesthood, must present God an offering. Paul said, "I beseech you therefore, brethren, by the mercies of God, that ye present your bodies a living sacrifice, holy, acceptable unto God, which is your reasonable service.

And be not conformed to this world: but be ye transformed by the renewing of your mind, that ye may prove what is that good, and acceptable, and perfect, will of God" (Rom. 12:1, 2).

The covenant partners also share a memorial meal of bread and wine. The bread is substituted for the flesh of the sacrificed animals and the wine is the substitute for the blood. The covenant partners serve one another this meal. Each man breaks off a portion of the bread and feeds it to his covenant partner. Next they serve each other the wine. This part of the covenant rituals is symbolic of becoming one with your covenant partner. They say to each other, "now I am in you and you are in me, we are now one with a new nature."

We see this part of entering into a blood covenant practiced at wedding receptions. The bride and groom feed each other a piece of the wedding cake. Then, they wrap their arms together to exchange sips of wine. At most weddings, this is usually made into a display of smearing the cake over each other's face. How sad! They have no idea how serious this part of the ceremony is in the marriage covenant.

Abraham shared a meal with the three men sent by the Lord to destroy Sodom (Gen. 18:1-8). God shared His plans to destroy Sodom with Abraham (Gen. 18: 17). After hearing God's plan, Abraham asked God (his covenant partner) to spare the righteous people in Sodom. God honored Abraham's request and spared Lot (Abraham's nephew) and his family. Lot was a member of Abraham's family and because God and Abraham were covenant partners, Lot and his family were spared (Gen. 18:22-37; 19:29).

The children of Israel shared a Memorial meal when they ate the Passover Lamb before leaving Egypt. The sacrificed lamb took the place of the first born of Israel. The Passover Lamb foreshadowed the Lamb of God (Yeshua) who became the final substitute for all humanity. God said, "And this day shall be unto you for a *memorial*; and ye shall keep it a feast to the Lord throughout your generations: ye shall keep it a feast by an ordinance *forever*" (Ex. 12:14; my emphasis).

The greatest of all Covenant Memorial meals is the one Yeshua established (Jn. 6:53-58). Yeshua fulfilled this portion of God's blood covenant, the covenant that started with Abraham, when He shared His last Passover meal with His disciples. Yeshua's flesh and blood became the substitute for man. He said "With desire I have desired to eat this Passover with you before I suffer. For I say unto you, I will not any more eat thereof, until it be fulfilled in the kingdom of God." He took the cup, blessed it, and said: "Take this, and divide it among yourselves: For I say unto you, I will not drink of the fruit of the vine, until the kingdom of God shall come." He took the bread, blessed it, and break it saying: "This *is my body* which is given for you: this do in remembrance of me." He took the final cup, after the meal and said: "This cup is the new testament in *my blood*, which is shed for you" (Lk. 22:14-20; my emphasis).

We are so very blessed to be able to share this Memorial Meal together every time we have communion, or celebrate Passover. Remember, when you eat of the sacraments, it is symbolic of becoming one with your covenant partner (Yeshua) and therefore you have a new nature. "Therefore if any man be in Christ, he is a new creature: old things are passed away; behold all things are become new" (2 Cor. 5:17).

Blood covenants require establishing a memorial to remind the covenant partners and their families of the terms and conditions of the covenant. One of the most common practices was to plant a memorial tree. Blood from the animals that were sacrificed is sprinkled on the tree. The bloodstained tree is a testimony of the covenant. The covenant between Abraham and Abimelech is a good example of this practice (Gen. 21:27, 28, 32, 33).

In God's Blood Covenant, the Cross of Calvary is the memorial tree. The blood of Yeshua, God's sacrificial Lamb, was poured out on the cross and when it was all spilled out,

Yeshua cried out with a loud voice, *it is finished* (Jn. 19:30). At last, God added His blood to the Covenant that started with Abram (Gen. 15:17). Now all of humanity can enter into God's Blood Covenant through Yeshua.

Yeshua on the cross (by Christa Shore)

After the memorial is established, the covenant partners refer to one another as friends. Yeshua said "Ye are my *friends*, if ye do whatsoever I command you. Henceforth I call you not servants; for the servant knoweth not what his lord doeth; but I have called you *friends*; for all things that I have heard of my Father I have made known unto you" (Jn. 15:14-15; my emphasis).

Abraham was the first man to be referred to as the friend of God (2 Chronicles 20:7; Isa. 41:8; Ja. 2:23. God told Abraham in advance, what his plans were for Sodom. Look how much better the covenant has become. Now, the Holy Spirit reminds the believer of every word spoken by Yeshua, which includes those that existed before the creation of the world. All of the knowledge of God is available with one stipulation, we must be obedient.

We have examined the procedures found in most blood covenants. But the God of all creation takes blood covenant even further. He has added something that only He could, resurrection from the dead.

In all other blood covenants death disannulled its terms, but with God, nothing is impossible. Yeshua is the first born from the dead, and because he ever lives, all who are in him live also. God added one final thing to his covenant. Man will receive an incorruptible body like that of Yeshua and live forever with Him (1 Cor. 15:50-54).

"Blessed be the God and Father of our Lord Jesus Christ, which according to his abundant mercy hath begotten us again unto a lively hope by the resurrection of Jesus Christ from the dead. To an inheritance *incorruptible*, and *undefiled*, and that fadeth not away, reserved in heaven for you. ... Being *born again*, not of corruptible seed, but of incorruptible, by the word of God, which liveth and abideth for ever" (I Pet. 1:3, 4, and 23; my emphasis)

Since God is a covenant-making covenant-keeping God, He surrounds His throne with memorial signs of the covenants found throughout the Bible. "And he that sat was to look upon like a jasper and a sardine stone: and there was *a rainbow round about the throne*, in sight like unto an emerald. And round about the throne were four and twenty seats: and upon the seats I saw four and twenty elders sitting, clothed in white raiment; and they had on their heads crowns of gold. And out of the throne proceeded *lightnings and thunderings* and *voices*: and there were *seven lamps of fire burning before the throne*, which are *the seven Spirits of God*" (Rev. 4:3-5; my emphasis).

The rainbow was given to Noah as a sign from God that He would never flood the earth again. Note: A bow is an instrument of war. From God's perspective, looking down from heaven, the bow is held backward. This was an ancient sign used by warriors to indicate that the battle was over (Gen. 9:8-17).

The seven lamps and the fire burning are symbolic of the covenant with Abraham. God the Father and God the Son walked together in the blood of the sacrificed animals. The burning lamp is descriptive of Yeshua and the smoking furnace is representative of God the Father.

The lightnings and thunderings and the voices are memorials of the covenant with the children of Israel at Mt. Sinai. Mt. Sinai is where God spoke the words of His marriage covenant (the Ten Commandments) to Israel. He appeared to Israel as flashes of lightening and His mighty voice sounded like thunder. The mountain shook at His awesome presence (Ex. 19:16-19; 20:18-22).

The seven Spirits of God are descriptive of the fullness of the Holy Spirit found in Isaiah chapter 11 (v. 2). The Holy Spirit is the seal of the covenant God made with all believers. The Holy Spirit is the fulfillment of God's promise, the earnest deposit or I like to think of Him as my engagement ring. The Holy Spirit is the promise that Yeshua will return and gather His people to the marriage supper of the Lamb (Rev.19:7-9).

If you understand blood covenant relationships, when you see the word friend or friends in the scripture, they are referring to those who are in a covenant relationship. Following are a few examples. A friend sticks closer than a brother (Pr. 18:24). A true friend would rather hurt you than see you fall to the enemy (Pr. 27:6). A friend loves at all times (Pr. 17:17).

There two other words that identify a covenant relationship, remember and remembered. The tense of the two words is important. The word remembered is most often used in relation to God. The past tense form of the verb shows that God's work is finished. The present active tense is applicable to man's response to God's commands. In the scriptures below, remember does not imply that God could forget His promise. He will never forget you! God's children are engraved in his hands; we are constantly before him (Isa. 49:14-16). God is continually looking for ways to bless his children. "For the eyes of the Lord run to and fro throughout the whole earth, to show himself strong in the behalf of them whose heart is perfect toward him" (2 Chronicles 16:9). God is looking for someone who will remember him and believe his promises.

Please note the tense of the verb in the following scriptures.

God *remembered* Noah (Gen. 6:18; 8:1). God *remembered* Abraham (Gen. 17:7; 19:29).

God *remembered* his covenant (Ex. 2:24). God said to *remember* Passover (Ex.13:3). God said to *remember* the Sabbath (Ex. 20:8). Yeshua said to *remember* his body and his blood (Lk. 22:19, 20).

Although every ritual found in the making of a blood covenant is not always present, to those familiar with such things, it is accepted that all are included. Since the Bible is the inspired word of God written by Jews to Jews, God revealed himself to them in ways that they would understand. The Western culture has caused many to miss the richness found in the customs of God's people ("Israel"). If you have accepted Yeshua as your savior, you have entered into a covenant with God, and you are entitled to the benefits of the common wealth of Israel. I encourage you to re-read the Bible and look for covenant words and ritual practices and explore the Jewish roots of your faith for yourself. If you do, you will be in awe of God's love for all of his children.

CHAPTER 2

The Journey to the Tabernacle

If you are asking yourself, why do I need to be familiar with the Tabernacle, its sacrificial system and its ceremonies? How are they applicable today? In order to answer these questions, we must start at the beginning and find out what happened to humanity. The journey to the Tabernacle will demonstrate how God's covenant continued to grow.

Our journey begins in Genesis. Genesis verse 1 says, "In the beginning God." This statement alone reveals that God has always existed. He is the self-existent eternal supreme God. Although God is holy, just, and righteous, He desires to demonstrate His love to and through man.

Genesis chapter 2 chronicles how God fashioned a special man by using the dust of the ground; his name was Adam. Adam is the first man, documented in the Bible, who had a relationship with his Creator. He was made alive by the very breath of God. The Bible says, "God breathed into his nostrils the breath of life and he became a living soul" (Gen. 2:7). When I read this, a picture of someone performing CPR comes to mind. God and his special man were nose to nose. What a picture of how close the Creator of the universe wants to be with His people.

Adam was made in the image of God; He was perfect. God placed him in a garden paradise and provided for his every need. He gave Adam power and authority over all of the other living creatures on the earth.

Once the relationship between God and Adam began, the name used to identify God changed from God, in Hebrew (*Elohim* – the Mighty One) to Lord God, in Hebrew (*Adonai Elohim* - the plural form of the supreme God) identifying the fullness of God (God the Father, God the Son and God the Holy Spirit). He is the self-existent or eternal supreme God. The addition of the word Lord indicates that every member of the Holy Trinity was a participant in the relationship with Adam.

God walked with Adam daily and taught him His ways. Everything in the garden was there for Adam's pleasure except the tree of the knowledge of good and evil that was located in the center of the garden, next to the tree of life. Even so, Adam was lonely. None of God's other creations could lessen Adam's loneliness. He needed someone, like himself, to love. God caused a deep sleep to fall upon Adam and while he slept, God performed the first surgery ever recorded. God took a rib from Adam's side and made a woman (Gen. 2:21-22). I have heard it taught that the word woman means (*man with a womb*). Whither that is accurate of not, God made Adam a wife. The relationship between Adam and his wife was one of intimacy. In the eyes of God, Adam and his wife were one, and that is why they were called Adam (Gen. 2:23-24). They were covered in the glory of God. The brightness of His glory shrouded their nakedness.

Adam's job was to maintain the garden. He was free to enjoy the beauty that surrounded him with one restriction. The restriction carried with it a severe consequence, death. He was not to eat the fruit of the tree of the knowledge of good and evil. That seems simple enough but Adam was unsuccessful; he ate of the forbidden fruit. Adam failed to realize how far-reaching the product of his disobedience would be. Through Adam's disobedience, sin and death entered the world and it touches every human being (1 Cor. 15:21-22).

Sin is what separated Adam from his creator, because God cannot look upon sin. "Thou art of purer eyes than to behold evil, and canst not look on iniquity" (Habakkuk 1:13a). Sin became the barrier between God and Adam.

As my daughter, Debbie, studied the book of Genesis, God allowed her to see His heart, in a vision. Her vision was that of the garden after Adam's sin. She watched as God entered the garden. He came to walk with Adam as He had done so many other times, but when God called out, Adam didn't answer; he was hiding. Adam covered himself with leaves, because now he recognized that he was naked. Debbie watched as God pressed His cheek against what appeared to be a glass barrier. She heard Him say, in a broken-hearted tone, "Oh! Adam where are you" (Gen. 3:8-9). Of course, God knew where Adam was; that is not why He asked the question. His heart was aching because sin had separated Him from the man he loved. He could no longer walk and talk with His beloved Adam.

Although Adam's physical body lived, the spirit within him died; sin had made him hopeless. It was at that time that Adam named his wife Eve (Gen. 3:20). There was nothing that Adam could do to make things right again. Only God could restore the lost relationship. Atonement must be paid for Adam's sin. This is where God began to reveal His Master plan for man's redemption. God killed an innocent animal to make coats for Adam and his wife (Gen. 3:21), and then they were expelled from the garden. The blood of the innocent animal temporarily paid the price for Adam's sin and allowed Adam and Eve to live. The animal's skin replaced the covering of God's Glory. Once again, the Lord could look at man, because the innocent blood covered sin, but man was cast out of the place of fellowship.

God longed for the lost moments of walking with Adam. His plan had begun, and when it was completed, God could once again dwell among the people He loved. Thus God's plan to give His Son for the sin of humanity began. "For the wages of sin is death; but the gift of God is eternal life through Jesus

Christ our Lord" (Romans 6:23). Forgiveness always precedes fellowship with God.

After the fall of Adam, the human race became increasingly evil and blinded to the need for a forgiving God. It was two hundred and thirty-five years before Enos, Adam's grandson, turned back to the Lord (Gen. 4:26).

By the time of Noah, the human race had become so evil that God bemoaned having created man. Genesis chapter 6 tells how God gave humanity one hundred and twenty years to repent before He ended life on the earth.

Noah was a man who loved God. His love and obedience is what kept God from destroying all of humanity. God gave Noah the instructions for building an Ark. The Ark was a large ship that was designed to carry hundreds of animals and their provisions. Once the Ark was finished, God sent animals, in pairs, to Noah. When the Ark was finally loaded, Noah took his family inside and waited. When the rain (God's judgment) started, God shut the door and sealed Noah and his family inside of the Ark (Gen. 7:16b). The Ark is how God chose to save Noah and his family. Noah's obedience gave the human race a new beginning.

The Ark is a *Shadow* of Yeshua and His saving power. Individuals who accept Yeshua as the Son of God are sealed by the power of the Holy Spirit and protected from the wrath of Gods' judgment, just as Noah and his family were protected in the Ark. Yeshua brought salvation to the world (Jn. 3:16). In Yeshua, every believer receives a new beginning (2 Cor.5:17).

One man's (Adam) disobedience brought spiritual death to all men, but Noah's obedience brought salvation to his family and a new beginning for the human race (Gen. 6:8). Note: All throughout the Scriptures the number *8* is associated with a *new_beginning.* God saved eight people inside the Ark to start fresh. God commanded His people to circumcise their sons on the eighth day of life. The new born-again man is to put on eight things--*bowels of mercies, kindness, humbleness of mind, meekness, longsuffering, forbearance, forgiveness, and love* (Gen. 17:10-14, Lk. 1:59, Col. 3:12-14). This is but a few examples. The Lord attends to the smallest detail to reveal His love. As our journey moves closer to the Tabernacle, God's redemptive plan grows. Two were cast out from the place of safety in the garden. Now, eight were saved in the Ark, and through them man has a new beginning.

Our journey brings us to Abraham, the man of faith. We have seen that Adam's disobedience brought death to all men, and Noah's obedience gave man a new beginning. Now we will see how one man's faith provided the way of salvation to all nations.

Abraham is often referred to as the father of the Jews, but Abraham was not Jewish. He was a man who answered the call of God by leaving his old pagan life and family behind, to follow God. Abraham became the father of all who believe. Abraham was the first man referred to as a Hebrew, which means *one from the other side* or *one who has crossed over* (Gen. 14:13). Because of Abraham's faith, we see God's redemption plan continuing to grow. God asked Abraham to do something that had never been done; to believe in something he could not see. Adam saw the forbidden fruit tree, and Noah built the Ark with his own hands. Abraham, on the other hand, was asked to simply believe God's promise that he would be the father of many nations (Gen. 17:5).

Abraham was an old man without children, and his wife, Sarah, was an old woman far past the age of child bearing. Their situation looked impossible; however:

"Is there anything too hard for the Lord? (Gen. 18:14). "With God nothing shall be impossible" (Lk. 1:37). The Lord caused the dead ninety-year-old womb of Sarah to conceive and bring forth life. Sarah gave her one hundred-year-old husband the son that God had promised. They named their son Isaac.

I stand in awe of Abraham's faith. After waiting all those years to have a son, God asked Abraham to offer Isaac on the altar. This meant that Abraham had to kill Isaac, the promised son. His willingness to sacrifice Isaac to the Lord made the way for the heavenly Father to sacrifice His only begotten Son, for the sin of man. Abraham, being a covenant-making man, knew how a blood covenant works. A covenant partner provides and protects. They are more than partners; they are friends. Abraham was a friend of God. He knew that God would not ask him to do anything that He was not willing to do Himself. This is evidenced in Abraham's words to Isaac as they went up the mountain. Isaac was between the ages of 17 and 27 when he and his father went up the mountain to offer a sacrifice to God. Isaac carried the wood for the fire on his back; providing a beautiful portrait of Yeshua carrying the cross. As they went along, Isaac turned to his father and said, "I have the wood, and you have the knife, but where is the lamb for the sacrifice?" Abraham answered his son with these words: "God will provide *Himself* a *Lamb* for a burnt offering" (Gen. 22:8; my emphasis). Abraham understood that through Isaac's descendants the Messiah would come and become the Lamb of God. Abraham knew, because he was the friend of God (Isa. 41:8, Ja. 2:23), and God talks with His friends face to face (Ex. 33:11). God talked with Abraham before destroying Sodom and Gomorrah (Gen. 18:22-23). Note: Yeshua also called His followers friends and taught them of His death and resurrection (Jn. 15:15). Abraham believed God's promise because God had already talked to him about his descendants. God told Abraham that his descendants would be in bondage for 400 years. He also had God's promise to deliver his children out of bondage and give them the land that God promised to give him (Gen.15:13, 14). God spared Isaac's life by providing a ram as the substitute. The ram is a shadow of God's Son, Yeshua, who became man's sacrifice. "The next day John seeth Jesus coming unto him and saith, Behold the *Lamb* of *God*, which taketh away the sin of the world" (Jn. 1:29; my emphasis).

Through Isaac's son Jacob, the family of God grows. The name Jacob means *supplanter.* God changed Jacob's name to Israel, which means *soldier of God.* Jacob/ Israel, like his grandfather, Abraham, and his father, Isaac, entered into God's blood covenant. God added Jacob's name to His by becoming the God of Abraham, Isaac, and Jacob. God gave the Tabernacle to Abraham's descendants. Israel had twelve sons and through them God would reveal His redemption plan for the world.

Moses is the next man in God's plan. Moses was the son of Levi, one of the twelve sons of Israel. He was the prophet chosen to deliver the children of Israel out of 400 years of Egyptian bondage and lead them to God's Promised Land (Ex. 3:9-23). Through Moses, the Egyptians learned that the God of Israel is the one true God.

From Adam to the present, God's requisite for deliverance from sin and death remains the same--the shedding of innocent blood. The children of Israel learned this lesson while they were in Egypt. God declared that every firstborn in the land of Egypt would die. The only protection from the curse of death was innocent blood.

Moses told the people to kill a lamb and place its blood on the door post and lintel of their homes. Why did they not question such a strange act? It is because they were familiar with blood covenants. It was a common practice to kill an animal and spread its blood on the *threshold* of the door when anyone of importance was expected to come by. When the guest sees blood on the threshold, he understands that the head of the household was saying, "you are welcome here, what I have is yours and I will serve you and treat you with respect". When the honored guest crossed the threshold, he was saying, "I come in peace and will do you no harm". Covenant people understand the blood is not a picture of death but rather it is a picture if life. This is called a Threshold Covenant. Let me explain.

3500 years ago there were no international peace treaties or mediators to settle disputes between peoples. The strong king or tribal leader would take what he wanted from the weaker. It was a way of life. So when a king defeated his enemy, he would march into the cities and put down any rebellion he found among the citizens. If they resisted, he killed them; simple as that. But remember, these are covenant people. If the defeated king happened to be one who was cruel or oppressive to his subjects, the people would welcome his overthrow. They would make their intentions known to the conquering king by killing their best sacrificial animal and spreading its blood on the threshold of their doorway. Thus, by inviting the king into the sanctuary of their home they preserved their lives. Imagine for a moment that you are the king standing on the outskirts of a city. You have declared war on the king of this country and you must decide to send either your army to wage war on the inhabitants, or your emissaries to comfort and protect them. Now, you see the blood of the "Threshold Covenant" on the door post. All is well for those who are in the house, for the Conquering King is come to deliver and save those who have been held in bondage. God had made it known that He was going to pass through the land that night and that the first born of everyone and everything that was not covered by this "Threshold Covenant" was going to die.

It is time for us to take a closer look at the word "pass" in the scripture. In Exodus 12:12, God says that He will pass through the land. The Hebrew word used there is "Abar" (צָבַר). It means *to be very angry, rage, to cause to perish.* But when we read in verse 13, I will pass over you (meaning those with the blood on the doorpost) the word used is "Pesach" (פֶּסַח). This word literally means *to bow down to cross a threshold.* The word Pesach has a second meaning in the Hebrew. It means to bow down in a limping dance of worship. So, in essence what God was saying to those who were under the blood was "When I see the blood, I will enter your dwelling and defend you from the death that lurks outside and we will worship together." This gives us a totally different meaning to the phrase "I will pass over you". We have been taught that it meant that God would skip over the house with the blood and not kill the first born who was there. We have made the mistake because we didn't understand Blood Covenant. God had given specific instructions to the Hebrews, and those who chose to join themselves to them, through Moses. They were to eat the Lamb, the bitter herbs, and the unleavened bread in haste, with their shoes on their feet and their staff in their hands. In other words, their deliverance was to come quickly---be ready! Note: In Exodus 12:22, the word *"basin"* used in this verse is in Hebrew, pronounced *sap (ps),* and means *Threshold or Doorway.*

A perfect lamb was killed for each household. The blood of the lamb was caught in a trough at the bottom of the door. The man of the house took a green branch and dipped it into the blood and raised the branch to the lintel above the door, then from side to side, forming the shape of the cross.

When the death angel came to kill all the firstborn, he passed over every house that was marked with the bloody cross. God *substituted* The Lamb for every firstborn of Israel (Ex. 12:24-47). What a beautiful shadow of the *Lamb of God, Yeshua,* who became the *substituted sacrifice* for all mankind by shedding His own blood on the cross.

Prior to leaving Egypt, God had His people go to their Egyptian neighbors and ask for gifts of gold, silver, brass, pure white linen, brightly colored yarn of blue, purple, and scarlet, precious gems, and animal skins. These items were gifts from God; and were payment for the work and the harsh treatment experienced during the 400 years spent in slavery.

God's people left Egypt strong and well, young and old alike, with their debt canceled and payment in their hands for all their labor. By the time of the exodus from Egypt, the children of Israel had grown to one million or more. Freed from bondage, they were on their way to the Promised Land (a "Shadow" of Salvation). Traveling first to the Red Sea, they crossed over to the other side on dry ground, leaving sin and death behind, and entering into a new life where they were free to worship the Redeemer, the Holy One of Israel (a "Shadow" of water baptism).

The children of Israel traveled for forty-seven more days until they came to Mt. Sinai. God told His people to purify themselves and be ready to experience His presence. At the end of three days, God appeared from the top of Mt. Sinai (a "Shadow" of the out pouting of the Holy Spirit).

Note: This was the *fiftieth* day following Passover or what is better known as *Pentecost.*

At Mt. Sinai, the sound and the sight of God's mighty presence caused the people to fear. They heard the thundering sound of God's voice as He spoke the words of His marriage covenant (the Ketuba or the Ten Commandments). There were flashes of lightning as God scrolled the words of His covenant into the tablets of stone with His finger (Ex. 20:1-22, 31:18). I believe God used stone to show us two things. First, His covenant is forever. He will not break it; *"It's written in stone."* The second was to reveal the hardened hearts of the people.

Because the people feared, Moses went before God on their behalf. He stayed in the presence of the Lord for forty days and forty nights (Ex. 24:15, 16). He sat for six days, not hearing one word but on the *seventh day* God began to speak with him and continued for the next thirty-three days showing him His plans for the Tabernacle.

Note: 40 - 7 = 33: For thirty-three days the Lord instructed Moses concerning His plans for the people He loved. *One day for each year of Yeshua's life on the earth.*

God gave Moses two things to give to the people, the *tablets of stone* and *the_instructions for the Tabernacle.*

Before Moses could return, God's beloved bride *(Israel)* had defiled the marriage covenant by worshipping another god *(the golden calf)* (Ex. 32:1-6). Sin was in the camp and God was jealous for His bride. Anger gripped Moses when he saw what the people had done and he broke the stone tablets that contained the promises of God's covenant relationship.

God's people were hopeless, doomed for death, because man had broken the covenant. God's requirement for sin had not changed; it required the shedding of innocent blood. There was none innocent or good enough to pay the price for their sin.

God's plan continues because Moses also carried with him the instructions for the *Tabernacle*. The Tabernacle and its sacrificial system is how God began to teach His people how to reestablish fellowship with Him through the blood sacrifice. Praise the Lord!

The sin of disobedience had spread from one person (Adam) to a nation of more than a million people. God's redemption plan has grown from one man to a nation. Through the children of Israel, God revealed Himself to the world as the only man worthy to pay the penalty for sin through the shed blood of Yeshua, His only begotten Son.

God spent thirty-three days showing and explaining to Moses every detail of the Tabernacle. Obviously, it is important to Him that we understand its design, because it is the *shadow of Yeshua and our relationship to the Father through Him* (Heb. 8:5). Through the Tabernacle in the wilderness, God was preparing man to recognize Yeshua, His True Tabernacle (Rev. 21:3). The Tabernacle was God's temporary dwelling place in the midst of His people (Ex. 25:8), foreshadowing the body of Yeshua who is His living presence in the earth (Jn. 1:1, 2, 14).

The Tabernacle along with the sacrifices and offerings teaches man at least four things: 1. God's way is the *only* way. 2. Through it God kept His people until the True Tabernacle was born. 3. It demonstrates how helpless man is without the Lord and that payment must be made for sin. 4. The shedding of innocent blood showed man that his righteousness is not good enough to re-establish fellowship with a Holy God. That is why God has given us One who can, Yeshua, the *last* Adam, the only begotten of the Father (1 Cor. 15:20-22, 44, 45). His blood is the only blood pure enough to take away the sin of the world forever (Heb. 9:11-14, 22-26). He, unlike the *first* Adam who had power and dominion over the earth, has ALL power in heaven, in the earth, and under the earth (Mat. 28:18, Phil. 2:10). Through His death and resurrection, life and eternal fellowship with God have been restored. Note: The *first* Adam was man clothed with God, and the *last* Adam was God clothed in man's flesh. The unsightly coverings of the Tabernacle concealed the boundless treasure inside, where the presence of God dwelt, just like the covering of flesh concealed the fullness of God, embodied in Yeshua (Co. 2:9).

Our journey has brought us to our destination, the Tabernacle in the wilderness, God's dwelling place. At last He could once again fellowship with the people He loved and teach them how to *know Him* and live in Him. The Tabernacle is the unfolding revelation of the Savior, who is God's ultimate gift of love to the world (Jn. 3:16).

He is who, I pray, you are able to see as we examine the Tabernacle.

CHAPTER 3

Numbers and Names

In the Hebrew language, each letter of the alphabet has a numerical value. We will be using numbers and their meanings as we examine the measurements God gave for the Tabernacle and its contents. This is not a study of numerology. However, the use of numbers in relation to scripture, especially with the study of the Tabernacle, aids in understanding what God is teaching. The following numbers and the application of their meanings will disclose God's design and purpose for Tabernacle.

ONE is the number of *unity. (Ekh awd')* God is the united one, and He said, "My people are one." The people in the upper room were said to have been in one accord (Gen. 11:6, Acts 2:1).

TWO is the number that represents *power, authority, and fellowship.* God made two lights, one to rule the day and one to rule the night. He said, "By two or three witnesses a matter is determined." Yeshua sent the disciples out two by two. God will give the earth two witnesses to testify of Him before the final judgment (Gen. 1:16, Mat. 18:16, Lk. 10:1, Acts 4:23, Rev. 11:6).

THREE is the number of *sufficiency*, or a sufficient number. There are three in the Holy Trinity--*God the Father, God the Son, and God the Holy Spirit.* There are also three in the anti-godhead--*Satan, the false prophet, and the false messiah.* Yeshua was three days in the grave. Jonah spent three days in the belly of the fish. There were three crosses at Yeshua's crucifixion. Three feasts of God required all males 20 years old and up to journey to Jerusalem annually--*Passover, Pentecost, and Tabernacles* (Deut. 16:16; Lev. 23:5-8, 16, 34-44).

FOUR is the number for the *earth.* The earth has *four* winds, four corners, four directions, and four seasons.

FIVE is the number for *grace*. There were five animals sacrificed in the covenant God made with Abraham--*a heifer, a she goat, a ram, a turtle dove, and a young pigeon.* Yeshua had five deep puncture wounds in his body--*His hands, feet, and side.* God established five offerings--*the Burnt offering, the Meat offering, the Peace offering, the Sin offering, and the Trespass offering* (Gen. 15:9; Lev. 1, 2, 3, 5, & 6).

SIX is the number for *man.* Man was created on the sixth day. The number 666 is the number of the name of the anti-messiah. Scripture says we will know him by his number (Rev. 13:18). There are 66 books in the Bible. When the number of the anti-messiah is written in fraction form, 6 over 66, it represents man putting himself above God's Word, or he is assuming the rightful place of God alone.

SEVEN is the number of *God's perfection.* On the seventh day God's work was complete. There are seven Spirits of God that describe His perfection--*the Spirit of the Lord, the Spirit of Knowledge, the Spirit of Counsel, the Spirit of Wisdom, the Spirit of Understanding, the Spirit of Might, and the Spirit of the Fear of the Lord* (Isa. 11:1, 2). In the book of Revelation we find seven churches, seven seals, and seven trumpets. In the book of Leviticus God established seven feasts to commemorate His holiness.

EIGHT is the number of a *new beginning.* Eight people were saved inside the Ark. God told His people to circumcise their sons on the eighth day. The new born-again man is to put on eight things--*bowels of mercies, kindness, humbleness of mind, meekness, longsuffering, forbearance, forgiveness, and love* (Gen. 17:10-14, Lk. 1:59, Col. 3:12-14).

NINE is the *self-repeating number*; it represents the eternal character of God. He has given us nine fruits of the Spirit and nine spiritual gifts; there are also nine beatitudes (Gal. 5:22, 1 Cor. 12:8-10, Mat. 5). The Bible says the gifts and calling of God are irrevocable, unchangeable, they begin with God, and as long as He is, they are. God repeatedly uses the Spiritual gifts to accomplish His will. They begin with Him and end with Him, just as the example below with the number nine.

According to Ervin N. Hershberger's book, *Seeing Christ in the Tabernacle:*

"Note: If 9 is multiplied by any number and the digits in the produce are added together, the sum is nine: 3x9 =27 (2+7) =9, 9x9 =81 (8+1) =9, 789x9 =7101 (7+1+0+1=9. In some cases, the addition process must be carried further to accomplish this: 11x9 = 99 (9+9 =81 [8+1=9], 546x9 =4914 (4+9+1+4 =18[1+8 =9], 951x9 =8559 (8+5+5+9 =27 [2+7 =9]. There are no exceptions.[3]

TEN is the number associated with *man's completeness.* For example, he has ten fingers and ten toes, etc. There were ten virgins and ten lepers. The metric system is based on tens. Ten is used as a standard of quality or perfection. For example, women are judged by men on a scale of one to ten with ten being the best. Born-again man is admonished to prepare for burial, an expression stronger than to put to death, ten things which had control of the flesh--*sexual vice, impurity, sensual appetites, unholy desires, all greed and covetousness, which is idolatry, anger, rage, bad feeling toward others, curses and slander, foul-mouthed abuse, and shameful utterances from your lips* (Col. 3:5-8).

ELEVEN is the number used to express several different things in scripture. It reveals human *failure, confusion, and judgment.* The symbolism found in the 11 strips used to make the goat hair covering of the Tabernacle expresses every use of the number 11 found in scripture.

Human failure God commanded the use of goats as the sin offering at least eleven times. Goats' hair is representative of our sin, which is why eleven strips of goats' hair made the second covering of the Tabernacle (Lev. 4:22-28, 9:3; Nu. 15:22-24; 28:11, 17, 22, 29; 29:5, 11, 16-38).

Confusion: Rebekah used goat's hair to confuse Isaac and cause him to bless Jacob instead of Esau (Gen. 27:1-29). Michal made a goats' hair pillow to deceive her father and save the life of her husband, David (1 Sam. 19:9-17). The Philistines paid Delilah eleven hundred pieces of silver to trick Samson (Judges 16:5). God confused the language of the people and disbursed them to different lands at the tower of Babel (*Babel* means *confusion).* The record of this event is found in the *"11th"* chapter of Genesis.

Judgments: The 11 strips that formed the goats' hair curtain of the Tabernacle foreshadowed Yeshua becoming the scapegoat for man's sin (Lev. 16:10, 20-22). God makes a distinction between sheep and goats at the final judgment. He blesses the sheep at his right hand, but the goats on his left will face the wrath of His judgment (Mat. 25:31-46).

TWELVE is the number used to express *earthly government and blessing.*

Earthly government: 3 (the number in the trinity) times *4* (the number of the earth) = *12* The 12 tribes of Israel revealed the governing ways of *the God of the Old Testament*, and 12 apostles reveal the ways of *the Lord of the New Testament.*

Blessing: There were 12 baskets left over after Yeshua fed the 5,000 (Jn. 6:13). God gave the 12 cakes of Showbread in the Tabernacle to the priest for food (Lev. 24:5). God put 12 kinds of fruit in the New Jerusalem (Rev. 22:2). God lead the children of Israel from Egypt to cross the Red Sea and camp at Elim, where there were 12 wells of water (Ex. 15:27).

FORTY is the number associated with *testing.* 40 Days: The length of the flood in Genesis, the number of days that Moses was on Mt Sinai, the number of days the spies where checking out the land of Canaan. Moses' prayer for the people lasted 40 days and 40 nights. It is the length of time that Goliath tormented Israel with his arrogance, the length of Elijah's fast, Nineveh's probation, Yeshua's temptations, and Yeshua's ministry after His resurrection (Gen. 7:17; Ex.24:18; Nu. 13:25; Deut.9:25-29; 1 Sam.17:16; I Kings 19:2, 8; Jonah 3:4; Lk. 4:1, 2; Acts1:3). 40 Stripes: The limit for scourging (Deut. 25:3). 40 Years: The number of years that Israel had to wander in the desert. For 40 years God sustained them with manna and extended the life of their shoes (Nu. 32:13, Deut. 29:5, Ex. 16:35).

FIFTY is the number of *God's timing for special acts of love.* Every 50th year is the year of Jubilee, a time of canceled debt, restoration of property, families reunited and rest for the land from cultivation (Lev. 25:8-17). Pentecost is the 50th day following Passover. The first Pentecost was fifty days after leaving Egypt. It was the time when the Lord spoke His marriage covenant to Israel from the top of Mt. Sinai. Fifty days after the resurrection of Yeshua, He fulfilled the promise of the Father and gave the gift of the Holy Spirit to every believer waiting in the upper room. The Holy Spirit is the earnest of our inheritance or the down payment. You might even refer to Him as the engagement ring to God's betrothed (2 Cor. 1:22; Eph. 1:13, 14). He is the assurance that Yeshua will return for His bride.

Names

Hebrew is not a language that can be translated word for word. Each letter has a numerical value and each word contains a complete thought, sometimes more than one thought. Hebrew names often contain a prophetic message, and we will be examining the names of those called by God concerning the things of the Tabernacle. Below are examples of this principle.

The first example is found in chapter five of the book of Genesis, in Adam's genealogy. The prophetic message is revealed in the connotations of the Hebrew names.

Adam means, *man*; Seth means, *appointed*; Enos means, *mortal*; Cainan means, *sorrow*; Mahalaleel means, *the blessed praised of God*; Jared means, *shall come down*; Enoch means, *teaching*; Methuselah means, *his death shall bring*; Lamech means, *the despairing*; Noah means, *rest/comfort*. Together their names prophesy the life and death of Yeshua. When we combine the meaning of the names they say: *Man is appointed mortal sorrow. The blessed praised of God shall come down teaching; his death shall bring the despairing rest and comfort.*

In this same passage of scripture, we find that *Methuselah* lived longer than any other man documented in the Bible (969 years); there is a reason for his longevity. Have you ever wondered why Methuselah lived so long? I did. As you can see above, his name prophesied that his death would bring something; that something was the flood of Noah. I will show you how I arrived at this conclusion by adding the age of Methuselah when his son, Lamech, was born, and the age of Lamech when his son, Noah, was born, and finally the age of Noah when the flood started. Methuselah was *187* when Lamech was born, *Lamech* was *182* when Noah was born, and *Noah* was *600* when the flood came. If we add the age of each man *187 + 182 + 600*, the total is *969*, which is the age of Methuselah at the time of his death. The Lord kept Methuselah alive until Noah finished the Ark (God's instrument of salvation for Noah and his family). Methuselah's death ushered in the flood that brought about a new beginning for the human race. The details in the Bible show us clearly the *depths*, *lengths*, *height*, and *breadth* of God's love if we will look. From the first words recorded in the Bible, God has been, and still is revealing His love.

After learning the prophetic message within Adam's genealogy, my spirit soared, ignited with enthusiasm. I launched a study of other genealogies in the Bible, searching for other prophetic messages in Biblical names. Through much prayer, the Lord allowed me to see a prophetic revelation in the names of the twelve tribes of Israel. After defining each name, I assumed the message was complete, but the Lord would not allow me to stop. I heard Him say, "go back and get Joseph's sons because they are also mine". He wanted to show me that His redemption plan included *all* men. The prophetic message is incomplete without Ephraim and Manasseh.

Please keep in mind that the Hebrew language cannot be translated word for word. One word can have several meanings and usually within the word is a complete thought. This concept is found within the names of Israel's sons. The order of the names is found in the forty- ninth chapter of the book of Genesis.

Reuben, means *behold a son*, Simeon, means *hearing,* Levi, means *joined,* Judah, means *praised*, Zebulun, means *dwelling*, Issachar, means *man of hire*, Dan, means *judge*, Gad, means *good fortune*, Asher, means *happy*, Naphtali, means *my wrestling* or *beating*, Joseph, means *may He* [*Jehovah*] *add*, Benjamin, means *son of the right hand.*

Israel added two other sons to this list, Ephraim and Manasseh (Gen. 48:5). It made no difference to Israel that Ephraim and Manasseh were half Egyptian (their mother was an Egyptian). Israel referred to them as his own sons, with the same status as Reuben and Simeon. Reuben and Simeon were Israel's first-born sons. It was customary to give a superior (double portion) blessing to the first-born. Israel's statement meant that Ephraim and Manasseh were entitled to the double portion. Israel's acceptance of Ephraim and Manasseh as his blood born sons provides a "shadow" of God adopting the Gentiles into His family. Just like Ephraim and Manasseh we (the Gentiles) are entitled to the same blessing and benefits as one blood born to Israel. The Bible tells us that in Yeshua, there is neither Jew nor Gentile, bond or free (1 Cor. 12:13; Gal. 3:28). Through Yeshua, we become something that never existed. We become *One New Man.*

The meaning of Ephraim is *doubly fruitful*, and Manasseh means *making to forget.* The prophetic message would be incomplete without the two adopted sons of Israel. Here is the message found in the names of the sons of Israel.

Behold a Son, hearing, joined to, and praised by God, dwelling as a man of hire to judge and bring good fortune and joy. His wrestling will beat the enemy; then God will add sons of His right hand. He is doubly fruitful, saving all those born of Israel (the Jew) and those adopted by Him (the Gentile), by refusing to remember their sins any more. Through Yeshua we have become *One New Man* (Eph. 2:11-22).

The number of letters in a name and the meaning of that number often reveal something about the person. The following are examples of this. Adam has 4 *letters; 4 is the number of the earth;* he was made from the ground (earth). Abram has *5 letters; 5 is the number of God's grace.* Abram believed God's promise and then God changed his name to Abraham. Abraham has *7 letters; 7 is the number of God's perfection.* God considered Abraham to be in perfect right standing with Him or that he was righteous.

Job has *3 letters; 3 is the number for sufficiency.* Job was God's suffering servant; his suffering foreshadowed the complete suffering of Yeshua. Everything the devil took from Job, God restored two-fold. Yeshua, like Job, had a two- fold blessing. Through Yeshua's complete suffering, both the Jew and the Gentile have been restored to a right relationship with the Father.

Matthew has seven letters; 7 is the number of God's perfection. Matthew wrote about the *Jewish Messiah*, the perfection of the Father. Mark, Luke and John all have four letters; 4 is the number of the earth. Mark wrote about the *suffering servant*. Luke wrote about the *Son of Man*. John wrote about the *Son of God*. Together these four men told the whole world that the Jewish Messiah would suffer as a man to reveal the love of God to all people.

The original text of the Bible was not divided into chapters and verses as we have them today. There are many translations that have made changes to the text, which has caused some to question the accuracy and truthfulness of the Bible. Even with all the changes, God's message remains the same. For example, in Genesis 2:7 you will find re-counted the *first Adam*; his sin became a part of all mankind. In Luke 2:7 is the birth of Yeshua, the *last Adam*, the man who would take away the sins of the world. Man's intervention cannot change the message of God to the world. It has always been His love for mankind revealed through His Son, our Savior, *Yeshua the Messiah.*

CHAPTER 4

Preparing to Build the Tabernacle

"And the LORD spake unto Moses, saying, Speak unto the children of Israel, that they bring me an offering: of every man that giveth it willingly with his heart ye shall take my offering. And this is the offering which ye shall take of them; gold, and silver, and brass, And blue, and purple, and scarlet, and fine linen, and goats' hair, And rams' skins dyed red, and badgers' skins, and shittim wood, Oil for the light, spices for anointing oil, and for sweet incense, Onyx stones, and stones to be set in the ephod, and in the breastplate. And let them make me a sanctuary; that I may dwell among them. According to all that I show thee, after the pattern of the tabernacle, and the pattern of all the instruments thereof, even so shall ye make it" (Ex. 25:1-9)."And the LORD spake unto Moses, saying, See, I have called by name Bezaleel the son of Uri, the son of Hur, of the tribe of Judah: And I have filled him with the spirit of God, in wisdom, and in understanding, and in knowledge, and in all manner of workmanship, To devise cunning works, to work in gold, and in silver, and in brass, And in cutting of stones, to set them, and in carving of timber, to work in all manner of workmanship. And I, behold, I have given with him Aholiab, the son of Ahisamach, of the tribe of Dan: and in the hearts of all that are wise hearted I have put wisdom, that they may make all that I have commanded thee; The tabernacle of the congregation, and the ark of the testimony, and the mercy seat that is thereupon, and all the furniture of the tabernacle, And the table

> and his furniture, and the pure candlestick with all his furniture, and the altar of incense, And the altar of burnt offering with all his furniture, and the laver and his foot, And the cloths of service, and the holy garments for Aaron the priest, and the garments of his sons, to minister in the priest's office, And the anointing oil, and sweet incense for the holy place: according to all that I have commanded thee shall they do" (Ex. 31:1-11).

Before beginning, there is one fact that must be determined. The "Tabernacle" was God's idea not mans'. He left no margin for error because the Tabernacle is a perfect "Shadow" of Yeshua. Man was not asked to make any decisions concerning its design or purpose. God alone gave the instructions to Moses in detail. God repeatedly told Moses to make everything according to the pattern that was shown to him on Mt. Sinai. The words *"all things according to the pattern showed Moses"* are used at least five different times (Ex. 25:9, 40; 27:8; Nu. 8:4; Acts 7:44; Heb. 8:5). God gave Moses the honor of seeing the "Heavenly Tabernacle", but with that privilege, came the tremendous responsibility of overseeing its construction and establishing its purpose. No other man except Yeshua has ever shouldered such responsibility. That is why God spoke with Moses face to face. "And the LORD spake unto Moses face to face, as a man speaketh unto his friend" (Ex. 33:11a).

Much of the Bible is devoted to the subject of the Tabernacle. There are *fifty* chapters in *five* different books--thirteen in Exodus, eighteen in Leviticus, thirteen in Numbers, two in Deuteronomy, and four in Hebrews. Obviously, the subject of the Tabernacle has a prominent place in the heart of God. We then, should make learning about it a priority.

God called His Tabernacle by different names; each name broadens its purpose. He called it Sanctuary; it was *the place set apart for a Holy God* (Ex. 25:8). He called it Tabernacle; it was *the dwelling place of God among His people* (Ex. 25:9). He called it Tent; it was *God's temporary dwelling place on the earth* (Ex. 26:36). He called it Tabernacle of the Congregation; it was *the place where God met with His people* (Ex. 29:42). And He called it Tabernacle of Testimony; it was where *Israel kept the covenant God made with them inside the Ark* (Ex. 38:21).

God selected two men to oversee the construction of the Tabernacle. He called them out by name and tribe (Ex. 31:1-11). These two men were anointed with superior wisdom and talent to reproduce the vision of the heavenly Tabernacle that was given to Moses. Their names are Bezaleel and Aholiab.

In the previous two chapters, the meaning of names was stressed in piecing together God's plan for the human race. God named John the Baptist, and Yeshua, and changed the name of Abram, Jacob and Peter just to mention a few. Hebrew names often reveal the persons character and calling, and that is certainly true of Bezaleel and Aholiab.

God chose Bezaleel, out of the tribe of Judah and Aholiab from the tribe of Dan (Ex. 31). He also gave reference to the father's names. The name of Bezaleel's father is Uri and the name of Aholiab's father is Ahisamach.

The Hebrew name Bezaleel means, *"under God's shadow"*. His father, Uri's, name means, *"Jehovah is Light"*. Their tribal name, Judah, means, *"Praised of God"*. The prophetic message in the Hebrew names is, *the "Shadow" of God reveals the light of Jehovah; the praised of God* (who is Yeshua). Yeshua is from the tribe of Judah. It was no coincidence that God chose Bezaleel, from the tribe of Judah, to oversee the building of the shadow of His Son. Bezaleel's tribal name draws attention to Yeshua, who is the Lion of the tribe of Judah.

The second man chosen by God was Aholiab. Aholiab's name means, *"Father's tent"*. His father, Ahisamach's name means, *my brother supports.* Their tribal name, Dan, means *judge or judgment.* The prophetic message found in Aholiab's name prophesied *that Yeshua would be the dwelling place of the Father* and his fathers name prophesied *that through Yeshua man would enter into a family relationship with Almighty God.* "One God and Father of all, who is above all, and through all, and in you all" (Eph. 4:6). Their tribal name, Dan, foretold the place of Yeshua as the judge of all men. "For the Father judgeth no man, but hath committed all judgment unto the Son" (Jn. 5:22).

The prophecies within the two tribal names, of Bezaleel and Aholiab, declare Yeshua the King of Kings and The Final Judge of All Men, and their given names reveal the Son of Man and the Son of God while at the same time declaring His purpose.

The Bible does not stipulate why God chose to include the father's names in this portion of scripture. Therefore, in my humble opinion, the father's names were recorded to show that God's plan for redemption encompassed those that had trusted in Him and had died before Yeshua came and fulfilled the covenant God promised to Abraham.

The Bible describes a place where the faithful were kept, called "Abraham's Bosom." In this passage of scripture, Luke is making a distinction between the rich man and Lazarus; a man who trusted in God. The rich man was in a place of torment while Lazarus was in a peaceful place (Abraham's Bosom); the two places were separated by a wide gulf (Luke 16: 22-31). The Bible teaches that Yeshua went and preached to the spirits in prison. "For Christ also hath once suffered for sins, the just for the unjust, that he might bring us to God, being put to death in the flesh, but quickened by the Spirit: By which also he went and preached unto the spirits in prison; Which sometime were disobedient, when once the longsuffering of God waited in the days of Noah, while the ark was a preparing, wherein few, that is, eight souls were saved by water" (1 Pet. 3:18-20). It also says that Yeshua led captivity captive. "Wherefore he saith, When he ascended up on high, *he led captivity captive*, and gave gifts unto men. (Now that he ascended, what is it but that he also descended first into the lower parts of the earth? He that descended is the same also that ascended up far above all heavens, that he might fill all things" (Eph. 4: 8-10; my emphasis). What does it mean to lead captivity captive? Yeshua descended into the bosom of Abraham where the faithful remained as described in the book of Luke (Luke 16: 22-31), and took all that were there with him at his resurrection. "And the graves were opened; and many bodies of the saints which slept arose, And came out of the graves after his resurrection, and went into the holy city, and appeared unto many" (Mat. 27: 52-53).

There is another revelation of Yeshua within the tribes of Bezaleel and Aholiab. God gave explicit instructions to Israel concerning the order of movement for each tribe's camp. Judah's camp moved out first, and Dan's camp moved out last (Nu. 2:9, 31). The prophetic revelation found in God's order is Yeshua the First and the Last, the Beginning and the End, the Alpha and the Omega, the Author and the Finisher of our faith (Isa. 44:6; Heb. 12:2; Rev. 1:8, 11, 17; 22:13). From the time of choosing the foremen, God began to reveal the "Shadow" of His Son. "Lift up your eyes on high, and behold who hath created these things, and *bringeth out their host by number: he calleth them all by names* and by the greatness of his might, for that he is strong in power; not one faileth" (Isa. 40:26; my emphasis). God speaks the end from the beginning (Isa. 46:10).

Prior to choosing the foremen, the Lord asked the children of Israel to bring an offering of gold, silver, brass, animal skins, precious gems, and beautiful colors of blue, purple, and scarlet, fine white linen, wood, oil, spices and sweet incense.

The children of Israel were in the middle of the wilderness when God asked them for this extravagant offering. How could they provide such things for Him? The Egyptian spoils gathered by Israel became the materials used to build God's dwelling place. God tried the heart of His people to see if they would willingly give back what was needed to build the Tabernacle, His dwelling place (Ex. 25:2-9). The people gave so much that Moses had to restrain them from giving (Ex. 36:6, 7). Each person gave something. Although God did not call each person by name, as He did Bezaleel and Aholiab, it took everyone working together with the Lord, to fulfill the "Shadow" of God's plan of redemption. God desires to have all believers participate with Him to accomplish His work in the earth. He provides everything needed, the believer's part is obedience. The completion of the Tabernacle meant that once again the Lord God could fellowship with His people (Ex. 25:8).

Every measurement of the Tabernacle, the gold, the silver, the brass, the colors, the pure white linen, the needlework, the different coverings, the wood, etc., are contributory in revealing the shadow of Yeshua, His life and His death. God uses every item to reveal His plan for restoring man's rightful position with Him through the blood of His Son, Yeshua.

God's Holy presence resided in the midst of his people inside the Tabernacle, above the Ark of the Covenant. The objective and design of the Tabernacle and its sacrificial system was to guide man to Yeshua, who was the embodied presence of God in the earth. Through Yeshua, God the Father once again walked and talked with His beloved creation teaching them His ways as He did in the beginning with Adam.

Do you realize that you, as a believer, are the habitation of God and you are a member of His household (1 Cor. 3:16, Eph. 2:19, Heb. 3:6)?

As we begin examining in detail the height, breadth, and length of the Tabernacle and its furnishings, I have chosen Paul's prayer for the Ephesians as the prayer for all who read this book. "For this cause I bow my knees unto the Father of our Lord Jesus Christ, of whom the whole family in heaven and earth is named, that He would grant you, according to the riches of His glory, to be strengthened with might by His Spirit in the inner man; that Christ may dwell in your hearts by faith; that ye, being rooted and grounded in love, may be able to comprehend with all saints what is the *breadth*, and *length*, and *depth,* and *height*; and to know the love of Christ, which passeth knowledge, that ye might be filled with all the fullness of God (Eph. 3:14-19).

The King James translation of the Bible best describes Yeshua as the True Tabernacle. The 35th chapter of Exodus refers to every article of furniture and the building as *HIS.*

> "The Tabernacle, HIS tent, and HIS covering, HIS thatches, and HIS boards, and HIS bars, HIS pillars, and HIS sockets, the ark, and the staves thereof, with the mercy seat, and the veil of the covering, the table, and HIS staves, and HIS vessels, and the showbread, the candlestick also for the light, and HIS furniture, and HIS lamps with the oil for the light, and the incense altar, and HIS staves, and the anointing oil and the sweet incense, and the hanging for the door at the entering in of the tabernacle. The altar of burnt offering, with HIS brazen grate, HIS staves, and all HIS vessels, the laver and HIS foot, the hangings of the court, HIS pillars, and their sockets, and the hangings for the door of the court, the pins of the tabernacle, and the pins of the court and their cords, the clothes of service, to do service in the holy place, the holy garments for Aaron the priest, and the garments for his sons, to minister in the priests' office" (Ex. 35:11-19).

As we continue, I will be using the word *"Shadow"* in reference to things found in the Tabernacle. Therefore, to help you understand what I mean by using the term, "Shadow", the following definition was taken from Strong's Exhaustive Concordance of the Bible. Strong's Concordance defines shadow, as used in Hebrews 8:5, as an *adumbration.* Webster's dictionary defines adumbration as (1) a sketchy outline, (2) to foreshadow, (3) to disclose partially or gradually. It defines foreshadow as to give a hint or suggestion of something beforehand, to represent beforehand.

As we begin our detailed look into the Tabernacle, you will begin to see the "Shadow"" of Yeshua. You will see Him as the place where the fullness of God dwelt in the Ark of the

Covenant. The Mercy Seat reveals that through Yeshua justice met grace. He is seen as the glory of His Father in the cloud above the Mercy Seat. The Candlestick portrays Yeshua as the Light of the World. The Table is the place of fellowship where the priest shared the Showbread. The Showbread is a shadow of Yeshua as the Bread of Life, the Living Bread. The hidden mystery of redemption is revealed through the four coverings of the Tabernacle. The coverings present Yeshua as the protected righteousness of the believer. He is the one who became sin for humanity, and paid the price of redemption for the world. His glory was hidden behind flesh so that man could look upon Him and live. The Cross of Calvary is revealed by the Brazen Altar. The cleansing power of the Word of God is found in the Laver. The power in the name Yeshua is seen in the Golden Altar of Incense. The enabling power of the Holy Spirit is represented in the Anointing Oil and the Incense. Yeshua's robe of righteousness that covers every believer is demonstrated through the Outer Court Hangings (the fence). The impartiality of God's love for the human race is manifested in the Cords used to support the Outer Court fence. The Nails or Pins that secured the Cords show that the judgment Yeshua suffered anchors the relationship between God and men. The Gate demonstrates that Yeshua is the only way to the Father. The Door is the entrance into the place of fellowship. Truth is the guide to fellowship. Yeshua is Truth. The Veil is the entrance to the throne of God; behind it is eternal life. Yeshua is Life. The priesthood established the need for an intercessor. Yeshua is the mediator between God and men (1Tim. 2:5).

The five offerings describe the complete surrender of Yeshua to become the sacrifice for humanity. He fulfilled the Whole Burnt Offering by yielding to the death sentence that rightfully belonged to man. The Meat Offering exposed Yeshua's perfect character and suffering. Through the Peace Offering He reconciled man's relationship with God. Yeshua suffered the penalty for sin and satisfied the Sin Offering.

Yeshua never trespassed any of God's law. He fulfilled the Trespass Offering by becoming the advocate for those who have trespassed and need forgiveness. The Atonement Money is the price that was required for redemption. Yeshua's death was the Atonement for the redemption of the world.

The Tabernacle was divided into three sections, the Outer Court, the Holy Place and the Holy of Holies. The Outer Court was where the sacrifices were burned on the Altar. The Holy Place was where the priest ate the showbread, tended the lamps and prayed at the Golden Alter of Incense; it was the place of fellowship. The Holy of Holies was where the Ark of the Covenant was kept; it was representative of God's throne. Each of the three sections of the Tabernacle distinguishes a different period of time. The Outer Court – yesterday, where His sacrifice was made. The Holy Place – today, where believers commune with God, and The Holy of Holies – where believers spend eternity in His presence.

There are specific materials and colors used throughout the Tabernacle, and they either describe characteristics of Yeshua or His purpose. Gold represents Deity, Silver represents Atonement, and Brass represents Judgment. The colors are blue, purple, scarlet, and pure white. Blue denotes heaven, purple represents royalty, scarlet signifies blood, and white is symbolic of righteousness. Goat's hair denotes sin. Ram's skin dyed red points to the blood of Yeshua. Badger's skin reveals the security found in Yeshua. Shittim wood is a picture of the incorruptible humanity of Yeshua. Oil is figurative of the Holy Spirit. Sweet spices are symbolic of the sweet smelling savor of Yeshua's sinless life. The Veil is representative of Yeshua's body of flesh.

With this foundational information, we are ready to begin an in-depth study of the Tabernacle.

CHAPTER 5

The Ark of the Covenant

"And they shall make an ark of Shittim wood: two cubits and a half shall be the length thereof, and a cubit and a half the breadth thereof, and a cubit and a half the height thereof. And thou shalt overlay it with pure gold, within and without shalt thou overlay it, and shalt make upon it a crown of gold round about. And thou shalt cast four rings of gold for it, and put them in the four corners thereof; and two rings shall be in the one side of it, and two rings in the other side of it. And thou shalt make staves of shittim wood, and overlay them with gold. And thou shalt put the staves into the rings by the sides of the ark that the ark may be borne with them. The staves shall be in the rings of the ark: they shall not be taken from it" (Ex. 25:10-15).

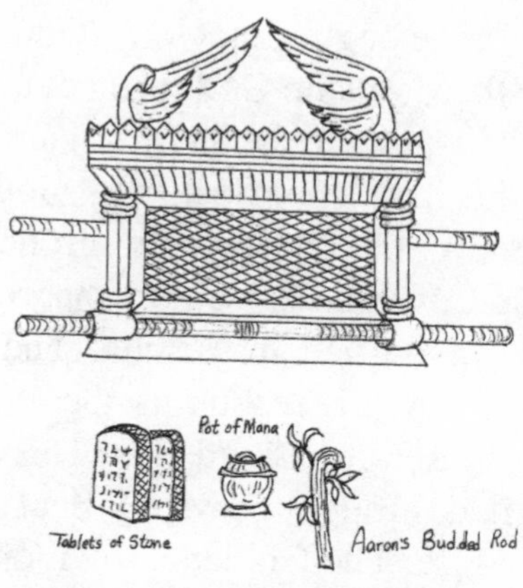

The Ark of the Covenant

The Ark of the Covenant was and still is precious to the people of Israel. It epitomizes the power and the presence of the Great I Am. The Ark always preceded the people as they moved from place to place. It was carried onto the field of battle, and when the enemy saw the Ark, they were terrified, because the presence of the Ark meant that God, the Holy One of Israel, was with His people. God's Holy presence filled the Tabernacle when Aaron was consecrated into the priesthood. God's Shekinah (glory) was so powerful that Moses was not able to enter the Tabernacle as long as it remained. The same thing happened when the priest carried the dismantled Tabernacle and the Ark of the Covenant into Solomon's temple (1 Ki. 8:4-11).

Our journey through the Tabernacle begins with the building of the Ark of the Covenant and its Mercy Seat. Most authors and lecturers, when presenting the Tabernacle, begin on the outside and make their way to the Ark of the Covenant. In order to comprehend the message of redemption found in the Tabernacle, it is important to begin as God did, with the Ark of the Covenant.

All things began with God. He gave the instructions for the Ark first, for Man must first believe that God is before he can accept what He has done (Heb. 11:6). The first words recorded in the Bible are, "In the beginning God" (Gen. 1:1) God said "I am he: before me there was no God formed, neither shall there be after me", and "Yes, before the day was I am he" (Isa. 43:10b, 13a). The Ark, with its Mercy Seat, was God's throne in the earth. It is a "Shadow" of His heavenly throne.

The Ark of the Covenant presents a shadow of the fullness of God that was personified in Yeshua. The contents in the Ark are representations of Yeshua as the Word of God, the Eternal High Priest, and the Bread from Heaven. We will see His purpose fulfilled through the Mercy Seat and His Glory in the Cloud and the Fire. The Golden Crown of the Ark reveals Yeshua's position as the eternal King of Kings.

Our travel through the Tabernacle will be visited from God's perspective. We will experience the passion of God's heart as He discloses more and more about Himself and His plan to redeem humanity. Sin separated all of humanity from their Creator, and God desired to show them how to reestablish a relationship with Him. That is precisely what He did, beginning with the Ark of the Covenant

God began with Himself making His way through the Tabernacle to the Gate where sinful man remains without hope. God, the Creator of the universe, stretches forth His loving and forgiving hands beckoning all men to come and enter with Him into an intimate relationship. He desires to guide them through the Tabernacle, as He reveals Himself little by little, until they come to the place behind the Veil, into His presence. God takes us from glory to glory until we reach our journey's end with Him for eternity. "But we all, with open face beholding as in a glass the glory of the Lord, are changed into the same image from glory to glory, even as by the Spirit of the Lord" (2 Cor. 3:18). "For now we see through a glass, darkly; but then face to face: now I know in part; but then shall I know even as also I am known" (1 Cor. 13:12).

With each step, you will learn more about Yeshua, God's gift of love (Jn. 3:16). The design of each item inside the Tabernacle discloses more about Yeshua, who is the only way back to the Father. "Jesus saith unto him, I am the way, the truth, and the life: no man cometh unto the Father, but by me" (Jn. 14:6). God made it simple; the only thing He requires of man is to trust Him enough to take hold of His hands and follow Him. God's heart is pictured in the smallest details. His love pervades in the height, depth, and length of the Tabernacle's furnishings beginning with the Ark of the Covenant.

The size and design of the Ark: The dimensions of the Ark are measured in Cubits. A cubit is the length of a man's arm from the elbow to the end of the middle finger, about eighteen inches. The Ark was two and a half cubits long, one and a half cubits wide, and one and a half cubits high. A close examination of the measurements of the Ark reveals the message of God's ultimate gift of love. That message is God will give man a new beginning through His Son, Yeshua the Messiah.

According to Ervin N. Hershberger's research concerning the size and design of the Ark, the Ark's ***vertical girth*** [height] is figured by multiplying its **4** sides by **1 1/2**, which equals **6** cubits. To figure the ***horizontal girth,*** we first need to multiply its **2** long sides by **2 1/2,** making the overall length **5** cubits; then multiply the remaining **2** sides by **1 1/2,** making the overall width **3** cubits. The horizontal girth is equal to the length plus the width (**5** + **3**), which is **8** cubits.[4] The meaning associated with each of these numbers is what reveals the prophetic message above. I will explain. The complete vertical measurement is ***6***, the number identified with ***man***. God became a man; that man was Yeshua. "And the Word was made flesh, and dwelt among us,(and we beheld his glory, the glory as of the only begotten of the Father, full of grace and truth" (Jn. 1:14).

The length of the Ark is ***5,*** the number associated with the ***grace of God***. Yeshua is the greatest gift of God's grace to man. "For God so loved the world that he gave his only begotten Son, that whosoever believeth in him should not perish, but have everlasting life" (Jn. 3:16). The width is ***3***, which characterizes the Holy Trinity. The fullness of God resided in Yeshua. "For in him dwelleth all the fullness of the Godhead bodily" (Col. 2:9). The combined horizontal measurement (5 + 3) is ***8***. Number eight stands for the ***new beginning*** that comes to every man through Yeshua the Messiah. "Therefore if any man be in Christ, he is a new creature: old things are passed away; behold, all things are become new" (2 Cor. 5:17). As you can see, the message in the measurement of the Ark is clear. *God gives man A NEW BEGINNING through His Son, Yeshua the Messiah.*

The Ark was made of *Acacia wood* and *Pure gold.* The materials draw attention to the person, position and character of Yeshua.

Wood throughout the Tabernacle depicts the human strength of Yeshua. He was a root out of dry ground (Isa. 53:2).

Acacia *wood,* the wood used to build the furniture of the Tabernacle, has indestructible qualities. It is an extremely hard wood resistant to heat and decay. Through it, we see the incorruptible strength of Yeshua. His body, like the burning bush, would see no corruption (Ex. 3; Ps. 16:10; Acts 2:27, 13:35, Acts 2:30-32). His body did not stay in the ground long enough to decay; He rose from the grave on the third day (Rom. 6:4; 2 Cor. 4:14; Eph. 1:20). Yeshua's body was preordained to be man's substitute on the cross (Heb. 10:5).

Pure gold is crystal clear. The book of Revelation describes the New Jerusalem as having streets of pure gold as clear as Crystal. Gold is known as the most precious metal in the earth. It is also a symbol of deity. Its use in the Tabernacle is a figure of the deity of Messiah and His Heavenly Kingdom. The Kingdom of Heaven is described as a pearl of great price; when a wise man finds it, he will give up all that he has to have it (Mat. 13:44-46). The Kingdom of God is not for sale. There is one way in and that is through Messiah Yeshua.

The design of the Ark foretells the eternal objective of the Messiah. The Ark had three layers; it was wood overlaid with pure gold inside and out. The *first layer of pure gold* is figurative of Yeshua's heavenly position; He is the Son of God. He was with the Father in the beginning. He began as deity. The *middle layer of wood* reveals the human quality of Yeshua. He is the Son of Man. He gave up His position in heaven to be made like us (Phil. 2:8), to be the representative of God to man (Heb. 2:17), and to be man's Advocate, standing between man and the Father's wrath (1 Tim. 2:5, 1 Jn. 2:1). Yeshua fulfilled His purpose through His humanity, not His deity. The *third layer of pure gold* denotes Yeshua's position now. He has ascended back to the Father and is seated at the Father's right hand (Col. 3:1).

There is another "shadow" within the gold and wood of the Ark. It is one of the believer. The believer, represented by (the wood), is sandwiched between (the Gold) the Lord of the New Covenant, and (the gold) the God of the Old Covenant. "for the LORD will go before you; and the God of Israel will be your rearward" (Isa. 52:12b).Praise His name! Our life is hidden with Messiah in God (Col. 3:3).

The ***crown*** of the Ark is a symbol of authority and majesty. God longed to reign over Israel as their king and relate to them through the high priest, but Israel rejected Him as king. The people appealed to God to give them a man to reign over them (I Sam. 8:4-7). God chose Saul to be the king. Saul's reign brought much suffering to the people of Israel. Rebellion always results in suffering. Many are quick to judge Israel's rejection of God as their king, but the generation that left Egypt had never related to God as their fathers had. Under the Egyptian rule, the Israelites were subjected to the pagan worship of gods made of wood, stone, gold, silver and brass, things both visible and physical. The God of Abraham, Isaac, and Jacob, the One True God is Spirit, therefore, the people could not relate to an invisible God. The children of Israel were removed from their place of safety, the only place they had ever known, to go into a foreign land to worship a God that they did not understand. Although God appeared to them in miraculous ways, unlike their ancestors, they had lost the intimate relationship with God. God knew it would take time for His people to come to know Him again. The Tabernacle and its sacrificial system is how he chose to reveal Himself, little by little. God tolerated Israel's rebellion, because He knew that one day Yeshua the Messiah would be the man who would reign over them as their King. " His appearing will be brought about in its own time by the blessed and sole Sovereign, who is King of Kings and Lord of Lords, who alone is immortal, who dwells in unapproachable light that no human being has ever seen or can see - to him be honor and eternal power. Amen" (1 Tim. 6:15-16).

The day is coming when all people will see Yeshua coming in the clouds, and He will be wearing the garments of a King.

On His robe and on His thigh is written KING of KINGS and LORD of LORDS (Rev. 19:12b, 13, 16). A good king provides for His subjects. He blesses and protects them as God's presence did for the children of Israel. Today, the life of every believer is kept and protected in Messiah Yeshua because He is both the Ark of the Lord and the Lord of the Ark.

Moses placed three items inside the Ark as a memorial for the children of Israel--*the tablets of stone, the golden pot of manna, and Aaron's rod* (Ex.16:32-33; Nu. 17:10; Heb. 9:3-4).

The *Stone tablets* were placed inside the Ark to remind Israel that God's promises are eternal. The tablets, often referred to as the Ten Commandments, are also known as the *Ketuba,* God's marriage covenant with Israel. The tablets are the hand-written promise of God's eternal love; they are His wise counsel for all who will obey them.

Generally, people don't read the Bible; therefore, it is impossible for them to know what God says, much less do as He says. Man was and still is unfaithful to his Creator. Yeshua is the only man who followed God's perfect council. He obeyed every word (Acts 10:38-39; Heb. 2:10, 5:8-9). The "shadow" revealed in the unbroken tablets is the sinless obedience of Yeshua. He is the WORD who was with God in the beginning; who became the LIVING WORD (Jn. 1:1-2, 14). Yeshua is the promised Prophet who revealed the certainty of God's Word to His people (Deut. 18:15; Mk. 6:4; Jn 6:14, 7:40; Acts 3:22, 7:37).

The *golden pot of manna* was placed inside the Ark to remind the people of God's sustaining power. Manna was food from heaven (Ex. 16:32-33). The children of Israel journeyed through the wilderness on their way to the Promised Land, and they became hungry. As a result, they griped and whined about leaving the succulent foods of Egypt behind. God heard their murmurings and told Moses to "speak unto them, saying, at even ye shall eat flesh, and in the morning ye shall be filled with bread; and ye shall know that I am the Lord your God" (Ex. 16:12). When evening came, quails covered the camp. The people continued to eat until the meat began to emanate from their nose. The next morning, when the dew had dried up, they saw small round things that resembled frost on the ground and said, "Manna", which means *what is this?* "It was white like coriander seed, and the taste of it was like wafers made with honey" (Ex. 16:31).

God continued to feed the children of Israel with the HEAVENLY BREAD called *"Manna"* until they entered into the Promised Land. Manna, the Bread from heaven, continued for forty years. The Manna was God's life sustaining gift to His people.

Through the Manna, God provided a "shadow" of Yeshua as THE BREAD OF LIFE, THE LIVING BREAD that came down from the Father in heaven. Yeshua said that His flesh is the gift of life to all who will receive it (Jn. 6:32-35, 48, 51, 58). Yeshua is God's eternal provision that is offered to all people.

Aaron's Rod was placed in the Ark to remind the people of God's resurrecting power (Nu. 17:3, 8, 10; Heb. 9:4). It was also to remind them of God's Sovereignty and of His everlasting covenant. You can read about Aaron's rod in Numbers 16 and 17. Chapters 16 and 17 record the rebellion against God's placement of Aaron in the office of the High Priest by three of Israel's leaders, Korah, of the tribe of Levi, Dathan and Abiram, of the tribe of Reuben. Their rebellion was not tolerated.

God commanded Moses to have the head of each of the twelve tribes inscribe their name on a rod and bring it to the Tabernacle. Aaron's name was inscribed on the rod for the tribe of Levi. Through the inscribed rods, the children of Israel would know, without question, who God had assigned the position of authority over the priesthood.

Aaron's rod was from the Almond tree. The almond tree is the first tree to produce fruit in Israel as early as January. The Lord had Moses put each of the twelve rods in front of the Ark. The next morning, when the people came to the Tabernacle, they saw that Aaron's rod had buds, blossoms, and yielded almonds. The power of God restored life to Aaron's dead rod; so there was no denying that God had chosen Aaron to be the High Priest. Aaron's rod provides man with the "shadow" of Yeshua as the Great High Priest. His High Priestly term will never end because He will never die (Heb. 7:21-28).

The second revelation found in Aaron's rod is the "Shadow" of resurrection. The restored life of Aaron's rod is the "shadow" of Yeshua's resurrected body. He was the first fruits from the dead. "But now is Christ risen from the dead, and become the firstfruits of them that slept. For since by man came death, by man came also the resurrection of the dead. For as in Adam all die, even so in Christ shall all be made alive. But every man in his own order: Christ the firstfruits; afterward they that are Christ's at his coming" (I Cor. 15:20-23).

Through Paul's writings, the Lord gave the following passage to comfort and instill hope that eternal resurrection belongs to everyone who believes. "But I would not have you to be ignorant, brethren, concerning them which are asleep, that ye sorrow not, even as others which have no hope. For if we believe that Jesus died and rose again, even so them also which sleep in Jesus will God bring with him. For this we say unto you by the word of the Lord, that we which are alive and remain unto the coming of the Lord shall not prevent them which are asleep. For the Lord himself shall descend from heaven with a shout, with the voice of the archangel, and with the trump of God: and the dead in Christ shall rise first: Then we which are alive and remain shall be caught up together with them in the clouds, to meet the Lord in the air: and so shall we ever be with the Lord. Wherefore comfort one another with these words" (1 Thess. 4:13-18).

The third revelation in Aaron's rod is the power and authority of Yeshua. A rod is a symbol of authority; another word for rod is *scepter*. When Jacob blessed his sons, he said of Judah, "The Scepter will not pass from Judah, nor the ruler's staff from between his legs, until he come to whom obedience belongs;

and it is He whom the peoples will obey" (Gen. 49:10). The prophetic words of this passage point to the future descendant of Judah, Yeshua; the one to whom obedience belongs. Before Him, every knee will bow and every tongue will confess that He is Lord (Phil. 2:10-11).

The forth revelation found in the inscribed rods is the prophetic message to all who have accepted Yeshua as Savior and Lord. Earlier, in chapter 1, I explained that exchanging names and symbols of authority are part of the process of entering into a blood covenant. The inscription of the tribal names on each rod represents the continuance of the covenant God entered into with Abraham and points us to Yeshua who is the fulfillment of that covenant. When God added one of the letters of His name to Abraham, the Hebrew letter He chose exemplifies *"His life's Breath"* (Gen. 17:5). So in essence, God breathed His life into Abraham. Yeshua followed the Fathers' example fulfilling God's covenant when He breathed on His disciples. "And when he had said this, he breathed on them, and saith unto them, Receive ye the Holy Ghost:" (Jn. 20:22).

It is essential that we catch on to this principal if we expect to live in the abundance God provides. Faith is how to appropriate the promises of God. For instance, God circumcises the heart of each believer by writing His WORD on each heart. Yeshua is synonymous with the "Word of God" (Jn. 1:1, 14; Jer. 31:33). Yeshua's name releases His power and the authority. All of the authority of heaven stands behind the name of Yeshua. His name is above every name that is named (Phil. 2:9). In other words, God exchanges names with those who believe. We cannot see the inscription of His name; therefore, we must believe His promise. The inscribed names were a "Shadow" of Gods' ever-growing Covenant to include the untold number of those still coming to believe in Messiah Yeshua.

Blood covenant is so powerful, even the descendents of the covenant partners have access to its promises. Here is an example, God changed Sarai's name to Sarah by adding the same

Hebrew letter He used in Abraham's name. Abraham and Sarah became one with God through faith in His blood Covenant. Just as Sarah was included in the relationship between God and Abraham, our children will also have the opportunity to enter into a relationship with God. God has promised to give His life to our children that His name might live on in them (Deut. 30:6). He has written the name of every person who has trusted in Him in the book of life (Phil. 4:3; Rev. 3:5, 21:27). Yeshua, the Great High Priest, carries the names of all who believe before the Father and the angels (Rev. 3:5). One day, Yeshua will write His NEW name on all of His children. When we enter into the covenant with God through Yeshua, we cannot see the mark that is made in our heart to prove that Yeshua's name is written there; therefore, we live by faith, just like Abraham (2 Cor. 5:7). Every time the Father looks upon a circumcised heart, He remembers His covenant, because He sees the name of His Beloved Son written there. The visible result of a circumcised heart is a changed life.

The rod, the inscription of Aaron's name, and the type of wood, reveal Yeshua as the Great Eternal High Priest, the Resurrected Redeemer, and the Eternal Covenant Partner of the Father. All of those who are in Yeshua have been given the benefits of His covenant. Yeshua has secured our salvation and sealed the covenant promise by giving the Holy Spirit as the guarantee that He will return for all who have received eternal life (Jn. 14:1-3; 2 Cor. 1:22; Eph. 1:13-14, 4:30).

SUMMARY OF THE CONTENTS:

1. **The Tablets of Stone** = *THE WORD OF GOD* = Yeshua the true PROPHET (Deut. 18:15, 18, 19; Jn. 12:49-50)
2. **The Golden Pot of Manna** = *THE BREAD OF LIFE* = Yeshua, the true BREAD that came from heaven. He is the giver of everlasting life, THE SAVIOR (Jn. 6:32, 33, 48-51)

3. **<u>Aaron's Rod that Budded</u>** = *RESURRECTED LIFE* = Yeshua the *RISEN LORD, THE TRUE HIGH PRIEST, MESSIAH, KING OF KINGS* and *LORD OF LORDS, THE ETERNAL COVENANT PARTNER OF GOD.* The scepter will continually be in His hand. (1 Cor. 15:20-23, Heb. 7:21-28, Gen. 49:10, Ps. 45:6, Heb. 1:8)

***<u>Note</u> * by the time of Solomon's Temple, the only item left inside the Ark was the tablets of stone [Ketuba] (1 Kings 8:9). How sad, Israel had lost to the enemy the "shadow" given by God to recognize He who gives everlasting life, the *One* who is the eternal High Priest, the Messiah, and King of Kings and Lord of Lords. Even so, God's marriage covenant [the Ketuba] is with Israel forever, and one day they ALL will recognize HIM.**

> **<u>The Mercy Seat</u>:** "And thou shalt make a mercy seat of pure gold: two cubits and a half shall be the length thereof, and a cubit and a half the breadth thereof. And thou shalt make two cherubim of gold; of beaten work shalt thou make them, in the two ends of the mercy seat. And make one cherub on the one end, and the other cherub on the other end: even of the mercy seat shall ye make the cherubim on the two ends thereof. And the cherubim shall stretch forth their wings on high, covering the mercy seat with their wings, and their faces shall look one to another; toward the mercy seat shall the faces of the cherubim be. And thou shalt put the mercy seat above upon the ark; and in the ark thou shalt put the testimony that I shall give thee" (Ex. 25:17-22).

The Mercy Seat was made from one piece of beaten gold. It fit securely inside the Crown of the Ark and was adorned with two cherubim. The Mercy Seat covered and protected the contents of the Ark that reveal the character of God in Messiah.

The cherubim reveal the ever-present ministry of the angels to God. Angels are ministering spirits to God and to his children (Heb. 1:13-14). The angels of God minister to those who are heirs to salvation, because the Spirit of God lives in every believer. Therefore, the protection overseen by the angels is a benefit because of God's Holy presence, not because of the believer's righteousness.

Angels always accompany God. The kneeling outstretched position of the cherubim on the Mercy Seat represents two things. First, kneeling is the position of worship. Second, their outstretched wings both concealed and protected the Ark and its contents. The presence of the cherubim revealed that God was there. The Mercy Seat was God's throne in the earth (Ex. 25:22). Thousands upon thousands of angels surround His heavenly throne; they act as a protective barrier against anything unholy, as they continually proclaim "HOLY, HOLY, HOLY, Lord God Almighty, which was and is, and is to come!" (Rev. 4:8).

Ezekiel saw God riding on the wind. He described the breathtaking appearance of the angels that surround God (Ezek. 1:1-28). They, like the Cherubim on the Mercy Seat, acted as a warning to anyone entering into the presence of the Holy One of Israel.

The cherubim on the Mercy Seat warned the High Priest not to enter without the cleansing blood of the sin offering. Yeshua is the sin offering for all mankind. He is the LAMB of GOD (Jn. 1:29). The angels ministered to Yeshua after the onslaught of the devil's temptations (Mt. 4:11). The manifestation of the angels with Yeshua declares the indwelling presence of God (Jn. 1:14). Yeshua could have, at any time, called upon the angels to help Him, but He chose not to for the sake of man (Mt. 26:53). It was the angel of the Lord that descended from heaven and rolled the stone away from Yeshua's tomb, revealing the LIVING MERCY SEAT OF GOD to Mary Magdalene. "But Mary Magdalene stood without at the sepulcher weeping: and as she wept, she stooped down, and looked into the sepulcher, *and seeth two angels in white sitting, the one at the head, and the other at the feet where the body of Yeshua had lain*" (Jn. 20:11-12; my emphasis).

The two angels that Mary saw were not kneeling anymore. They did not have their wings stretched out concealing anything, because the One they worshipped, their Creator, Messiah Yeshua, was not there any more. He had risen from the grave to live forever. Yeshua's blood fulfilled the purpose of the Mercy Seat of the Tabernacle.

Yeshua blessed Mary with the privilege of delivering the first gospel message. Yeshua sent Mary to those He referred to as His brethren. She had the privilege of telling them things have changed; God is still your God, but He has also become your Father (Jn. 20:17). You are no longer the people of God; you are the family of God (Eph. 2:19-22; Heb. 3:6).

God provided no measurement for the thickness of the Mercy Seat. The omission of a measurement unveils the boundless mercy of God. His mercy lives forever through Yeshua. Yeshua's Sacrifice paid the penalty required by God for ALL sin revealing the boundless gift of God's mercy.

Annually the high priest of the Tabernacle sprinkled blood from the sin offering on the Mercy Seat, for himself first and then for the people. Yeshua, operating in the office of the Great High Priest, carried His own blood into the heavenly Holy of Holies and poured it on the Mercy Seat, once and for all times, for the sin of the world (Heb. 9:12, 22-28).

The angels no longer pose a threat to those who enter by the blood of Yeshua. Yeshua is God's gift of mercy offered to every man without measure (Jn. 3:16; I Jn. 2:2, 4:10; Acts 4:12; 1 Tim. 2:5).

The three dimensional design of the Mercy Seat, made from one piece of beaten gold, reveals the unity of God and the singleness of His purpose. Finally, God was re-united with His creation. "Let us therefore come boldly unto the throne of grace, that we may obtain mercy, and find grace to help in time of need" (Heb. 4:16).

* **A DAY IS COMING WHEN GOD WILL POUR OUT HIS WRATH WITHOUT MERCY** * (Rev. 19:11-21) **Please don't let this happen to you! You can receive mercy today by asking the Father to forgive you and accepting His gift of eternal life that comes through believing that Yeshua is the Son of God and that He died for your sin and rose from the grave. He took your place and gave you His. Yeshua is the FATHER'S GIFT TO YOU.** "For God so loved the world, that he gave his only begotten Son, that whosoever believeth in him should not perish, but have everlasting life" (Jn. 3:16).

The Pillar of the Cloud and the Pillar of the Fire: God called Israel out from the other nations and set them apart to teach them His ways so that He could show Himself to the world through them. Israel was the smallest of all nations (Deut. 7:6-11). The Israelites numbered between 2,500,000 and 3,000,000. Their campsite around the Tabernacle is estimated to have covered twelve square miles. The daily provisions needed to feed and provided water for that many people would fill thirty railroad boxcars with food and three hundred tank cars with water. When they moved from place to place, if they traveled fifty abreast, the procession would stretch for forty miles. I think we fail to appreciate the extent of God's miraculous power that kept His people for forty years. They were in the middle of the desert wilderness; water obviously was limited, but God caused water to flow out of the rock at Meribah (Ex. 17:5-7). Archeologist located the place where they believe this event took place. The pressure of the water flow was so powerful that the rocks in the area are smooth. A deep river bed exists there today, however, the water has long since dried up. God provided three million people with water for forty years until they entered the Promised Land.

God used the pillar of the cloud and of the fire to reveal His heart to His people. The manifestation of the pillars showed the people that God was always with them. He used the pillars as a means to *guide, shelter, and protect* His people. "And the LORD went before them by day in a pillar of a cloud, to lead them the way; and by night in a pillar of fire, to give them light; to go by day and night: He took not away the pillar of the cloud by day, nor the pillar of fire by night, from before the people." (Ex. 13:21-22)

A pillar signifies power. According to Webster's Dictionary, "1) it is an upright, slender structure used as a building support or as a monument: 2) it is also a person who is a chief supporter of a state, institution, etc."[5]

The sight of the pillar of the cloud and of the fire comforted God's people. The pillars extended to the heavens so that all of the people, no matter how far their tents were from the Tabernacle, could see them. The pillars acted as shields from the blistering heat of the desert sun, and provided warmth in the cold desert night. At night, the Pillar of the fire concealed the stars and the moon, so that the people of Israel were protected from the influence of the surrounding nations who were worshipers of such things. God put Himself between His people and those things that would cause them to sin, just as He does today. He is a jealous God and His desire is for all of His people to stay focused solely on Him. God requires holiness because He is holy: "Sanctify yourselves therefore, and be ye holy: for I am the LORD your God (Lev. 20:7). "As obedient children, not fashioning yourselves according to the former lusts in your ignorance: But as he which hath called you is holy, so be ye holy in all manner of conversation; Because it is written, Be ye holy; for I am holy" (1 Pet. 1:14-16).

God also commands obedience; the people were not to move unless He did. "And when the cloud was taken up from over the tabernacle, the children of Israel went onward in all their journeys: But if the cloud was not taken up, then they journeyed not till the day that it was taken up. For the cloud of the LORD was upon the tabernacle by day, and fire was on it by night, in the sight of all the house of Israel, throughout all their journeys" (Ex. 40:34-38, Nu. 9:15-23).

Many churches mistakenly teach new believers that everything will be rosy if they are following God. However, that is not always the case as we see with the children of Israel. As they followed the Lord, the pillar would sometimes stop in unpleasant places. At other times, the people rested where things were good; nevertheless, the people did not move until God moved.

The process of learning how to trust is often difficult. God's leading is not always to pleasant places. He moves the believer out of his/her comfort zone so that they will learn to be dependent on Him. Sometimes in our zealousness to do "work for the Lord", we move too fast and get ahead of Him, or through fear we fail to move at all. Failure to keep our eyes on the Lord makes us vulnerable to the temptations of sin, and we find ourselves in places He never intended for us to be. Moving out without Him is like walking about in total darkness.

As a Man, Yeshua was tempted in all ways, yet he did not sin (Heb. 4:15). We must strive to be like Yeshua who did nothing unless he heard the voice of His Father (Jn. 8:26, 38). "For I have not spoken of myself; but the Father which sent me, he gave me a commandment, what I should say, and what I should speak. And I know that his commandment is life everlasting: whatsoever I speak therefore, even as the Father said unto me, so I speak" (Jn. 12:49-50).

The children of Israel heard God's voice speak out of the fire and smoke from the top of Mt. Sinai (Ex. 19:9, 17-19; 20: 18-21). They also heard His voice coming from the cloud above the Mercy Seat (Ex. 25:22, 33:9-11; Nu. 7:89). At Yeshua's baptism, the voice of God spoke from the cloud. "This is my beloved Son, in whom I am well pleased" (Mt. 3:16-17). A bright cloud overshadowed Peter, James and John when they witnessed the transfiguration of Yeshua. They heard the voice of God coming out of the cloud saying, "This is my beloved Son, in whom I am well pleased; hear ye him" (Mt. 17:5).

The third member of the Holy Trinity, the Holy Spirit, is man's guide now (Jn. 14:16, 26). He is like the bright glow from the Pillar of fire that illuminated the path for Israel. The ancient oriental custom of strapping oil lamps on the feet to light one's way in the night is descriptive of the Holy Spirit's work. John 14:26 teaches that the Holy Spirit will bring to remembrance every word spoken by Yeshua. "The Word of God" is synonymous with Yeshua; the psalmist said of Him: "Thy Word is a lamp unto my feet, and a light unto my path" (Ps. 119:105). The Holy Spirit illuminates every word that Yeshua spoke.

Another vivid example of the guiding power of the Lord is in Proverbs. "Trust in the Lord with all thine heart; and lean not unto thine own understanding. In all thy ways acknowledge him, and he shall DIRECT thy paths" (Pr. 3:5-6; my emphasis). The word translated direct in this passage implies to plow open a path. Not only does God's word light our way; it moves like a bulldozer, plowing up anything hindering the one following Him. Yeshua is the Light that removes all darkness; His light causes darkness to flee (Jn. 8:12). The cloud and the fire were only "shadows" of Yeshua the Messiah. Just as the Father promised never to forsake the children of Israel, Yeshua promises to never leave or forsake you (Josh. 1:5, Heb. 13:5).

Shelter is another benefit found in the cloud and fire of the Lord. "The Lord is thy keeper: the Lord is thy shade upon thy right hand. The sun shall not smite thee by day, nor the moon by night" (Ps. 121:5, 6).

According to Webster's Dictionary, an Old English definition of cloud is rock. We have a wonderful example of the ROCK sheltering Moses. Moses sought to see the glory of the Lord. The Lord granted his request. The Lord protected Moses by sheltering him in the cleft of a *rock* as the He passed by (Ex. 33:21-23). Later in the song of Moses found in Deut.

32:4, Moses said the *Lord is the Rock*. The ROCK in the song of Moses is the Messiah (1 Cor. 10:4; Ps. 31:3, 20). He was the Rock that provided a hiding place for Moses, and that same Rock hides us. Our lives are hidden with Messiah in God (Col. 3:3). The Bible is full of passages that speak of the shelter provided by the Lord. I urge you to look them up and take comfort in God's provisions.

The cloud and the fire also protected Israel. When Pharaoh's chariots pursued God's people, the cloud and the fire got between Israel and the Egyptians. "And the angel of God, which went before the camp of Israel, removed and went behind them; and the pillar of the cloud went from before their face, and stood behind them: And it came between the camp of the Egyptians and the camp of Israel; and it was a cloud and darkness to them, but it gave light by night to these: so that the one came not near the other all the night "(Ex. 14:19, 20).

God's presence appeared to the enemy as darkness, but to His people it was light. The Lord still gets between the believer and his enemy. He protects on all sides--the Lord goes before and the God of Israel is behind (Isa. 52:12). Yeshua, the incarnate person of God, is the manifested presence of the PILLAR of God to all people. "Who being the brightness of his glory, and the express image of his person, and upholding all things by the word of his power, when he had by himself purged our sins, sat down on the right hand of the Majesty on High." (Heb. 1:3; my emphasis) Yeshua is LIGHT, He is SALVATION, and He is STRENGTH (Ps. 27:1).

There are so many other things I could say about the glory of God, but instead I'll give you a few facts from the Bible, and you can investigate them for yourselves. First, the glory of God did not appear over the Tabernacle until the sin offering had been made (Ex. 40:34, 35). Second, His glory departed from the Mount of Olives and was not seen again until the birth of Yeshua (Ezek. 11:23, Lk. 2:9). Third, forty days after the resurrection of Yeshua, He was carried up into heaven from the Mount of Olives, the same place the Glory of God left six hundred years earlier (Acts 1:9-11).

Fourth, He is coming back to stand on top of the same mountains, and His appearance will be so great that the mountains will divide (Zech. 14:4, 5). Fifth, during Eli's term as high priest, the Ark of the Lord was taken from Israel, and the glory of the Lord left. That same day Eli's grandson was born. His name was Ichabod, which means the glory of the Lord has departed (I Sam. 4:21, 22). Sixth, Yeshua prophesied that He would return in full Glory (Mt. 16:27, 25:31; Mk. 8:38). Seventh, His Glory will fill the temple again (Rev. 15:8). Eighth, His glory has a permanent city to dwell in (Rev. 21:11).

Violating the holiness of the Ark was punishable by death, just as denying the deity of Messiah is eternally fatal! The Ark did not protect Israel, the Lord of the Ark was their protector and He is ours. His name is Yeshua.

SUMMARY

THE ARK: *The person of Yeshua*
THE MERCY SEAT: *The purpose of Yeshua*
THE CROWN OF GOLD: *The man, Yeshua the Messiah, promoted and exalted KING of KINGS and LORD of LORDS.*

CHAPTER 6

The Table and the Showbread

"Thou shalt also make a table of shittim wood: two cubits shall be the length thereof, and a cubit the breadth thereof, and a cubit and a half the height thereof. And thou shalt overlay it with pure gold, and make thereto a crown of gold round about. And thou shalt make unto it a border of a handbreadth round about, and thou shalt make a golden crown to the border thereof round about. And thou shalt make for it four rings of gold, and put the rings in the four corners that are on the four feet thereof. Over against the border shall the rings be for places of the staves to bear the table. And thou shalt make the staves of shittim wood, and overlay them with gold, that the table may be borne with them. And thou shalt make the dishes thereof, and spoons thereof, and covers thereof and bowls thereof, to cover withal: of pure gold shalt thou make them. And thou shalt set upon the table showbread before me always" (Ex. 25:23-30).

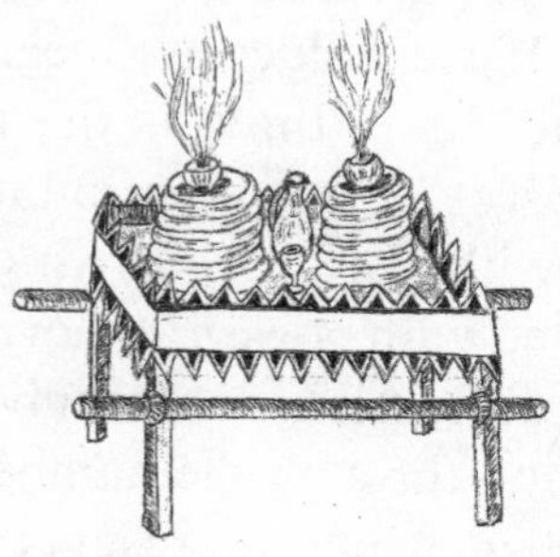

The Table of Showbread

We started our journey looking at the Tabernacle from God's perspective. We began with God. He was behind the Veil above the Ark of the Covenant and the Mercy Seat. God stepped down from His throne and walked through the Veil to enter into the holy place. There we find the Table of Shewbread, the Altar of Incense, and the Golden Candlestick; through them God reveals the other two persons of the Holy Trinity, God the Son and God the Holy Spirit. God is one; therefore, each person in the Godhead is ALL God. However, each has a distinctive purpose with a common goal, and that goal is to bring man into a personal relationship with His Creator. The Holy Place is the "Shadow" of where God the Father will interact with man in the person of Yeshua. He will reveal His plan for fellowship through the duties of the priests. The intimacy of that fellowship is made known as the priests eat portions of the bread and drink the wine of the offerings, directing us to the body and the blood of Yeshua. We saw the "Shadow" *of the Son in the Father* in the Ark of the Covenant. The Table and the Shewbread are "Shadows" of *the Father in the Son.*

Other "Shadows" of Yeshua will emerge as we examine the design, the size and the materials used to make the Table. We will look closely at the double crown and the band that divided them, the position of the rings used to carry it, and the Bread that was always present.

The Size: The Table, as well as the other furnishings of the Tabernacle, was measured in cubits. It was one and a half cubits high. If we reduce its measurement into half cubits, it is equal to three (three is the number associated with the Holy Trinity). It was one cubit wide (one is the number identified with unity), and two cubits long (two is the number associated with power, authority, and fellowship). As we study each dimension, the numbers will reveal the steadfast heart of God through the number nine. Nine is the self-repeating number, which represents God's unchanging character. God gave us nine Spiritual gifts to reveal His power in the world; they each begin with Him and point man back to Him. There are nine beatitudes, which show the progression of our walk with God. The beatitudes show how man moves from hopelessness to a faith in Yeshua that will eventually lead to persecution.

To see the consistent everlasting revelation of God, I am going to convert the measurements of the Table from cubits to inches. One cubit equals 18 inches. Two cubits equals 36 inches. One and a half cubits equals 27 inches. When you divide each measurement of the Table that has been converted into inches by 3 (the number of its dimensions), and add the quotients you will see that they always return to 9, revealing that God never changes.

> 18" divided by 3 = 6, 36" divided by 3 = 12, 27" divided by 3 = 9
>
> Now if we add the quotients the sum is equal to the height of the Ark.
>
> 6 + 12 + 9 = 27 (2 + 7 = 9)
>
> If we add the total number of inches, 18 + 36 + 27 = 81 (8 + 1 = 9)
>
> Even if we use the measurements as they appear in Scripture the result is the same.
>
> 1.5 cubits + 1.0 cubits + 2.0 cubits = 4.5 cubits or 4 + 5 = 9

God has revealed Himself in many ways, the Tabernacle being one of them. Regardless of the method He uses, they always lead man back to Him, and that is what I pray you see in the number nine. It does not matter how we rearrange the numbers found in the measurements of the Table; they always return to nine because God is revealing the singleness of His purpose.

God reveals the unity and equality shared by the Father and Son through the identical height of the Table and the Ark.

He is *Ekh awd'* (God is the united one). The Bible, speaking of Yeshua, says, "Who being in the form of God, thought it not robbery to be equal with God" (Phil. 2:6). Yeshua's own words also confirm His unity with the Father. "Have I been so long with you, and yet hast thou not known me, Philip? He that hath seen me hath seen the Father; and how sayest thou then, Show us the Father? (Jn. 14:9). "I and my Father are one" (Jn. 10:30). Of course, the Table and the Ark are the same height because God is the same yesterday, today, and forever (Heb. 13:8). Later, you will see this same principal in the Brazen Altar. As we continue, you will see that each piece of furniture foreshadowed a characteristic of Yeshua, who is the image of the invisible God (Col. 1: 15-20).

The "Shadows" revealed through the measurements of the Table go beyond the revelation of Yeshua. They serve as patterns for the believer's life, encouraging each of us to grow up into Yeshua's image (Eph. 4:11-13). "Till we all come in the unity of the faith, and of the knowledge of the Son of God, unto a perfect man, unto the measure of the stature of the fullness of Christ" (v. 13).

We are to have the mind of the Messiah (Phil. 2:5). The Ark and the Table are three dimensional, and so is man. God wants to bring the length, breadth, and height of our beings--spirit, soul, and body--into oneness with Him (Jn. 17:21-23).

The materials: Gold and Wood: The Table was made of wood overlaid with gold. The wood reveals the Son of Man, Yeshua's human character, and the gold reveals the Son of God, His deity. Yeshua is ALL God and ALL man. He had to be to reunite fallen man with the Holy God. "For there is one God, and one mediator between God and men, the man Christ Jesus" (1 Tim. 2:5). "Who, being in the form of God, thought it not robbery to be equal with God" (Phil. 2:6).

The double crown: The feature of the double crown was unique to the Table. In it, we have the revelation of the double-portion blessing given to the firstborn son. "But he shall acknowledge the son of the hated for the firstborn, by giving him a double portion of all that he hath: for he is the beginning of his strength; the right of the firstborn is his" (Deut. 21:17). Part of the double blessing bestowed on Yeshua was a double crown. God crowned Him with *Glory* and *Honor* to experience death for every man (Heb. 2:9). The double crown is a "Shadow" of the power, authority, and position of Yeshua. Yeshua's *Power:* He left His place with the Father to become a man, so that He could pay the sin debt that man could not. "But made himself of no reputation, and took upon him the form of a servant, and was made in the likeness of men: And being found in fashion as a man, he humbled himself, and became obedient unto death, even the death of the cross" (Phil. 2:7-8). Yeshua came to die for you and me. He surrendered to death on a cross and received the punishment we deserved. He was given the power to look past the shameful way He had to die to the end result of what He came to do. "Looking unto Jesus the author and finisher of our faith; who for the joy that was set before him endured the cross, despising the shame, and is set down at the right hand of the throne of God. (Heb. 12:2).

Yeshua's *Position: Yeshua* is the *Sin Sacrifice and the Risen Redeemer*, the *Eternal High Priest and the Prince of Peace*. He, as the Eternal High Priest, intercedes and makes our worship acceptable to the Father. "Wherefore he is able also to save them to the uttermost that come unto God by him, seeing he ever liveth to make intercession for them" (Heb. 7:25). "Having predestinated us unto the adoption of children by Jesus Christ to himself, according to the good pleasure of his will, to the praise of the glory of his grace wherein he hath made us accepted in the beloved" (Eph. 1:5-6).

Yeshua became the Sin Sacrifice for all men and rose from the grave to give them eternal life. As the Prince of Peace, Yeshua has restored the relationship between man and God (Isa. 43:25, Isa. 44:22, Ps. 103:12). Yeshua's *Authority:* God the Father crowned Yeshua the *King of Kings* and the *Lord of Lords*

(Rev. 19:16). ALL of heaven stands behind Him. "And Jesus came and spake unto them, saying, All power is given unto me in heaven and in earth" (Mat. 28:18). As our King, Yeshua protects us from the wicked one. "He that committeth sin is of the devil; for the devil sinneth from the beginning. For this purpose the Son of God was manifested, that he might destroy the works of the devil" (1 Jn. 3:8). As our Lord, He provides us with everything we need to sustain our relationship with the Father. Paul Said, "For I know whom I have believed, and am persuaded that he is able to keep that which I have committed unto him against that day" (2 Tim. 1:12). "Wherefore let them that suffer according to the will of God commit the keeping of their souls to him in well doing, as unto a faithful Creator" (1 Pet. 4:19).

Yeshua has equipped every believer with the power and authority to do the work He commanded us to do. He said, "Go and teach all nations, baptizing them in the name of the Father, and of the Son, and of the Holy Ghost: Teaching them to observe all things whatsoever I have commanded you: and, lo, I am with you always, even unto the end of the world. Amen" (Mt. 28:19-20).

God the Father gave Yeshua one other double portion blessing. Through the shed blood of Yeshua, Jew and Gentile have been re-united with the Father to become ONE NEW MAN. Yeshua, "Having abolished in his flesh the enmity, even the law of commandments contained in ordinances; for to make in himself of twain one new man, so making peace; And that he might reconcile both unto God in one body by the cross, having slain the enmity thereby" (Eph. 2:15-16). The Jews and the Gentiles are the two sheepfolds spoken of by Yeshua. "As the Father knoweth me, even so know I the Father: and I lay down my life for the sheep. And other sheep I have, which are not of this fold: them also I must bring, and they shall hear my voice; and there shall be one fold and one shepherd" (Jn.10:15-16).

The Band: God chose a handbreadth to measure the band that separated the double crowns of the Table. A handbreadth is the width of four fingers, or about three inches. This is the only place in the Tabernacle that a handbreadth is used as a measurement. God chose the handbreadth to narrow the path that points man to the Messiah. Yeshua is from the tribe of Judah. The handbreadth of the table reveals how Yeshua fulfilled the prophecy of Moses concerning the hands of Judah (Deut. 33:7). Judah's hands, in this passage, speak of the keeping power of Yeshua. "And I give unto them eternal life; and they shall never perish, *neither shall any man pluck them out of my hand.* My Father, which gave them to me, is greater than all; *and no man is able to pluck them out of my Father's hand.* **I and the Father are one"** (Jn. 10:28-30; my emphasis). Nothing can separate you from the love of Messiah (Rom. 8:35-39).

The rings: The position of the golden rings used to carry the Table is another feature that set the Table apart. The rings were located underneath the bottom crown, somewhere on the four legs (Ex. 25:26). The staves (gold overlaid poles) were inserted into the rings by the priests before moving the Table. When the priests lifted the Table, the placement of the gold rings caused the Table to tower above their shoulders.

God commanded that the Showbread remain on the Table at all times, even when it was being carried. He gave explicit instructions for preparing the Table and the Showbread for travel. First, the Priest covered them with a cloth of blue; the blue color revealed their heavenly origin. The next covering was a cloth of scarlet; the red color points to the blood that Yeshua shed for man. The top covering was a badger's skin; the outer covering of badgers' skin is a "Shadow" of the outer covering of Yeshua's flesh. The preparation, along with what the priest carried, provides a glorious picture of the gospel message. That message is this; Yeshua came down from the Father in heaven to shed His blood for the sin of humanity. He put on flesh to die in man's place upon the Cross of Calvary.

God placed the responsibility of carrying that message upon the shoulders of the priest (Nu. 7-9). The elevated Table with the Showbread revealed a "Shadow" of Yeshua. He was high and lifted up for the entire world to see.

God used the Table and the Shewbread as visual aids to teach His children about Himself. We, who are believers, need to take notice of the method God planned to deliver the message of Salvation to the world. Yeshua said, "And I, if I be lifted up from the earth, will draw all men unto me" (Jn. 12:32).

At the time of the Tabernacle, the Levites were the only ones authorized to enter the office of priest. Now, through Yeshua's position as Eternal High Priest, God declares that all believers belong in His royal priesthood as members of His Holy Nation. "But ye are a chosen generation, a royal priesthood, an holy nation, a peculiar people; that ye should show forth the praises of him who hath called you out of darkness into his marvelous light: Which in time past were not a people, but are now the people of God: which had not obtained mercy, but now have obtained mercy" (1 Pet. 2:9-10).

As you can see from this passage of scripture, the responsibility of delivering the gospel message to a lost and dying world is the responsibility of each believer. We, the new priesthood, like the priest of the Tabernacle, must lift up Yeshua so that the world can see Him. How are we to do that? By sharing the things he has done in our own lives and allowing the Holy Spirit to draw others into the family of God. "Blessed be God, even the Father of our Lord Jesus Christ, the Father of mercies, and the God of all comfort; Who comforteth us in all our tribulation, that we may be able to comfort them which are in any trouble, by the comfort wherewith we ourselves are comforted of God." (2 Cor. 1:3-4)

Generally, people have sin, hurts, and disappointments from the past that keep them in bondage. Things like lust, hate, resentment, and bitterness just to name a few. We, who God delivered from such things, can tell others of Yeshua's power to break the yoke that once held us in bondage. "And it shall come to pass in that day, that his burden shall be taken away from off thy shoulder, and his yoke from off thy neck, and the yoke shall be destroyed because of the anointing" (Isa. 10:27). The atoning power of Yeshua destroys the yoke of sin. Yeshua said. "Take my yoke upon you, and learn of me; for I am meek and lowly in heart: and ye shall find rest unto your souls. For my yoke is easy, and my burden is light" (Mt. 11:29-30).

Webster's Dictionary defines yoke several ways, "1) A frame resting on a person's shoulders to carry two loads, as a pair of buckets, one at each end, 2) Something that binds; bond or tie, 3) A shaped and fitted piece in a garment, especially at the shoulders, 4) To join, couple, link, or unite."[6] Therefore, Yeshua wants us to recognize that our burdens rest upon His shoulders. If we will learn of Him and accept what He has done for us, we will find rest.

Yeshua was a carpenter and He knows how to make a yoke that perfectly fits each individual. Whatever the burden is that you are carrying, when you unite with Yeshua, His yoke, designed exclusively for you, provides rest. When we lift Him up, by telling others what He has done in our lives and that He will do the same for them, we create a way for the Holy Spirit to woo them into God's family. Please, with boldness, share your testimony with others and watch the Lord honor His Word. When we lift Him up, He draws men unto Himself.

The Showbread: Why do you think God called this bread "Showbread"? There are many very good reasons that you will see as we examine its use, ingredients, and preparation. God reveals the pure sinless life of Yeshua and His suffering through the Showbread. The Showbread also teaches how God perceives redeemed man.

The first mention of Showbread is in Ex. 25:30. The ingredients and method of preparation for making the Showbread, the Meat offering, and the Meal offering are the same (Lev. 24:5-9). An individual could present his offering cooked or uncooked. If he brought it uncooked, a portion of it was burned on the Altar, and the remainder was a gift from God to Aaron's family; it was their food. If one brought his offering cooked, it was prepared one of three ways--*baked in an oven, cooked in a covered pan on an open fire*, or *cooked in a frying pan.* Each method required molding or shaping with the hands, as well as other instruments. The molding and shaping process exposes the different forms of Yeshua's suffering at the hands of man.

(1). **Baked in an oven**. When food is cooked inside an oven it's hard to see what is being prepared. This method of preparation is symbolic of the personal suffering of Yeshua that was hidden within His heart. He knew that He was preordained to taste the bitter cup of God's wrath, which was intended for us (Isa. 51:22). He understood accepting our sin would separate Him from His Father. The thought of that caused Him to suffer intense agony, to the point of sweating drops of blood, yet He yielded to the will of the Father. "And being in an agony he prayed more earnestly: and his sweat was as it were great drops of blood falling down to the ground" (Lk. 22:44).

(2). **Cooked in a covered pan on an open fire**. A pan on an open fire makes known that something is being cooked, but the lid of the pan conceals what is inside. This form of preparation is figurative of the suffering of Yeshua that was witnessed by those who did not understand. Many people watched as He was tortured. Although His wounds were fully visible, they could not comprehend the purpose for His suffering. Yeshua said, "You have eyes but you don't see and ears yet you don't hear"; that is why He cried out to the Father, "Father, forgive them; for they know not what they do" (Lk. 23:34).

(3). **Cooked in a frying pan on an open fire.** Frying in a pan is usually done without a lid. Therefore, the observer can readily see the contents. Preparing the bread in this manner is representative of the undeniable deliberate torture of Yeshua. He was beaten, pierced, spat upon, and His beard was ripped out. His suffering was not only seen but was also understood. Many recognized Him as the Messiah while others rejected Him. Each method of preparation publicized the progression of suffering, which leads up to Yeshua's death. He is the fine flour of the meat offering and the meal offering. To help us understand this, He spoke of Himself as a grain of wheat saying, "Except a corn of wheat fall into the ground and die, it abideth alone: but if it die, it bringeth forth much fruit" (Jn. 12:24).

Today, the preparation of (*Matzah*), the unleavened bread used during the Passover season in the homes of both traditional Jews (those who have not yet accepted Yeshua as the Messiah) and Messianic Jews (those who have accepted Yeshua as their Messiah) provides many symbolisms of the suffering of the Lord.

To make *Matzah,* a sharp instrument is used to score and pierce the dough. The piercing process produces multiple holes in the bread and scoring leaves impression that resemble stripes. Yeshua suffered at the hands of the Roman soldiers who beat Him with a whip designed to tear away the flesh from His body. His side was pierced with a spear, and nails large enough to support the weight of His body were hammered into His hands and feet, pinning Him to the cross. The prophet Isaiah said of Him, "He is despised and rejected of men; a man of sorrows, and acquainted with grief: and we hid as it were our faces from him; he was despised, and we esteemed him not. Surely he hath borne our griefs, and carried our sorrows: yet we did esteem him stricken, smitten of God, and afflicted. But

he was wounded for our transgressions; he was ***bruised for our iniquities***: ***the chastisement of our peace was upon him***; and ***with his stripes we are healed***" (Isa. 53:3-5; my emphasis). The stripes He received provide healing. He was bruised for our iniquities; a bruise is bleeding underneath the skin. The Hebrew word translated iniquities is *Avon,* pronounced *Aw-vone.* Avon means perversity, i.e. (moral) evil. Yeshua's bruises teach that His blood is powerful enough to reach down into the depths of man's soul to bring even our hidden sins to the surface.

In the Garden of Eden, God took Adam's bride from his side foreshadowing the way Messiah's bride would come. "But for Adam there was not found a help meet for him. And the LORD God caused a deep sleep to fall upon Adam, and he slept: and *he took one of his ribs, and closed up the flesh instead thereof; And the rib, which the LORD God had taken from man, made he a woman, and brought her unto the man***.** And Adam said, *This is now bone of my bones, and flesh of my flesh:* she shall be called Woman, because she was taken out of Man. *Therefore shall a man leave his father and his mother, and shall cleave unto his wife: and they shall be one flesh*" (Gen. 2:20-24; my emphasis).

A Roman soldier pierced Yeshua's side, causing blood and water to gush out ushering forth the birth of His bride, the community of believers ("the church"). We, like Adam's bride, belong to Yeshua. We, "the church" are, *"members of his body, of his flesh, and of his bones. For this cause shall a man leave his father and mother, and shall be joined unto his wife, and they two shall be one flesh. This is a great mystery: but I speak concerning Christ and the church"* (Eph.5:30-32).

Yeshua is the LAST ADAM; "And so it is written, The first man Adam was made a living soul; the last Adam was made a quickening spirit" (1 Cor. 15:45). The first Adam's wife was his helpmeet; she worked with him. We, who are believers, work with Yeshua as His help meet doing the will of the Father. "We then, as *workers together with him*, beseech you also that ye receive not the grace of God in vain" (2 Cor. 6:1; my emphasis).

The ingredients: The Showbread had three ingredients--fine flour, oil, and salt.

Fine flour: To obtain the quality of flour needed to make Showbread, the grain was ground into a fine powder. The grinding process gives a "shadow" of Yeshua's suffering.

"Though he were a Son, yet learned he obedience by the things which he suffered" (Heb.5:8). He had to suffer the grinding of the mill to become the **"Living Bread"** for all men. "I am the living bread which came down from heaven: if any man eat of this bread, he shall live forever: and the bread that I will give is my flesh, which I will give for the life of the world" (Jn. 6:51).

Oil: The oil of the bread is the "shadow" of the Holy Spirit. He is the operating power of God that gave Yeshua the strength to withstand all temptation and suffering. Yeshua is the only man to receive the Holy Spirit without measure. "For he whom God hath sent speaketh the words of God: for God giveth not the Spirit by measure unto him. The Father loveth the Son, and hath given all things into his hand" (Jn. 3:34-35).The Holy Spirit drove Yeshua into the wilderness where Satan tempted Him with every aspect of Sin. Adam and Eve fell into the same trap and failed (Gen. 3:6).

All sin can be summed up in three categories; the lust of the flesh, the lust of the eyes and the pride of Life (1 Jn. 2:16).

The devil tempted Yeshua with food when He was hungry *(the lust of the flesh*). He caused Yeshua to look down upon the Holy city from the highest point in Jerusalem (*the lust of the eyes)*. Finally, he tempted Yeshua with power and possessions (*the pride of life*), yet Yeshua did not sin (Mt. 4:1-11; Mk. 1:12: Heb. 3:13).

The same power that helped Yeshua is a gift from God to every believer. The anointing power of the Holy Spirit makes it possible to overcome the trials, temptations, and pressures that we face every day.

Salt: Salt is the final ingredient. Salt is a symbol of Gods' covenant promise to Aaron, his sons, and to the children of Israel. Salt preserves and purifies. God's covenant of salt preserved the rightful place of Yeshua as both the High Priest and the King. Yeshua is a direct descendant of both Aaron and David. Therefore, He is entitled to inherit the provisions of Gods' SALT COVENANT (Mt. 1:1; Lk. 3:23-24). Yeshua's position as our High Priest was promised through the SALT covenant God made with Aaron. "All the heave offerings of the holy things, which the children of Israel offer unto the LORD, have I given thee, and thy sons and thy daughters with thee, by a statute for ever: *it is a covenant of salt for ever before the LORD unto thee and to thy seed with thee*" (Nu. 18:19; my emphasis). The guarantee that Yeshua would be the KING came through God's SALT covenant with David. "Ought ye not to know that *the LORD God of Israel gave the kingdom over Israel to David for ever, even to him and to his sons by a covenant of salt"?* (2 Chro.13:5; my emphasis).

God decreed that every offering burned on the altar have salt applied to it (Lev. 2:13). The meat offering and the meal offering, as mentioned earlier, are prepared the same way as the Showbread. The *Meat* (grain) offering also points to Yeshua (Lev. 2:10). The suffering Yeshua experienced purified his flesh to become the MEAT OFFERING for humanity; He became the "Living Bread" to give eternal life. Yeshua said, "Whoso eateth my flesh, and drinketh my blood, hath eternal life; and I will raise him up at the last day" (Jn. 6:54).

God gave the remainder of the Showbread offering to Aaron's family. Only the chosen servants of God were entitled to share in God's Holy offerings (Lev. 24:9) Now, everyone who enters into the family of God, by accepting Yeshua as the Messiah, has the privilege of participating in God's Holy offering. Yeshua is the Holy Offering.

Yeshua is the living bread which came down from heaven. He said, "The bread that I will give is my flesh, which I will give for the life of the world" (Jn. 6:51). Just as salt adds flavor to food, Yeshua is the flavor of every new life (Ps 119:103. 34:8). Salt induces thirst and adds flavor (Mt. 5:6; Ps. 81:10).

The Priests of the Tabernacle salted each offering before placing it on the altar. Yeshua, our High Priest, salts each believer with salt and with fire (Mk. 9:49-50). What does it mean to be salted with fire? The Bible teaches that God is a consuming fire. His purifying fire is what molds us into the image of Yeshua (Heb. 12:29). Purifying comes through test and trials. God knows the extent of our faith, but often we don't. As we experience the fire of His testing, we will either turn to Him or away from Him. Turning to Him shows our strengths and turning away from Him reveals our weaknesses. Every believer must experience the fire of testing (1 Pet. 4:12-13). I feel the lack of teaching on this subject has brought about a misconception concerning Grace. True, Grace and faith in Yeshua is the means to Salvation, but that does not disannul the trying of our faith. Many new believers fall away when trials and temptations come, because they were lead to believe that once saved, life becomes easy; the times of suffering are over. We, like Yeshua, learn obedience through suffering. The Bible is full of passages that teach about suffering. Suffering is necessary to grow into the image of Yeshua. Every trial presents the opportunity to be changed if we obey Him. If not, we will continue to go through the same trials and temptations until we get it right. James, the brother of Yeshua, said, "Those who endure trials will receive the crown of life." The key word is endure (suffer without yielding). The way this passage reads implies that those who love the Lord practice steadfast endurance. James also says that God tempts no man; the temptations of man are the result of his own lust (Ja. 1:12).

Works is another area subject to the fire of God. Works do not produce salvation. Salvation comes through Grace and faith, and faith produces works. Grace is the empowerment that gives the ability to do the works God calls us to do. Every individual is answerable for his/her works to determine if they are self seeking or pure of heart. The fire of God is what decides the quality of our works. "Every man's work shall be made manifest: for the day shall declare it, because it shall be revealed by fire; and the fire shall try every man's work of what sort it is. If any man's work abide which he hath built thereupon, he shall receive a reward. If any man's work shall be burned, he shall suffer loss: but he himself shall be saved; yet so as by fire" (1 Cor. 3:13-15).

The fire of testing changes us into the image of Yeshua, but how does the salt of the Holy offerings apply to us today? Yeshua said, "Ye are the salt of the earth" (Mt.5:13).

What does it mean, "Ye are the salt of the earth"? It means you have the flavor of God's grace living in you. Every word you speak needs the seasoning of His grace. "Let your speech be alway with grace, seasoned with salt, that ye may know how ye ought to answer every man (Col. 4:6) Yeshua is the flavor in every believer's life, He is the salt that makes thirsty, He is the one who preserves and purifies. The Salt Covenant is still in existence today and it belongs to the believer. We, as members of Yeshua's Royal Priesthood have access to the Salt Covenant (1 Pet. 2:9-10).

We, the Royal Priesthood, like the priests of the Tabernacle, need an offering. "I beseech you therefore, brethren, by the mercies of God, that ye present your bodies a living sacrifice, holy, acceptable unto God, which is your reasonable service. And be not conformed to this world: but be ye transformed by the renewing of your mind, that ye may prove what is that good, and acceptable, and perfect, will of God " (Rom. 12:1-2). God requires total surrender. That means dying to self that He might live through you. We must never loose the flavor of Yeshua's manifested presence. If we do, we become "good for nothing, but to be cast out, and to be trodden under foot of men". Therefore, we must count it joy when we suffer trials, knowing that Yeshua is salting us with the flavor of God's love and burning it into our lives.

Forbidden ingredients: Leaven and honey were the two forbidden ingredients in the Showbread (Ex. 12:15, I Cor. 5:6-8, Gal. 5:9). "No meat offering, which ye shall bring unto the LORD, shall be made with leaven: for ye shall burn no leaven, nor any honey, in any offering of the LORD made by fire" (Lev. 2: 11).

God prohibited the use of leaven in the Showbread, because throughout the Bible He uses leaven to describe sin. It is particularly descriptive of the deception of false doctrine, because the product of false doctrine is the sin of hypocrisy. Yeshua warned his followers about such things. "Then Jesus said unto them, Take heed and beware of the leaven of the Pharisees and of the Sadducees. How is it that ye do not understand that I spake it not to you concerning bread, that ye should beware of the leaven of the Pharisees and of the Sadducees? Then understood they how that he bade them not beware of the leaven of bread, but of the doctrine of the Pharisees and of the Sadducees (Mt. 16:6, 11-12). "Beware ye of the leaven of the Pharisees, which is hypocrisy" (Lk. 12:1).

Hypocrisy is a sin that puffs up, just like the presence of leaven in bread dough. We protect ourselves against false teachers by studying the Bible for ourselves. If we know the truth, we will quickly recognize a lie. "Study to show thyself approved unto God, a workman that needeth not to be ashamed, rightly dividing the word of truth. But shun profane and vain babblings: for they will increase unto more ungodliness" (2 Tim. 2:15-16). "All scripture is given by inspiration of God, and is profitable for doctrine, for reproof, for correction, for instruction in righteousness: That the man of God may be perfect thoroughly furnished unto all good works" (2 Tim. 3:16-17).

It is obvious why God did not want leaven in the Showbread, but why do you suppose He did not want it to contain honey? Honey is a natural product used as a sweetener to enhance the taste of bread, etc. Since the Showbread was a symbol of the sinless body of Messiah, who is the perfection of the Father, a natural product like honey could not enhance or improve it. Man can never improve on God's perfection by the omission or addition of any thing. We find this principle again in the book of Revelation where God describes Yeshua the Messiah in His glory. The entire book is written in Yeshua's honor, revealing Him as the conquering King of Kings and the Lord of Lords. There we find a warning to the reader much like the warning concerning the Showbread. "For I testify unto every man that heareth the words of the prophecy of this book, If any man shall add unto these things, God shall add unto him the plagues that are written in this book: And if any man shall take away from the words of the book of this prophecy, God shall take away his part out of the book of life, and out of the holy city, and from the things which are written in this book" (Rev. 22:18-19).

Man can neither diminish nor improve on the perfection of God's Word. Nothing man does will alter or prevent the fulfillment of one word, and to try is eternally fatal.

There is another aspect of the Showbread. The twelve loaves of Showbread are representative of the twelve tribes of Israel. From God's perspective, the twelve unleavened loaves (one from each tribe) are symbolic of the nation of Israel; those that have been forgiven by the blood of the sin sacrifice. They also point to those cleansed by the blood of Yeshua. The unleavened Showbread is representative of all of God's redeemed children. If the blood of Yeshua's sacrifice saved you, you are part of a new lump, an unleavened lump. The old leaven (sin nature) is gone, destroyed by His blood. In God's eyes, you are as pure as the unleavened Showbread, because you have partaken of "The Bread of Life". "Purge out therefore the old leaven, ***that ye may be a new lump***, as ye are unleavened. For even Christ our Passover is sacrificed for us: Therefore let us keep the feast. Not with old leaven, neither with the leaven of malice and wickedness; but with the unleavened bread of sincerity and truth" (1 Cor. 5:7-8; my emphasis)

God never intended to start a new religion, or any religion for that matter. His desire has always been to establish relationship with the human race. Jew and Gentile, united in Messiah, become ONE BREAD. "For we being many are ONE BREAD and ONE BODY: for we **are all partakers of that one Bread**" (1 Cor. 10:17; my emphasis).

The priests (the Levites), unlike the other tribes, did not receive an inheritance; God was their portion. One of the benefits of the priesthood was the privilege of partaking of God's holy offerings. God gave the priests portions of the Showbread (*the Meat offering*) and the drink offerings (Lev. 6:16-19, 7:34, 8:31), foreshadowing the day when Yeshua would become man's portion. "Verily, verily, I say unto you, except ye eat the flesh of the Son of man, and drink his blood, ye have no life in you. Whoso eateth my flesh, and drinketh my blood, hath eternal life; and I will raise him up at the last day. For my flesh is meat indeed, and my blood is drink indeed. He that eateth my flesh, and drinketh my blood, dwelleth in me, and I in him. As the living Father hath sent me, and I live by the Father: so he that eateth me, even he shall live by me" (Jn. 6:53-57).

Matzah, today's unleavened bread (like the Showbread), is part of the Passover meal. Yeshua always celebrated the feast of Passover. In the book of John chapter six, we find Yeshua making arrangements to celebrate Passover with his disciples. The stage was being set for Yeshua to reveal Himself as the Passover Lamb, the Covenant Promise, and the Living Bread (Jn. 6:51).

Luke records the events of Yeshua's final Passover. It was during the Passover meal that Yeshua revealed Himself as the Covenant Partner of the Father. Yeshua's deepest desire was for His followers to understand the extent of Gods' love by showing them that He is the fulfillment of God's covenant. Yeshua said, "With *desire* I have *desired* to eat this Passover with you before I suffer: For I say unto you, I will not any more eat thereof, until it be fulfilled in the kingdom of God" (Lk.

22:15-16; my emphasis). The Greek word translated desire and desired is *epithumia*, which comes from *epithumeo* meaning to long for or to lust after. Yeshua yearned for His followers to understand what He was about to do for them and the world. Keep in mind; Yeshua was talking to Jewish believers that were familiar with blood covenants. They understood what the division of the sacrificial animals and walking in the blood was about. They also knew that after walking through the blood of the sacrificial animals, the covenant partners shared a meal that consisted of bread and wine, which represented the body and the blood of the covenant partners. It is the most intimate part of the covenant because it symbolized the union of two entities as one new person.

Sharing the bread and wine of the Passover meal is much like this part of the blood covenant, it is perhaps the most intimate part of the meal. During Yeshua's final Passover meal, as the unleavened bread passed from hand-to-hand, each man broke off a portion to eat. Afterward, Yeshua stood and said, "This is my body which is given for you: this do in ***remembrance*** of me" (Lk. 22:19; my emphasis). Then He took the cup of wine and said, "This cup is the new testament in my blood, which is shed for you" (Lk. 22: 20).

REMEMBER is a blood covenant word, and Yeshua desperately wanted His followers to understand that He was about to shed His own blood to complete the covenant promise made to Abraham so many years earlier. At last, there was a man with blood pure enough to enter covenant with his creator for all mankind. Yeshua was telling His disciples that His body and His blood fulfilled Abraham's and God's part of the covenant that was made in Genesis 17:7. His blood not only sealed God's covenant with Abraham; it also fulfilled the purpose of the Passover Lamb. Yeshua is the seed of Abraham, and as the Passover Lamb, He has redeemed man from the curse of death and has given, all who will believe, eternal life (Lev. 17:11, Ex. 12:13-15, 1 Cor. 5:7-8). Yeshua is also the fulfillment of the "shadow" of the Showbread; those who feed on Him will be sustained until He returns to reign as the King of Kings and Lord of Lords.

Each loaf of Showbread was offered with pure frankincense. **Frankincense** is a fragrant gum that comes from a tree. It was one of the ingredients used to make the incense for the Golden Altar. Fire releases the sweetness of bread; the burning frankincense represents that sweet aroma. As it burned in the censers placed on top of the Showbread, white smoke rose up towards heaven. Its sweet aroma along with that of the bread was pleasing to God, because it represents Yeshua's sacrifice and His indwelling presence in every believer. "And walk in love, as Christ also hath loved us, and hath given himself for us an offering and a sacrifice to God for a sweet smelling savour" (Eph. 5:2). "For we are unto God a sweet savour of Christ, in them that are saved, and in them that perish (2 Cor. 2:15).

The Showbread is referred to as *the bread of presence, the bread of faces, the bread of ordering,* and *the continual bread.* *The bread of presence* indicates its location (Ex. 25:30). It was always on the Table just outside the Holy of Holies where God dwelt. Its location teaches that God desires to keep His children close. *The bread of faces*--this name serves a dual purpose. First, it teaches us that the sinless life of Yeshua reveals the face of God.

"He that hath seen me hath seen the Father" (Jn. 14:9). "Who is the image of the invisible God, the firstborn of every creature (Col 1:15). Second, the twelve cakes of unleavened bread symbolize the redeemed children of God. From God's perspective, the bread on the Table foreshadowed the time when He would live inside of His children. The Lord said, "Can a woman forget her sucking child, that she should not have compassion on the son of her womb? Yea, they may forget, yet will I not forget thee. Behold, I have graven thee upon the palms of my hands; thy walls are continually before me" (Isa. 49:15-16; my emphasis). *The bread of ordering*--God gave the method of order for the placement of the bread to teach us that He is the one who puts our lives in order. "The steps of a good man are ordered by the Lord" (Ps. 37:23). There is only one way a man can know the order of his steps; he must stay close to the Lord and trust Him (Pr. 3:5-6). Finally, we come to the *continual bread* (2 Chr. 2:4). Every Sabbath the priests replaced the Showbread with fresh cakes. Yeshua, like the continual bread, is always present. He said, "I will not leave your comfortless: I will come to you" (Jn. 14:18). He is always fresh, and ready to give freely of the Bread of Life to all who will come and eat. "It is of the Lord's mercies that we are not consumed, because his compassions fail not. They are new every morning: great is thy faithfulness" (Lam.3:22-23).

Even the place of Yeshua's birth pointed to Him as the Bread of Life. BETHLEHEM means "HOUSE OF BREAD".

SUMMARY

THE SIZE *Yeshua and the Father are one.*
THE MATERIALS *Yeshua was all God and all man.*
THE DOUBLE CROWNS *Yeshua's power and authority.*
THE BAND *The keeping power of Yeshua's hands.*
THE RINGS *Yeshua's elevated position as the redeemer of all mankind.*
THE SHOWBREAD *Yeshua is the Living Bread, the Bread of Life.*

I. **The method of preparation** = *Yeshua's suffering*
II. **The ingredients** = *Yeshua's death, the anointing power of the Holy Spirit, and the flavor of the goodness of God.*
III. **Forbidden ingredients** = *Yeshua's life was sinless, and His sweetness is beyond nature.*

THE FRANKINCENSE = *Yeshua's sacrifice is a sweet aroma to the Father.*

CHAPTER 7

The Golden Candlestick

"And thou shalt make a candlestick of pure gold: of beaten work shall the candlestick be made; HIS shaft, and HIS branches, HIS bowls, HIS knobs, and HIS flowers, shall be the same. And six branches shall come out of the sides of it; three branches of the candlestick out of the one side, and three branches of the candlestick out of the other side: Three bowls made like unto almonds, with a knob and a flower in one branch; and three bowls made like almonds in the other branch, with a knob and a flower: so in the six branches that come out of the candlestick. And the candlestick shall be four bowls made like unto almonds with their knobs and their flowers. And there shall be a knob under two branches of the same, and a knob under two branches of the same, and a knob under two branches of the same, according to the six branches that proceed out of the candlestick. Their knobs and their branches shall be of the same: all it shall be ONE BEATEN WORK OF PURE GOLD. And thou shalt make the seven lamps thereof: and they shall light the lamps thereof, that they may give light over against it. And the tongs thereof, and the snuffdishes thereof, shall be of pure gold. Of a talent of pure gold shall he make it, with all these vessels. And look that thou make them after their pattern, which was showed thee in the mount" (Ex. 25:31-40; my emphasis).

The Golden Candlestick

The Candlestick was made from one piece of gold that weighed approximately ninety pounds. It was the most extravagant, ornate piece of furniture in the Tabernacle; its appearance must have been breathtaking. Its elaborate design was fashioned after the almond tree. The gold was beaten and formed into groupings of buds, blooms, and the mature meat of the almond. In today's market, it would be worth millions.

The image of Yeshua (the Messiah) and His suffering as the Son of God emerges through the gold, the size, the location, and the method used to create the Candlestick. The illuminating power of the Holy Spirit is revealed through the Oil. The complete Word of God and the Hebrew language is shown in its design.

Gold is descriptive of deity. The gold of the Candlestick is representative of the divine nature of Yeshua; He is the Son of God. The gold was not melted and poured into a mold. It was beaten and formed into the shape of the almond tree. Beating and shaping the gold are "Shadows" of the suffering experienced by the Yeshua, as the Son of God.

The location of the Candlestick draws attention to Yeshua's Son- ship. It was on the south wall of the Tabernacle, nearest to the camp of Reuben. Reuben's Hebrew name means ***Behold a Son***. The writer of the book of Hebrews said of Yeshua, "Even though he was the Son, He learned obedience through His suffering" (Heb. 5:8).

The Holy Spirit, often referred to as Oil, is the person of the Godhead who brings to light the words of Yeshua. "But the Comforter, which is the Holy Ghost, whom the Father will send in my name, he shall teach you all things, and bring all things to your remembrance, whatsoever I have said unto you" (Jn. 14:26). The pure olive oil that was used in the lamps of the Candlestick is a "Shadow" of the Holy Spirit's illuminating power. The Candlestick was the only source of light inside the Tabernacle, without it, the priests could not do their work. Through the Candlestick, we see the synchronization of the Holy Trinity. The Holy Spirit reveals the Son and the Son reveals the Father. Yeshua is the *LIGHT*, He was present with God in the beginning and it was the *Spirit of God* who caused His *LIGHT* to make known the glory of His *Father*. "And the earth was without form, and void; and darkness was upon the face of the deep. And the ***Spirit of God moved upon the face of the waters. And God said, Let there be light: and there was light*"** (Gen. 1:2-3; my emphasis). ***"Who is the image of the invisible*** God, the firstborn of every creature" (Col. 1:15; my emphasis).

The placement of the furnishings of the Tabernacle forms the shape of a cross, displaying God's divine plan for the redemption of man. From God's heavenly vantage point, He sees the end from the beginning (Isa. 46:10). When God looked down at the Tabernacle, He saw Yeshua on the cross. His head is crowned with the Ark of the Covenant and the Mercy Seat; He alone fulfilled God's Covenant. Therefore, all JUDGEMENT will come through Yeshua. His judgments are true and righteous, revealing the steadfast mercies of God. Yeshua held the Table of Showbread in His left hand, revealing the power of His COMMANDMENTS to keep and defend all who will follow them. ***His right hand holds the Candlestick,*** which illuminates His STATUTES. Yeshua's ways are pure like the oil of the lamps; they enlighten every man. The Golden Altar of Incense is over His heart showing His desire to lead and direct by His PRECEPTS. The good of man has always been on God's Heart. The Brazen Laver, at the bend of His knees, speaks of the life changing cleansing power found in the Word of His TESTIMONY. His feet stand on the Brazen Altar foretelling that His innocent blood would be the atonement for sin, and fulfill the LAW of GOD. As we continue our journey, the "shadow" of Yeshua's finished work emerges.

The design: The Candlestick consisted of one central shaft and six connecting branches. Some scholars believe the central shaft fed oil to the connecting branches. The validity of this remains questionable. However, scripture is clear on the significance of the central shaft. According to B. R. Hicks, the Hebrew word translated "shaft" is ***Yarekh*** (Ex. 25:31, 32). The same word was translated "thigh" in Gen. 24:2 and "loin" in Gen. 46:26.[7]

The word ***Yarekh,*** in the design of the Candlestick, points to the procreative power of God, which is found inYeshua. "All things were made by him; and without him was not anything made that was made. In him was life; and the life was the *Light of Men*" (Jn. 1:3, 4; my emphasis). Through Him, man is born into the family of God. If the Light of Yeshua is in you, you have the power to become the *Sons of God.* "But as many as received him, to them gave he power to become the sons of God, even to them that believe on his name" (Jn. 1:12). You are the Children of Light, "Then Jesus said unto them, yet a little while is the light with you. Walk while ye have the light, lest darkness come upon you: for he that walketh in darkness knoweth not whither he goeth. While ye have light, believe in the light, that ye may be the children of light" (Jn. 12: 35 – 36a). "For ye were sometimes darkness, but now are ye light in the Lord: walk as children of light."(Eph. 5:8). As a child of God, the light in you shines to glorify the Father (Mt. 5:-16). We, the children of light, like the branches of the Candlestick, are connected to the central shaft, (Yeshua, *the vine*), and are a product of His fruit. "I am the vine, ye are the branches: He that abideth in me, and I in him, the same bringeth forth much fruit: for without me ye can do nothing" (Jn. 15:5).

If you are not a child of God and you want to be. You must first repent and acknowledge Yeshua as the Son of God and believe that He died so that you can live. If you ask Him to forgive you, He will. Yeshua is the only way to the Father. "Jesus saith unto him, I am the way, the truth, and the life: no man cometh unto the Father, but by me" (Jn. 14:6).

Moses used the Hebrew language to describe the Tabernacle, and for one to see the significance of the revelation of Yeshua found in the design of the Candlestick, you must have some knowledge of the language. The Hebrew alphabet has twenty-two letters, from which came the complete Word of God.

The Candlestick was designed to resemble the almond tree. It had *twenty-two* sets of buds, blooms and fruit; four *sets* in the central shaft, and *three sets* in each of the *six branches*. Its twenty-two set design delivers a portrayal of how God gave humanity His written word through the Hebrew language, and points the way to Yeshua, the Living Word. The Candlestick is a "Shadow" of Yeshua who is the perfect incarnate WORD of God, and the LIGHT of the world.

According to B. R. Hicks' research, the almond is like the Word of God; it is eatable in two different stages.[8] (1) .The green pods: The tender pod of the almond is a "Shadow" of the *Milk of the Word*, which provides nourishment for the newborn babes in Messiah. "As newborn babes, desire the sincere *milk* of the *word* that ye may grow thereby" (1 Pet. 2:2; my emphasis). (2). The ripened nutmeat: The meat of the almond is harder to chew and digest than the tender pod, and is a "Shadow" of the s*trong meat* of the Word of God.

As children born into the family of God mature; their appetite increases. The Word of God continues to satisfy their hunger. "But *strong meat* belongeth to them that are of full age, even those who by reason of use have their senses exercised to discern both good and evil" (Heb. 5:14; my emphasis). No matter where you are in your development, He is always there to give you what you need. His Word is alive, providing nourishment for all stages of development. His desire is for all of His children to grow to maturity. "For one that useth *milk* is unskillful in the word of righteousness: for he is *a babe*. But *strong meat* belongeth to them that are *of full age*, even those who *by reason of use* have their senses exercised to discern both good and evil" (Heb. 5:13, 14; my emphasis).

Choosing the almond tree as the pattern for the Candlestick teaches man to feed on **ALL** of GOD'S WORD, because it is essential for growth. It provides the nourishment that feeds the spirit of man. Yeshua said, "Man shall not live by bread alone, but by every word that proceedeth out of the mouth of God" (Deut. 8:3, Mt. 4:4).

John saw Yeshua, the Heavenly Candlestick and said, "And I turned to see the voice that spake with me. And being turned, I saw seven golden candlesticks and in the midst of the seven candlesticks ONE LIKE UNTO THE SON OF MAN" (Rev. 1:12- 13; my emphasis). Yeshua said, "I am the light of the world: he that followeth me shall not walk in darkness, but shall have the light of life" (Jn. 8:12). He is the Light that lights every man. He is the vine and the redeemed are the branches. If we abide in Yeshua, His procreative power will produce much fruit (Jn. 15:5).

"The spirit of man is the candle of the Lord" (Pr. 20:27). If Yeshua is the Light of your life, the Spirit of the Living God lives in you to teach you His ways (1Cor. 3:16; Ps. 18:28). We, the believers, have the tremendous responsibility to be the LIGHT OF THE WORLD (Mt. 5:14-16). If Yeshua has never become your light, He can, and will, if you will repent and believe. To have your spirit ignited by the Lord, you must be born again (Jn. 3:3). When an individual accepts Yeshua as the Son of God, the regenerating power of the Holy Spirit gives life to his/her dark dead sinful spirit. The Holy Spirit baptizes each new believer into the body of Messiah; and then the believer becomes His dwelling place (1 Cor. 12:13; 2 Cor. 6:16). The Holy Spirit sets the believer's new spirit ablaze, as He did the Candlestick of the Tabernacle. Yeshua, who is represented by the central shaft of the Candlestick, unites with you (the branch), to be the single source of Light in your life (Eph. 5:8). Your new spirit and the Spirit of God become one for eternity.

The **Location:** The Candlestick was on the southern side of the Tabernacle next to the camp of Reuben, who is the firstborn son of Israel. From God's perspective, Yeshua held the Candlestick in His right hand. The traditional right hand blessing over the firstborn son was and still is a custom performed by the patriarch of Middle Eastern families. The father places his right hand on the head of his son and proclaims the blessings that are imparted to him. It is customary to give the firstborn male a double portion of the father's possessions. Yeshua, being the first and only begotten Son of God, was entitled to this blessing (Jn. 3:16) He also received a double portion blessing from His Father. God the Father gave His Son the lives of all the Hebrews (Israel) and the nations (the Gentiles). "The Lord GOD which gathereth the outcasts of Israel saith, Yet will I gather others to him, beside those that are gathered unto him" (Isa. 56:8), and "And other sheep I have, which are not of this fold: them also I must bring, and they shall hear my voice; and there shall be one fold, and one shepherd" (Jn. 10:16).

The Heavenly Father restored Yeshua to His original position in heaven; He is seated at the Father's right hand (Col. 3:1). At the trial before the crucifixion, the high priest asked Yeshua, "Art thou the Messiah the Son of the Blessed?," and Yeshua answered with these words, " I am: and ye shall see the Son of man sitting on the right hand of power, and coming in the clouds of heaven" (Mk. 14:62). His position is secured for ALL eternity.

Believers receive a three-fold double blessing through Yeshua. (1) Through Him sin is forgiven and forgotten. "As far as the east is from the west, so far hath he removed our transgressions from us" (Ps. 103:12) "I, even I, am he that blotteth out thy transgressions for mine own sake, and will not remember thy sins" (Isa. 43:25). "For I will be merciful to their unrighteousness, and their sins and their iniquities will I remember no more" (Heb. 8:12)

(2) Each believer receives a *new heart* and a *new spirit* (Ezek. 11:19, 36:26-27; Jer. 24:7).

(3) As a new creation, the believer is blessed with the Lord's indwelling presence here in the earth and one day face to face to share everlasting life with Him (Jn. 14:3; 17:11, 21, 23-24; 2 Cor. 5:17) If you are a believer, you are seated with Yeshua in heavenly places and the wealth of Heaven is available to you. "And hath raised us up together, and made us sit together in heavenly places in Christ Jesus" (Eph. 2:6). Yeshua has given you a three-fold double blessing; please don't wait to enjoy your new life in Messiah. Today is the day to begin living in the abundant life He provided.

The Oil for the lamps: "And thou shall command the children of Israel that they bring *pure olive oil beaten* for the light, to cause the lamp to burn always" (Ex. 27:20; my emphasis).

The process for making pure olive oil serves as another "shadow" of suffering. The olives were either ground or beaten to render oil. One method entailed grinding the olives on a millstone and straining the impurities through a cloth filter. This method left small fragments in the oil, rendering it unfit for use in the Candlestick. To produce the pure clean oil needed for the Candlestick, harvesters placed the olives in a cloth bag made of several pieces of cloth. A cord was used to tie the cloth together forming a bag for the olives, much like a drawstring bag. Next, the olives were beaten to release the oil and finally, the bag was hung from a tree branch. A vessel was placed beneath the bag to catch the oil. This process produced the Pure Beaten Olive Oil needed for the Candlestick.

God required the purest quality oil because it is the "Shadow" of the Holy Spirit. It represents His indwelling presence in the life of Yeshua. The Holy Spirit was present at Yeshua's conception. "And the angel answered and said unto her, The Holy Ghost shall come upon thee, and the power of the Highest shall overshadow thee: therefore also that holy thing which shall be born of thee shall be called the Son of God" (Lk. 1:35). He was with Him at His baptism and His power raised Him from the grave. "And Jesus, when he was baptized, went up straightway out of the water: and, lo, the heavens were opened unto him, and he saw the Spirit of God descending like a dove, and lighting upon him" (Mt. 3:16). "But if the Spirit of him that raised up Jesus from the dead dwell in you, he that raised up Christ from the dead shall also quicken your mortal bodies by his Spirit that dwelleth in you" (Rom. 8:11). Each of the seven lamps of the Candlestick represents an attribute of the Holy Spirit's power operating in the life of Yeshua. "And there shall come forth a rod out of the stem of Jesse, and a Branch shall grow out of his roots: And the spirit of the LORD shall rest upon him, the spirit of wisdom and understanding, the spirit of counsel and might, the spirit of knowledge and of the fear of the LORD" (Isa. 11:1-2). His seven-fold ministry was active in Yeshua's life without measure (Jn. 3:34-35). "How God anointed Jesus of Nazareth with the Holy Ghost and with power: who went about doing good, and healing all that were oppressed of the devil; for God was with him" (Acts 10:38).

The lamp of the central shaft of the Candlestick is a "Shadow" of the ***Spirit of the Lord***. The remaining six lamps reveal how the Holy Spirit functions in the earth. He is the ***Spirit of Wisdom***, the ***Spirit of Understanding***, the ***Spirit of Counsel,*** the ***Spirit of Might***, the ***Spirit of Knowledge***, and the

Spirit of Reverence. The Holy Spirit's work continues through the children of God.

The Pure Oil of the Candlestick foretold of the indwelling presence of the Holy Spirt in the lives of believers. He is the one who enlightens the things concerning the Word of God. Yeshua said, "But the Comforter, which is the Holy Ghost, whom the Father will send in my name, he shall teach you all things, and bring all things to your remembrance, whatsoever I have said unto you" (Jn. 14:26). The Holy Spirit illuminates the written Word and His power brings it to pass. The Holy Spirit reveals that God's Word produces *Wisdom* and *Understanding*. Through Him the Word of God becomes the *Counsel* that directs and supplies the *Power* and *Might* to stand against the enemies' attacks. The Holy Spirit takes residence in every believer and brings with Him the *Knowledge* of Yeshua's love, which produces a *Reverential Respect* for God the Father. "But when the Comforter is come, whom I will send unto you from the Father, even the Spirit of truth, which proceedeth from the Father, he shall testify of me (Jn. 15:26). "All things that the Father hath are mine: therefore said I, that he shall take of mine, and shall show it unto you" (Jn.16:15).

The Holy Spirit has always been the operating power of God in the earth. He reveals the sin of unbelief that separates man from God. He also reveals the righteousness of God in Messiah and convicts those who reject God's free gift of salvation of the forthcoming judgment (Jn. 16:8-11). New birth comes through Him (Jn. 3:3-6, 1 Cor. 12:12-13). His anointing power supplies everything needed to serve in the Kingdom of God (1 Cor. 12:7-11, 27-30; Eph. 4:11). He empowers us to be witnesses (Acts. 1:8, 1 Cor. 6:19). The power of His light reveals sin and changes us into the image of Messiah (Rom. 8:29). His indwelling presence is what confirms that we are members of the family of God (Rom. 8:9).

There is another aspect of the Candlestick that warrants our attention. God said the Light was NEVER to go out.

Every morning and evening the priests had the responsibility of adding fresh oil and trimming the wicks. If they failed to trim the wicks properly or add fresh oil, the light would eventually go out and prevent the priests from completing their assigned task.

Do you realize that as priests in the Kingdom of God, you are also responsible for tending the Light that dwells in you? "But ye are a chosen generation, a royal priesthood, an holy nation, a peculiar people; that ye should show forth the praises of him who hath called you out of darkness into his marvelous light" (1 Pet. 2:9). For certain, we don't want to become like the five virgins who found themselves unprepared to meet the bridegroom because they failed to buy oil for their lamps (Mt. 25:1-13). We must tend the Light within by spending time with Him and receiving His fresh oil daily. Every experience with the Lord is wonderful, but we need to always be moving forward. Paul said, "Brethren, I count not myself to have apprehended: but this one thing I do, forgetting those things which are behind, and reaching forth unto those things which are before, I press toward the mark for the prize of the high calling of God in Christ Jesus" (Phil. 3:13-14). The spirit of the believer is the candle of the Lord. The wick of our spirit is trimmed as we have new experiences with Him daily. Without the Pure Oil of the Holy Spirit flowing through you, the fire will go out. The fire of the Lord ignites our newborn spirit as He did the Candlestick, but we are responsible for keeping it burning (Pr. 20:27). The only way to keep the fire of God burning is to get to know Him intimately and obey His commandments. Yeshua said, "He that hath my commandments, and keepeth them, he it is that loveth me: and he that loveth me shall be loved of my Father, and **I will love him, and will manifest myself to him"** (John 14:21; my emphasis) The book of Proverbs teaches, "For thy commandment is a <u>lamp</u>, and thy law is <u>light</u>; and reproofs of instruction are the way of life" (Pr. 6:23; my emphasis) The Psalmist says this, "The entrance of thy words giveth light; it giveth understanding unto the simple" (Ps. 119:130). The more you fall in love with the Lord, the more you want to obey Him. Obedience not only keeps the fire of God burning, it produces His manifested presence.

The size: God excluded the measurement for the Candlestick, because to do so would place limitations on the Holy Spirit. The size and purpose of the Candlestick is a "Shadow" of the Holy Spirit's power to illuminate the WORD of GOD, and there is no limit to His power. He is the person of the Holy Trinity who moves on the spoken Word to bring it to pass. His light in the Tabernacle illuminated the Table of Showbread, revealing Yeshua as the LIVING BREAD (Lk. 24:27, 30-31; Jn. 6:53-58; 14:26). The brightness of the Holy Spirit's lights shining on the Golden Altar of Incense makes known the power of prayer that comes through the name of Yeshua. The Holy Spirit searches the heart and takes our feeble insufficient prayers before the Father. His prayers are always in accordance with the will of God. "Likewise the Spirit also helpeth our infirmities: for we know not what we should pray for as we ought: but the Spirit itself maketh intercession for us with groanings which cannot be uttered. And he that searcheth the hearts knoweth what is the mind of the Spirit, because he maketh intercession for the saints according to the will of God" (Rom. 8:26-27).

God anoints His children with the same powerful anointing that belonged to Yeshua. As a result, His work continues and is multiplied. Yeshua said, "Verily, verily, I say unto you, He that believeth on me, the works that I do shall he do also; and greater works than these shall he do; because I go unto my Father" (Jn. 14:12). If every believer surrenders to the Spirit's LIGHT, there is no limit to what the Father can accomplish in the earth.

God put the size of the Candlestick in the hands of man, much like the working of the Holy Spirit. He is here without measure; His only limitation is YOU. God said, "Be FILLED with the Holy Spirit to show the world the Light of His love" (Eph. 5:18). We must never quench the Spirit of God, because

He restores sight to the blind, heals the sick, instructs, gives wisdom and knowledge, and brings forth new life; and He has chosen to do those things through the life of every believer who yields to Him (1 Thess. 5:19; 1 Cor. 12:7-11).

The only light: The Candlestick was the single source of light inside the Tabernacle.

It was during the Feast of Tabernacles that Yeshua declared Himself the Light of the World (Jn. 8:12). The feast of Tabernacles (*Sukkot* in Hebrew) is one of the three annual feast that required every Israeli male (twenty years old and up) to travel to Jerusalem and appear before the Lord (Ex. 23:14-17). Through four different events during the Feast of Sukkot, recorded in the book of John, Yeshua not only revealed Himself as the Light of the World; He also declared that He is the Living Water, and the Savior.

God's feasts are for ALL people to celebrate. Although He gave them to Israel, they were never for Israel only. "Speak unto the children of Israel, and say unto them, concerning **the feasts of the LORD**, which ye shall proclaim to be holy convocations, even **these are my feasts"** (Lev. 23:2; my emphasis). "One law shall be to him that is homeborn, and unto the stranger that sojourneth among you" (Ex. 12:49).

God called His feasts Holy Convocations, which means to assemble together. During each of God's feasts, the people recalled and rehearsed the blessings that God had given them, and looked forward to a new year of blessing. God's feasts are perhaps the greatest of all tools for teaching our children His faithfulness. Oh, how the "Church" has missed out on this part of our heritage!

As we examine some of the ways the Feast of Sukkot is celebrated, you will see why Yeshua chose the days of this feast to reveal Himself.

The Feast of Sukkot is celebrated for eight days. It begins on the fifteenth day in the seventh month (the month of *Tishrei*) (Lev. 23:34-36). The First, seventh and eighth days are Sabbath days. It takes place at the end of the agricultural season, with great expectation for a new and better year. During the first seven days the people lived in three-sided booths made from various tree branches, such as willow and palm, to remind them of the time spent in the desert wilderness and that they were strangers and pilgrims on the earth (Lev. 23:42 -43; Heb. 11:13, 16).

The city of Jerusalem and the nearby countryside overflowed with people who had gathered to celebrate God's feast. They set up booths throughout the area; there were people as far as the eye can see resembling the campsites around the Tabernacle (Lev. 23:43). Joy and anticipation filled their hearts as the priest set up extra candlesticks in the Temple court. The city glowed in their bright light. The stage was set for God to make Himself known. On the final day of the feast, when the light from the candlesticks grew dim, and the city became dark Yeshua stood and said, "I **am the light of the world:** he that followeth me shall not walk in darkness, but shall have the light of life" (Jn. 8:12; my emphases). He revealed Himself as the LIGHT of GOD that was foreshadowed by the Candlestick of the Tabernacle.

God used the wicks of the extra candlesticks to reveal Yeshua as the incarnate WORD of GOD (the *LIVING TORAH*). The wicks were made from the discarded white linen robes of the priests and the Levites. The priests received a new white robe upon completion of their annual term in the temple. The name commonly used for the linen strips is "Swaddling cloth".

Celebrating the Torah (in Hebrew *Simchat Torah*) is another event the takes place during Sukkot. Reading the same scriptures aloud in the Synagogues each year is a special time of celebration. The people rejoice and thank God for giving His Word to preserve them. Since ancient times, the scribes continue to copy the Torah to preserve it, (*Torah is the first five books of the Bible*). The finished scroll is wrapped in

"Swaddling cloth". We have the written Word of God today because of their efforts.

When Yeshua was born, His mother, Mary, wrapped Him in "Swaddling cloth". "And she brought forth her firstborn son, and wrapped him in *swaddling clothes*, and laid him in a manger" (Lk. 2:7; my emphasis). Her action revealed that the child born in Bethlehem that day is the LIVING TORAH OF GOD; "And *the Word was made flesh*, and dwelt among us" (Jn. 1:14; my emphasis).

Did you ever wonder where Mary got the "Swaddling cloth"? The "Swaddling cloth" used to wrap Yeshua points to the lineage of Mary. She was a descendent of Aaron, the high priest of the Tabernacle. Her Cousin Elizabeth's husband was also in the priesthood. He served at the Altar of Incense. "There was in the days of Herod, the king of Judaea, a certain priest named Zacharias, of the course of Abia: and his wife was of the daughters of Aaron, and her name was Elisabeth" (Lk. 1:5). "And it came to pass, that while he executed the priest's office before God in the order of his course, According to the custom of the priest's office, his lot was to burn incense when he went into the temple of the Lord" (Lk. 1:8-9).

The Bible does not say where Mary got "Swaddling cloth" and perhaps it is not important. However, Yeshua's lineage is. He is the Great High Priest appointed by God not man. His priesthood is after the order of Melchizedek. "Without father, without mother, without descent, having neither beginning of days, nor end of life; but made like unto the Son of God; abideth a priest continually" (Heb. 7:3).Yet, through His mother, Yeshua qualified as a Levitical priest as well.

In answer to where Mary got "Swaddling cloth", perhaps her cousin Elizabeth gave them to her. Mary visited her as Zechariah, Elizabeth's husband, completed his course in the temple. The custom required Zechariah to discard his white robe, giving Elizabeth access to "Swaddling cloth". God revealed the Deity of the baby within Mary's womb to Elizabeth so, it is befitting that she would give Mary "Swaddling cloth" to wrap Yeshua in. "Swaddling cloth" teaches two things about Yeshua, He is the Living Torah, and He is the Great High Priest.

The second event, during Sukkot, took place on the seventh day, (the last day), of the feast during the ceremony of water drawing, (in Hebrew *Nissuch Ha-Mayim).* The seventh day of the feast is referred to as the great celebration. The priests leave the temple and travel to the pool of Siloam to draw out water. As they traveled, an entourage of people followed waving willow branches, stirring the air to signify the breath of God. Arriving back at the temple, before the water was poured out, they circled the altar seven times shouting Hosheanah (save now). On the previous six days, the priest circled the altar only once saying, "Save now, I beseech thee, O LORD: O LORD, I beseech thee, send now prosperity!" (Ps. 118:25). As the priest poured the water around the altar to commemorate the blessing of rain for the new crop, the people beat the willow branches bare and saved them to kindle the fire that would cook their next Passover Lamb. "But the land, whither ye go to possess it, is a land of hills and valleys, and drinketh water of the rain of heaven: A land which the LORD thy God careth for: the eyes of the LORD thy God are always upon it, from the beginning of the year even unto the end of the year. And it shall come to pass, if ye shall hearken diligently unto my commandments which I command you this day, to love the LORD your God, and to serve him with all your heart and with all your soul, That I will give you the rain of your land in his due season, the first rain and the latter rain, that thou mayest gather in thy corn, and thy wine, and thine oil" (Deut. 11:11- 14). Pouring the water is also a "Shadow" of the Holy Spirit being poured out on all flesh (Joel 2:28; Acts 2:1-21). This was, in all probability, the exact moment that Yeshua said, "If any man thirst let him come unto me, and drink. He that believeth on me, as the scripture hath said, out of his belly shall flow rivers of living water. (But this spake he of the Spirit which they that believe on him should receive: for the Holy Ghost was not yet given; because that *Yeshua* was not yet glorified.)" (Jn. 7:37-39; my emphasis).

As mentioned earlier, celebrating the Torah (in Hebrew *Simchat Torah*) is an important part of the celebration of Sukkot. Specific portions of scripture commemorating the festivities are read aloud during the synagogue services. One of them is, "O LORD, the hope of Israel, *all that forsake thee shall be ashamed, and they that depart from me shall be written in the earth, because they have forsaken the LORD, the fountain of living waters.* Heal me, O LORD, and I shall be healed; save me, and I shall be saved: for thou art my praise" (Jer.17:13-14; my emphasis)

Eight is the number identified with a new beginning; therefore, I am of the opinion that the third and fourth events took place on the eighth day of the feast. Both lives of the individuals associated with the latter events received NEW BEGINNINGS.

The first event is the woman who was caught committing adultery. The Scribes and Pharisees brought her before Yeshua. Their intent was to entrap Him with their questions; however, as it turned out, they fell into their own trap (Jn. 8:1-12). The Pharisees, of all men, knew the written word, and had they considered the events of the previous seven days along with the scripture readings; they would not have challenged Yeshua. They would have recognized Him as the "Thirst Quenching Water of God", and the "Light of the World". Instead, with hard hearts, they came pointing an accusing finger at the adulteress. Once again the stage was set, this time, for Yeshua to reveal Himself as the Fountain of Living Waters. Without speaking a word, Yeshua stooped and began to write in the earth. No one knows what He wrote that day, however, the events of the week, along with the annual reading of Jer. 17:13-14 leads me to believe that He may have written these two verses on the ground. "O LORD, the hope of Israel, all that forsake thee shall be ashamed, and they that depart from me shall be written in the earth, because they have forsaken the LORD**, the fountain of living waters"** (Jer. 17:13-14; my emphasis). He stood up and gave the accusers the opportunity to repent before he stooped down again and continued to write. Although we cannot be certain what He wrote, it had to be words of conviction. I believe, He did exactly what the scripture said and wrote each of their names exposing their sin and at the same time revealing Himself as "The Hope of Israel" and the "Fountain of Living Water". Afterwards, He spoke saying, "He that is without sin among you, let him cast a stone at her" (Jn. 8:7). Each man, in silence, turned and walked away beginning with the oldest. Not one cast a stone at the woman. Forgiven, the woman had a new life with a NEW BEGINNING.

The final event is the young man who was born blind in John chapter 9. Since both the seventh and eighth days of the feast are Sabbath days, it is uncertain which day the young man was healed. We begin with Yeshua being questioned about the cause of the young man's blindness; some thought that it was either his sin of that of his parents. However, as with the previous events that led to the revelation of Yeshua, this was His opportunity to manifest the works of God. "Jesus answered, Neither hath this man sinned, nor his parents: but that the works of God should be made manifest in him." (Jn. 9:3)

God's timing is always perfect; He waited until Jerusalem was filled with untold numbers of people celebrating His Feast to reveal His power to save and to heal. Yeshua made clay with His own spittle (since man is made of clay, perhaps Yeshua formed eyes out of the clay, just food for thought) and put it on the boy's eyes, and told him to go and wash it off in the pool of Siloam; the same pool of water used by the priest for the water ceremony in the temple. The young man obeyed and returned seeing, but not knowing who healed him. Later, Yeshua appeared to him and revealed Himself as Messiah, the Savior, and the young man immediately believed and worshipped Him (Jn. 9:1-39). Remember, at the water pouring ceremony, the people shouted "Hosheanah" (save now). The young man's life would no longer be lived in darkness; the Light of the World had opened both his physical eyes and his spiritual eyes. Yeshua, The Living Water, washed him and gave him drink; he was clean, and he would never thirst again because he also received a new beginning. I hope you see how incredible our God is! His timing is always perfect.

My husband and I once had the privilege of celebrating the Feast of Sukkot with a combined group of Messianic believers from congregations throughout Tennessee. Although different from the ancient celebration, in many ways it was similar. There was dancing, worship, teaching, preaching, and prayer. Marty Goetz, a very talented Messianic musician, was there providing awe-inspiring worship music. People of all ages attended; the youngest was about a month old and the oldest was in her eighties. Services were in an outdoor facility, an open tent. One evening during the worship service, several people spontaneously began to walk through the congregation waving large leafy branches. Everywhere they walked people fell unable to stand in the presence of God. My husband and I were standing outside of the tent and the overwhelming presence of God was so strong that it reached beyond the tent and we fell to our knees. That night, I witnessed the power of God as He healed the sick, delivered people from bondage, restored relationships, and called men, women, and children into His ministry.

I take this opportunity to encourage you to find a congregation who celebrates the Feasts and join with them. You will see the works of Messiah Yeshua in all of them.

You will see *the crucifixion* and *redemption* in *(Pesach)* **Passover** (1 Pet. 1:18, 19); you will see *sanctification* (1 Cor. 5:7) and *justification* (2 Cor. 5:21) in (*Hag HaMatzah*) **Unleavened Bread;** the *resurrection of Messiah* is revealed (1Cor. 15:20-22b) in (*Sfirat Haomer*) **First fruits;** the *coming of the Holy Spirit* (Acts 2:1-4, 41b) and the *birth of the Church* is seen in the (*Shavuot*) **Feast of Weeks/** Pentecost (Heb. 10:16). The summer feasts represent the time of preparation for the FINAL HARVEST or the Church age. They have been fulfilled. Some of the remaining fall feasts have not yet been fulfilled. **The Feast of Trumpets** (*Rosh Hashanah*) reveals three things, *Israel regathered* (Jer. 32:37), *the rapture of the Church* and *the return of Messiah* (1 Thess. 4:16-17, 1 Cor. 15:52). **The Day of Atonement** (*Yom Kippur*) is not yet complete. Yeshua has paid the ATONEMENT for the world. Although, not all have believed. Those who believe that He is the Messiah have been forgiven (Heb. 9:28). Many of Israel's children are still looking for the Messiah. When ALL Israel turns to her Messiah, this feast will be fulfilled (Zech. 12:10. 13:1). **The Feast of Booths** (*Sukkot*) represents the final harvest, *The Kingdom of God on the Earth* (Zech.14:16).

SUMMARY

THE CANDLESTICK = Yeshua, the Light of the World
THE OIL = the anointing of the Holy Spirit
THE DESIGN = Yeshua the vine = the procreative power of God that brings forth His family. Yeshua is the complete Word of God.
THE LOCATION = the blessing of the right hand of God
THE SIZE = the unlimited illuminating power of the Holy Spirit to reveal the written word.

CHAPTER 8

The Coverings

Moreover, thou shalt make the tabernacle with ten curtains of fine twined linen, and blue, and purple, and scarlet; with cherubim of cunning work shalt thou make them. The length of one curtain shall be eight and twenty cubits, and the breadth of one curtain four cubits: and every one of the curtains shall have one measure. The five curtains shall be coupled together one to another; and other five curtains shall be coupled one to another. And thou shalt make loops of blue upon the edge of the one curtain from the selvedge in the coupling; and likewise shalt thou make in the uttermost edge of another curtain, in the coupling of the second. Fifty loops shalt thou make in the one curtain, and fifty loops shalt thou make in the edge of the curtain that is in the coupling of the second; that the loops may take hold one of another. And thou shalt make fifty taches of gold, and couple the curtains together with the taches: and it shall be one tabernacle. And thou shalt make curtains of goats' hair to be a covering upon the tabernacle: eleven curtains shalt thou make. The length of one curtain shall be thirty cubits, and the breadth of one curtain four cubits, and the eleven curtains shall be all of one measure. And thou shalt couple five curtains by themselves and six curtains by themselves, and shalt double the sixth curtain in the forefront of the tabernacle. And thou shalt make fifty loops on the edge of the one curtain that is outmost in the coupling, and fifty loops in the edge of the curtain which coupleth the second. And thou shalt make fifty

> taches of brass, and put the taches into the loops, and couple the tent together that it may be one. And the remnant that remaineth of the curtains of the tent, the half curtain that remaineth, shall hang over the backside of the tabernacle. And a cubit on the one side, and a cubit on the other side of that which remaineth in the length of the curtains of the tent, it shall hang over the sides of the tabernacle on this side and on that side, to cover it. And thou shalt make a covering for the tent of Rams' skins dyed red, and a covering above of badgers' skins (Ex. 26:1-14).

The Tabernacle surrounded by the people's tents (Christa Shore)

Four very different coverings protected the Tabernacle and its furnishings from the outside elements. Four, being the number associated with the earth, indicates that the Creator of all things is about to reveal more of Himself to His people through the coverings of the Tabernacle. Within each of the four coverings is a revelation of Yeshua. The "Shadows" of

Yeshua become unmistakable, as we examine each curtain and covering. As with the furnishings, the numbers associated with the measurements, the assembly, and placement of each will reveal something about Yeshua.

First, we will look at the ***white*** curtain.

> "Moreover, thou shalt make the tabernacle with ten curtains of fine twined linen, and blue, and purple, and scarlet; with cherubim of cunning work shalt thou make them. The length of one curtain shall be eight and twenty cubits, and the breadth of one curtain four cubits: and every one of the curtains shall have one measure. The five curtains shall be coupled together one to another; and other five curtains shall be coupled one to another. And thou shalt make loops of blue upon the edge of the one curtain from the selvedge in the coupling; and likewise shalt thou make in the uttermost edge of another curtain, in the coupling of the second. Fifty loops shalt thou make in the one curtain, and fifty loops shalt thou make in the edge of the curtain that is in the coupling of the second; that the loops may take hold one of another. And thou shalt make fifty taches of gold, and couple the curtains together with the taches: and it shall be one tabernacle" (Ex. 26:1-6).

The white linen curtain is the first covering over the Tabernacle. It spanned the entire length of the structure and was the most beautiful of the four. It hung nearest to the most holy things, those things that represent the deity of the Son of God. It was wide enough to hang over the sides and it extended beyond the backside of the building. It took anointed hands, skilled in needlework, to produce this beautiful covering made of white, blue, purple and scarlet threads interwoven with the image of Cherubim.

Through this curtain, the correlation between the number *four* and the earth appears several different ways. First, fine linen is the fabric that was used to make it. Linen comes from flax, a plant whose very existence comes from the earth. Second, the artisans used Linen to make *four* features of the Tabernacle; the white linen curtain being the first. Each of the others, the Veil, the hanging for the door, and the gate consisted of white linen interwoven with blue, purple and scarlet. Third, within the *four* colors we have "Shadows" of Yeshua. White reveals His pure righteous, Blue reveals His heavenly origin, Purple reveals His position of royalty, and Scarlet points to His shed blood.

Two features separate the White Curtain from the other three.

(1) White was the predominate color. The bright white color is the "Shadow" of Yeshua's PURE RIGHTEOUSNESS. His righteousness supersedes His position in heaven, and that He is royalty. It even supersedes His blood. The Father accepted His blood because He is righteousness not because of His Son-ship or His royal position.

This particular linen was Egyptian, the finest quality ever known. Even with today's modern technology, man cannot reproduce its pure white color. The rare quality and color make it the most valuable and desirable of all linen. Its pure quality is a "Shadow" of the righteousness of Messiah, the bridegroom, arrayed in His triumphant robe of righteousness. "Lift up thine eyes round about, and behold: all these gather themselves together, and come to thee. As I live, saith the LORD, thou shalt surely clothe thee with them all, as with an ornament, and bind them on thee, as a bride doeth" (Isa.49:18b). "I will greatly rejoice in the LORD, my soul shall be joyful in my God; for he hath clothed me with the garments of salvation, he hath covered me with the robe of righteousness, as a bridegroom decketh himself with ornaments, and as a bride adorneth herself with her jewels" (Isa.61:10).

The fine quality of the linen also points to the adornment of the believers (the bride). "Let us be glad and rejoice, and give honor to him: for the marriage of the Lamb is come, and his wife hath made herself ready" (Rev. 19:7). "Fine linen, bright and clean, was given her to wear." (Fine linen stands for the righteous acts of the saints)" (Rev. 19:8) NIV.

How glorious are these passages of scripture to those who have been redeemed. Our wedding dress is Yeshua's righteousness.

(2) The image of cherubim: From God's position, above the Ark of the Covenant, the angels of heaven surround Him on the White Linen Curtain. Angels are always present with God to defend His righteousness and to declare His holiness. Their image on the White Curtain reminded the priests of the holiness of the God they served. Behind the Veil was the Holy of Holies, the holiest place in the Tabernacle. It symbolizes the throne of God where the angels minister continually saying, "Holy, holy, holy, Lord God Almighty, which was, and is, and is to come" (Rev. 4:8; Isa. 6:3). Their presence warns all who enter into the presence of God to proceed with caution YOU ARE STANDING ON HOLY GROUND, **ENTER ONLY WITH THE BLOOD!** Nadab and Abihu, Aaron's sons, failed to heed the warning and offered strange fire before the Lord and perished (Lev. 10:1). Ezekiel saw God's war chariot surrounded with angels coming to destroy the sinful men who had entered God's Holy Place without the blood (Ezek. 1). God sends His angels to minister to those who are the heirs of salvation (Heb. 1:13, 14). The "Shadow" of angels surrounding the redeemed children of God is revealed through the White Linen Curtain. It is God's indwelling presence that commands the presence of the angels (1 Cor. 6:19). "The angel of the Lord encampeth

round about them that fear him, and delivereth them" (Ps. 34:7). Just as God was surrounded by the angles on the White Linen Curtain of the Tabernacle, the angels of heaven surround those who have been redeemed.

There are two types of angels found in the Bible, Cherubim and Seraphim. Their descriptions are found in Ezekiel chapter 1verses 5-14 and chapter 10; also Revelation chapter 4 verses 7-9. All angels are immortal and holy created beings, their vast number is beyond man's ability to comprehend. The angels have an organized rank system (Isa. 6:2, I Thess. 4:16). They also have emotions and are concerned with human activities in relation to their interaction with the things of God (Lk. 15:10, 1 Pet. 1:12). They have, at times, taken on human form (Gen. 18:2-8). Following are a few examples of their work. God sent an angel with Eliezer, the servant of Abraham, to find a wife for Isaac (Gen. 24:7, 40). The angel of God prepared food for Elijah three times (1 Ki. 19:5-8). God sent His angel to shut the mouth of the lions to protect Daniel (Dan. 6:22). The angel of the Lord was sent to deliver Peter from prison (Acts 12:7-10). The angel of the Lord spoke to Philip and told him where to go to share the gospel (Acts 8:26). The angel of the Lord was sent to comfort Paul before he was shipwrecked (Acts 27:23, 24).

Believers can enter into the presence of God and His angels without fear THROUGH THE BLOOD OF YESHUA (Heb. 10:19- 20). A day is coming when all men will see the Lord with His angels coming to take vengeance on those who reject Him. "And to you who are troubled rest with us, when the Lord *Yeshua* shall be revealed from heaven <u>with his mighty angels</u> in flaming fire taking vengeance on them that know not God and they obey not the gospel of our Lord *Yeshua the Messiah*; who shall be punished with everlasting destruction from the presence of the Lord, and from the glory of his power" (2 Thess. 1:1-9; my emphasis). **You do not have to be one of them if you receive Him now!**

God reveals His perfect grace through the assembly, the pure quality of the linen, and the meaning of the numbers associated with this curtain. The White Linen Curtain consisted of *Ten* strips, each strip was *twenty-eight cubits* long, and *four* cubits wide. It was assembled in two sections of *five strips*, and connected by *fifty* blue loops and *fifty* golden clasps. The parallels in the numbers associated with the White Linen Curtain unfold the Grace of God. *Twenty-eight*, the length of each strip, reveals the quality of the pure white linen and its origin. Number *seven*, the number identified with God's perfection, represents its pure quality. Number *four*, the number for the earth, which produces the flax used to make linen, reveals its origin. *Four* is also the width of each strip. If we multiply God's perfection times the number for the earth (the origin of the linen) 7 x 4 = 28, it is equal to the length of each strip. God, through the written WORD, attends to the smallest detail to reveal His love for man.

Ten, the number of strips used to make the curtain, is the number identifying man's completeness (ten fingers, ten toes etc.) *Five*, the number of strips that formed each section reveals the Grace of God. Using these two numbers God shows how His Grace completed every requirement to re-unite man with his Creator, and make redeemed man His dwelling place. Gods' Grace multiplied by man's completeness 5 x 10 = 50; fifty is the number of loops and clasps on each section that held the curtain together. *Fifty* loops of blue reveal the heavenly might of the Holy Spirit, who connects redeemed man to the Son of God. "For as the body is one, and hath many members, and all the members of that one body, being many, are *one body: so also is Christ. For by one Spirit are we all baptized into one body,* whether we be Jews or Gentiles, whether we be bond or free; and have been all made to drink into one Spirit" (1Cor. 12:12-13; my emphasis). The *fifty* golden clasps reveal God's divine nature. The fullness of God's completed Grace is made known by the fifty loops and fifty clasps; 50 + 50

= 100. One hundred is one number made up of three units, a "Shadow" of the Holy Trinity. When the loops and the clasps connect, it becomes one; God and man are reunited through His Grace. Through the combined efforts of the Holy Trinity, it becomes "ONE Tabernacle WHEREIN GOD DWELLS" (Ex. 26:6; my emphasis). Could the use of these numbers be a coincidence? You are the judge. I believe God used the exact numbers needed to reveal the perfection of His Son. Through Yeshua, all humanity can come to know God the Father and be clothed with Yeshua's pure white robe of righteousness that was foreshadowed by White Linen Curtain of the Tabernacle. Yeshua is pure like the quality of the Egyptian linen; His righteousness cannot be duplicated.

The fifty blue loops and fifty gold clasps also reveal another mystery. God declared the 50th year the year of *Jubilee;* it is the year of release. Through it, God revealed His *Redemptive Grace*. In the year of Jubilee, God exonerated His people from all debt and restored their inheritance. Yeshua fulfilled the year of Jubilee at Calvary, when He paid the debt that man could not pay, thereby restoring the relationship between God and man.

The 50th day following Yeshua's resurrection is *Pentecost.* On this day, God poured out the Holy Spirit, who is His *Enabling Grace*, on all flesh "Even the mystery which hath been hid from ages and from generations, but now is made manifest to his saints: To whom God would make known what is the riches of the glory of this mystery among the Gentiles; which is Messiah in you, the hope of glory" (Col. 1:27). Through *faith* in Yeshua, God's *Redemptive* grace unites with His *Enabling* grace, *"it shall be ONE Tabernacle WHEREIN GOD DWELLS"* (Ex. 26:6; my emphasis).

The *second* curtain over the tabernacle was made of *goats' hair.*

> "And thou shalt make curtains of goats' hair to be a covering upon the tabernacle: eleven curtains shalt thou make. The length

> of one curtain shall be thirty cubits, and the breadth of one curtain four cubits, and the eleven curtains shall be all of one measure. And thou shalt couple five curtains by themselves and six curtains by themselves, and shalt double the sixth curtain in the forefront of the tabernacle. And thou shalt make fifty loops on the edge of the one curtain that is outmost in the coupling, and fifty loops in the edge of the curtain which coupleth the second. And thou shalt make fifty taches of brass, and put the taches into the loops, and couple the tent together that it may be one. And the remnant that remaineth of the curtains of the tent, the half curtain that remaineth, shall hang over the backside of the tabernacle. And a cubit on the one side, and a cubit on the other side of that which remaineth in the length of the curtains of the tent, it shall hang over the sides of the tabernacle on this side and on that side, to cover it" (Ex. 26:7-13).

Before the Lord cast Adam and Eve out of the Garden of Eden, He killed an animal to make coverings for them. This is the first reference to the shedding of innocent blood to cover sin. Although the Bible doesn't say what type of animal God killed, later, goats were accepted as sin offerings (Lev. 4:23, 27). Can you imagine the emotions suffered by Adam and Eve as they watched an innocent animal die because of what they had done? They deserved to die but the mercy of God spared them by substituting their blood for that of the sacrificed animal. God taught them the consequences of sin; death and innocent blood is the only acceptable payment. "For the wages of sin is death; but the gift of God is eternal life through Jesus Christ our Lord" (Rom. 6:23). God made the first sacrifice for sin with the blood of an animal, and the final sacrifice with His own blood in the body of His Son. He is the only one qualified to make such a sacrifice.

Before Adam sinned, he was clothed with the glory of God. After his sin, the glory of God departed and he was naked. God cannot look upon sin, so he killed an animal (I believe a goat) and made coverings for Adam and Eve. The hairy skin signified the presence of sin while at the same time revealed the mercy of God. God revealed His mercy when He exchanged our sin for His righteousness through His Son, Yeshua. "For he hath made him to be sin for us, who knew no sin; that we might be made the righteousness of God in him" (2 Cor. 5:21). "For if by one man's offence death reigned by one; much more they which receive abundance of grace and of the gift of righteousness shall reign in life by one, Jesus Christ" (Rom. 5:17).

The hairy curtain of the goats' hair was quite a contrast to the beautiful white linen curtain that lay beneath it. Anointed hands spun the goats' hair into yarn and weaved it into strips that were thirty cubits long and four cubits wide. Woven hair is heavy and the odor from the goats' hair must have been dreadful. The goats' hair curtain is diametrically different from the white linen covering. White linen is a "Shadow" of the righteousness of God, and the goat's hair is a "Shadow" of the totality of SIN. Everything about it is different. It consisted of uneven sections, five strips in one section and six in the other, for a total of eleven strips. The two sections were connected with brass clasps. As we look at the elements and numbers used to make this curtain, you will see a prophetic message emerge. Brass represents judgment. "And Moses made a serpent of brass, and put it upon a pole, and it came to pass, that if a serpent had bitten any man, when he beheld the serpent of brass, he lived" (Nu. 21:9).

Six is the number identified with man and five, God's Grace. Eleven reveals confusion and human failure. The prophetic message found within the goats' hair curtain is this, THE GRACE OF GOD REUNITES FALLEN MAN TO HIMSELF BY THE JUDGMENT YESHUA BORE.

The section of six strips is a "Shadow" of sin-ravaged man. God told Moses to, "Double the sixth curtain in the forefront of the Tabernacle" (Ex. 26:9b). By doing this, the ugly sight of the goats' hair was visible from the Brazen Altar. The goats' hair curtain acted as a reminder to every man bringing a sin offering to the Tabernacle that *his* sin is what caused the death of the animal he was bringing to sacrifice. The section of the curtain that was divided into five strips (5) reveals God's grace. Grace is God's unmerited favor; it is the gift that gives man the ability to live a holy life. God spared man by giving him a substitute to pay the price for his sin. Untold numbers of goats gave up their lives to make the goats' hair curtain to help us understand the extent of Gods' love. The "goats' hair" curtain and the innocent blood that was shed pointed the way to the Son of God, Yeshua the Messiah, who is the final sacrifice for ALL sin.

Eleven strips formed the goat's hair curtain. Eleven is the number associated with human failure and confusion. We see the application of this principle several times in the Scriptures. The ***first*** time is in Genesis chapter 11. The entire chapter is devoted to the sinfulness of the people who tried to be equal with God by building the Tower of Babel (*Babel means confusion*). The gravity of their sin provoked God to cause the people to speak in different languages. The result was mass confusion. God divided the people according to their language and scattered them throughout the earth. The ***second*** is in Gen. 27:11, 16. After Isaac and Rebekah's son Esau gave up his birthright for a bowl of soup, Rebekah seized the opportunity to get the double portion blessing for her favored son, Jacob. Jacob and Esau were opposites. Esau was a rugged hairy man who loved to hunt and Jacob was of a softer nature. Rebekah knew the only way to get Isaac to bless Jacob rather than Esau required deception. She prepared Isaac's favorite meal and had Jacob pretend to be Esau. She made a "goats' hair" covering for Jacob's arm so that he would appear to be hairy like Esau to the dimming eyes of his father. Confused and deceived, Isaac gave Jacob the blessing that rightfully belonged to Esau. The ***third*** example is in 1 Samuel 19:9-17. Here again, we see deception in the use of goats' hair. King Saul's daughter, Michal, used a goatskin to make a pillow to fool her father and protect her husband, David. The *fourth* example is in Judges 16:5. Goats' hair was not used in this passage, but the number eleven is; Delilah received eleven hundred pieces of silver as payment to deceive and betray Samson.

Eleven times goats are used for the sin offering. 1) For a ruler (Lev. 4:22-24), 2) the common people (Lev. 4:27-28), 3). the children of Israel (Lev. 9:3), 4) the land of promise (Nu. 15:22-25), 5) the beginning of months (Nu. 28:11, 15), 6) Passover (Nu. 28:17, 22), 7) Pentecost (Nu. 28:26-30), 8) the first day of the seventh month (Nu. 29:7, 11), 9) the tenth day of the seventh month (Nu. 29:7, 11), 10) one each day from the fifteenth to the twenty-first day of the seventh month (Nu. 29:16-24), and 11) the eighth day of the feast of Tabernacles (Nu. 29:35-38). In each of these passages the goat sacrifice reveals the "Shadow" of YESHUA as our atonement. He became the SIN OFFERING for MAN (Isa. 53:10). Yeshua did no sin, knew no sin, is holy, harmless, undefiled, and separate from sinners; in Him is no sin (1 Pet. 2:22, 2 Cor. 5:21, Heb. 7:26, 1 Jn. 3:5).

The goats' hair curtain was long enough and wide enough to completely cover the white linen curtain. It foreshadowed the ugliness of man's sin that obscures the righteous beauty of our Lord. Each strip was *thirty* cubits long and *four* cubits wide. Using the numbers associated with the goats' hair curtain points to the totality of man's sin. When we multiply the width of the goats' hair curtain by its length 4 x 30 = 120, which is the precise number of years that God gave the human race to repent before the flood began. "And the LORD said, My spirit shall not always strive with man, for that he also is flesh: yet his days shall be an hundred and twenty years" (Gen. .6:3). The ugly goats' hair completely covered the beautiful white linen hidden beneath it; the same way our sin made the beauty of Yeshua's righteousness unrecognizable, as He hung on the cross.

The number fifty is the only common feature shared by the first two curtains of the Tabernacle. Fifty clasps of brass connected the two sections of the goats' hair curtain and fifty clasps of gold connected the white linen curtain. Even the clasps are diametrically different. Brass symbolizes judgment while gold symbolizes deity.

One of the best examples of brass as judgment is in Numbers 21:4-9; in this passage of scripture, the children of Israel had sinned. The Lord sent fiery serpents among the people and many were bitten and died. He told Moses to make a brass serpent and put it on a pole. Individuals who had been bitten by the serpents lived if they looked upon the brass serpent. The serpent on the pole is the "Shadow" of Yeshua who hung on the cross receiving the wrath of God's judgment for us. Yeshua said, "And as Moses lifted up the serpent in the wilderness, even so must the Son of man be lifted up. That whosoever believeth in him should not perish, but have eternal life" (Jn. 3:14-15). Yeshua, like the brass serpent, is the only deliverance from God's wrath.

Goats are also used to represent *judgment*. Once a year the sins of the people were symbolically transferred to a scapegoat; foreshadowing the transfer of our sin to Yeshua. The scapegoat was led out into the wilderness and banished forever (Lev. 16:10, 20-22). It was OUR sin that separated Yeshua from His Father. This is the only time He and the Father were apart. The agony of that separation caused Yeshua to cry out from the cross, "Eloi, Eloi, lama sabach thani? Which is being interpreted, *My God, my God, why has thou forsaken me?"* (Mk. 15:34; my emphasis). Yeshua, unlike the scapegoat of the Tabernacle times, did not remain separated from His Father. His separation was temporary. Isaiah, speaking of Yeshua said, "Thus saith thy Lord the LORD, and thy God that pleadeth the cause of his people, behold, I have taken out of thine hand the cup of trembling, even the dregs of the cup of my fury; thou shalt no more drink it again" (Isa. 51:22). Although forsaken for the moment, He was able to look beyond His suffering to see the victory that gave man eternal rest. Therefore, it is said of Him, "Who for the joy that was set before him endured the cross, despising the shame, and is set down at the right hand of the throne of God" (Heb. 12:2b). Yeshua defeated sin and death and gave everlasting life to the world. He said "I am he that liveth, and was dead; and, behold, I am alive for evermore, Amen; and have the keys of hell and of death" (Rev. 1:18). Because of Him, we are forgiven. Our sin is blotted out and cast behind His back; MAN HAS BEEN REDEEMED! "Behold, for peace I had great bitterness: but thou hast in love to my soul delivered it from the pit of corruption: for thou hast cast all my sins behind thy back" (Isa. 38:17). "I have blotted out, as a thick cloud, thy transgressions, and, as a cloud, thy sins: return unto me; for I have redeemed thee" (Isa. 44:22).

During the final judgment, the sheep will be separated from the goats. The sheep, which represent the believers, will have eternal life in the presence of the Lord, but the goats, which represent unbelievers, will be cast into the lake of fire, separated from Him forever (Mt. 25:31-46).

God referred to the goats' hair curtain as a TENT, meaning it was temporary (Ex. 26:11). The sin that separated man from God was temporary. Note: In a blood covenant, the parties exchange coats, and that is what Yeshua did. He took the ugly, filthy covering of man's sin and in exchange gave man His beautiful robe of righteousness. Yeshua defeated sin along with its consequences, death and hell. Man and God were once again connected, but unlike the glory that covered Adam and his wife, now the glory of God lives inside each believer. God and man will never be separated again.

The prophetic message found within the goats' hair curtain is this, BY HIS GRACE GOD REUNITES FALLEN MAN TO HIMSELF BY THE JUDGMENT YESHUA BORE.

SUMMARY

Yeshua is the scapegoat and the *sacrifice*. The ***fifty*** clasps of ***brass*** are symbolic of the judgment He <u>bore at Calvary</u> that connects ***six***, redeemed man, to ***five, and the*** grace of God, who is the *Redeemer* ***(Yeshua), "that they may be one"*** (Ex. 26:11, Jn. 17:21).

The *third* covering was ***rams' skin dyed red***.

"And thou shalt make a covering for the tent of rams' skins dyed red" (Ex. 26:14).

God said very little about this covering but within it, we find many revelations. Its red color points to the blood of Yeshua. God said, "For the life of the flesh is in the blood: and I have given it to you upon the altar to make an atonement for your sins" (Gen. 9:4, Lev. 17:11). His blood gives new life to humanity. The RAM not only demonstrates Yeshua's sacrifice, it also reveals His ministry as the Great High Priest. Only the High Priest could enter behind the Veil with the blood of the sin offering. As the High Priest of the final sin sacrifice, Yeshua carried His own blood into the heavenly Holy of Holies and presented it to His Father.

The consecration of Aaron and his sons included rams. (Ex. 29, Lev. 8). The first ram was a whole burnt offering; the entire animal was consumed by the fire of the altar. The second ram was different, the application if its blood signified purification.

God chose to use the first ram in this offering to remind His people of His promise to Abraham. "And Abraham said, "My son, God will provide himself a lamb for a burnt offering" (Gen. 22:8; my emphasis) A ram was substituted for Abraham's son, Isaac (Gen. 22:13). Through Isaac, God revealed that He would (HIMSELF) become the SACRIFICE for the human race. The ram is a "Shadow" of Yeshua, God's only begotten Son, who fulfilled the Covenant promise made to Abraham; He is the whole burnt offering.

God used the second ram to illustrate holiness. Moses applied some of the ram's blood to the right ear, the right thumb, the right toe, and the garments of Aaron and his sons. The priests were set apart to serve a Holy God and His people. They were the representatives of God to the people, and mediators for the people. God required purity in everything they heard, touched or held, as well as their walk. The holiness of the priesthood provides a "shadow" of Yeshua, the Great High Priest who is the mediator between God and men: "For there is one God and one mediator between God and men, the man Christ Jesus" (2 Tim. 2:5.) Yeshua's priestly ministry, unlike the Levitical priesthood whose office ended when the priest died, is forever. "For those priests (meaning the Levites) were made without an oath; but this with an oath by him that said unto him (speaking of Yeshua), *The Lord swear and will not repent, thou art a priest forever after the order of Melchizedek.* By so much was Yeshua made a surety of a better testament" (Heb. 7:21-22; my emphasis). Yeshua was born to be the representative of God to the world, and as a man, He was the mediator for man before God. His absolute surrender to His Father's will fulfilled the purpose of the application of the ram's blood; and demonstrates how the believer is to live up to his position in the royal priesthood (1 Pet. 2:9).

The Breast of the second ram was the portion of the offering that God gave to Moses. Moses represented God to Aaron and his sons. "And thou shalt speak unto him, and put words in his mouth: and I will be with thy mouth, and with his mouth, and will teach you what ye shall do. And he shall be thy spokesman unto the people: and he shall be, even he shall be to thee instead of a mouth, <u>and thou shalt be to him instead of God</u>" (Ex. 4:15-16; my emphasis). Moses took the breast of the second ram and waved it before the Lord. The breast of the ram symbolized two things. <u>First</u>, it signifies the surrendered heart of Aaron and his sons to the service of the Lord. <u>Second</u>, the breast of the ram is a "Shadow" of Yeshua's heart towards His heavenly Father. He said, "Verily, verily, I say unto you, The Son can do nothing of himself, but what he seeth the Father do: for what things so ever he doeth, these also doeth the Son likewise. I can of mine own self do nothing: as I hear, I judge: and my judgment is just; because I seek not mine own will, but the will of the Father which hath sent me" (Jn. 5:19, 30). We, as members of the Royal priesthood need to follow Yeshua's example and surrender our hearts to the heavenly Father. Romans chapter 12 verse 1, declares that it is our reasonable service.

Only the high priest could offer the sacrificial blood before God. Caiaphas, the officiating high priest at the time of Yeshua's trial, became angry and tore *(rent)* his priestly robe; and broke God's law. "And he that is the high priest among his brethren, upon whose head the anointing oil was poured, and that is consecrated to put on the garments, shall not uncover his head, nor REND his clothes" (Lev. 21:10). His actions made him unfit to serve as the high priest during that Passover season. Rending his clothes opened the door for Yeshua to assume His lawful position as the officiating High Priest over His own sacrifice. It was previously determined that Yeshua, through His mother's lineage, is a descendent of Aaron. Therefore, He had a robe like the one worn by Caiaphas, and His robe remained whole. The guards gambled for it at the foot of His cross "Then the soldiers, when they had crucified Jesus, took his garments, and made four parts, to every soldier a part; *and also his coat: now the coat was without seam, woven from the top throughout. They said therefore among themselves; Let us not rend it,* but cast lots for it, whose it shall be: that the scripture might be fulfilled, which saith, they parted my raiment among them, and for my vesture they did cast lots. These things therefore the soldiers did" (Jn. 19:23-24; my emphasis). Therefore, Yeshua was the only one qualified to officiate at His sacrifice, and carry His own blood into heaven, and sprinkle it on the Mercy Seat before the Father (Heb. 7:26-28).

According to Jewish tradition, after the high priest offered the blood of the final sacrifice to the Lord, He would shout aloud, ***" IT IS FINISHED".*** [9] Yeshua used the same words to declare the end of His work on the cross. "When Yeshua therefore had received the vinegar, he said IT IS FINISHED: and he bowed his head, and gave up the ghost" (Jn. 19:30; my emphasis).

God withheld the measurement for the rams' skin covering. As the third covering; it had to extend farther than the first two to reach the ground. Its size and color foreshadowed the Sacrifice of Yeshua's Blood. The Ram's Skin covering was placed over the goats' hair curtain (the "Shadow" of sin). Its location points to the untold cleansing power of Yeshua's blood. His Blood goes beyond covering sin; it eradicates it.

SUMMARY

(1) No measurement: *the **boundless power** of Yeshua's blood.* (2) Rams' skins: *the suffering of Yeshua as **our sacrifice*** (Eph. 5:2) (3) The color: ***Yeshua's own blood**, without which there is **no remission*** (Lev. 17:11, Heb. 9:22).

The *fourth* and final covering was *badger's skin.*

There are many opinions about the type of animal referred to here as badger. The Hebrew word translated badger is *tachash.* Strong's Exhaustive Concordance defines it as a clean animal with fur, probably a species of antelope. Others have suggested that it was porpoise skins that were acquired at the crossing of the Red Sea. The kind of animal is not important, but the quality of its skin is. It had to be tough enough and strong enough to withstand the elements, because it is a "Shadow" of the outward covering of Yeshua's flesh. God covered Himself with human flesh, through the birth of Yeshua, His Son, to save the human race (Jn. 3:16, Heb. 2:9-10, 1 Pet. 3:18).

The badger's skin was perhaps the most unsightly of all the coverings. It was the outer covering, exposed to all the elements of nature. The pounding desert winds blasted it with sand and the scorching sun bleached its color. Although it appeared tattered and worn by the abuse of the elements, hidden beneath it was the treasure of God. A priceless treasure of 8,400 pounds of brass, 8,400 pounds of sliver, 2,400 pounds of gold, and hundreds of yards of the finest linen made.[10] The strength of the outer covering provided protection for all that was hidden inside.

The Bible, speaking of Yeshua's outward appearance, says, "He had no form nor comeliness; no beauty that we should desire him" (Isa. 53:2). Yet, we know that inside, underneath His flesh, dwelt the fullness of God (Col. 2:9). The only unsightly part of Yeshua was the part that came from man (His flesh). His own people did not recognize Him as the Son of God (Jn. 1:11). Perhaps they could not see past the tattered badger's skin of His flesh. Even Satan tried to tempt Him into throwing back the outer covering and displaying the glory underneath (Mt. 4:1-11). All that God is was contained inside the outer covering of Yeshua's flesh, just like the treasure inside the Tabernacle underneath the badger's skin.

If we stay in Yeshua, He keeps us through the devastating storms of life. There is nothing that we go through that Yeshua does not understand; He senses all that we feel (Heb. 2:17-18). He is our hiding place (Ezek. 16:8-10, Ps. 91). "Thou art my hiding place; thou shalt preserve me from trouble; thou shalt compass me about with songs of deliverance. Selah" (Ps. 32:7). "Thou art my hiding place and my shield: I hope in thy word" (Ps. 119:114).

When the nations that surrounded Israel saw the Tabernacle, they understood that the God of Israel was in their midst, but they could not see the hidden treasure concealed by its outer covering. A lost person often believes in God but is not able to see the real treasure until he accepts THE MAN, Yeshua the Messiah, and enters into His protection. "Jesus said, Verily, verily, I say unto thee, except a man be born again, he cannot see the kingdom of God" (Jn. 3:3)

God chose not to give a specific measurement for this covering either, because it is a "Shadow" of the boundless protection that comes to man through MessiahYeshua. "He that dwelleth in the secret place of the most High shall abide under the shadow of the Almighty. I will say of the LORD, He is my refuge and my fortress: my God; in him will I trust (Ps. 91:1-2).

SUMMARY

BADGER SKIN = *Yeshua's flesh concealed the beautiful treasure of God*

COMPLETE SUMMARY OF THE COVERINGS

WHITE LINEN: *The protected righteousness of God*
GOATS' HAIR: *The sin of man*
RAMS' SKIN DYED RED: *The boundless cleansing blood of Yeshua*
BADGERS' SKIN: *The never-ending protection for the redeemed*

The four coverings of the Tabernacle reveal God's Great LOVE and the results of His covenant. Two of the coverings, the badger's skin and the goats' hair represent the things Yeshua took upon Himself. He took the two things that a lost person cannot control, his flesh and sin. The rams' skin dyed red and the pure white linen represent Yeshua's Blood and His righteousness; the two things he gives in exchange. The exchange has been made; the covenant is sealed. "Blessed be the name of the Lord from this time forth and for evermore. Who is like unto the Lord our God, who dwelleth on high, who humbleth himself to behold the things that are in heaven, and in the earth!" (Ps. 113:2, 5-6).

CHAPTER 9

The Structure

"And thou shalt make boards for the tabernacle of shittim wood standing up. Ten cubits shall be the length of a board, and a cubit and a half shall be the breadth of one board. Two tenons shall there be in one board, set in order one against another: thus shalt thou make for all the boards of the tabernacle. And thou shalt make the boards for the tabernacle, twenty boards on the south side southward. And thou shalt make forty sockets of silver under the twenty boards; two sockets under one board for his two tenons, and two sockets under another board for his two tenons. And for the second side of the tabernacle on the north side there shall be twenty boards: And their forty sockets of silver; two sockets under one board, and two sockets under another board. And for the sides of the tabernacle westward thou shalt make six boards. And two boards shalt thou make for the corners of the tabernacle in the two sides. And they shall be coupled together beneath, and they shall be coupled together above the head of it unto one ring: thus shall it be for them both; they shall be for the two corners. And they shall be eight boards, and their sockets of silver, sixteen sockets; two sockets under one board, and two sockets under another board. And thou shalt make bars of shittim wood; five for the boards of the one side of the tabernacle, And five bars for the boards of the other side of the tabernacle, and five bars for the boards of the side of the tabernacle, for the two sides westward. And the middle bar in the midst of the boards shall reach from end to end. And thou

> shalt overlay the boards with gold, and make their rings of gold for places for the bars: and thou shalt overlay the bars with gold. And thou shalt rear up the tabernacle according to the fashion thereof which was showed thee in the mount" (Ex. 26:15-30, 36:20-38).

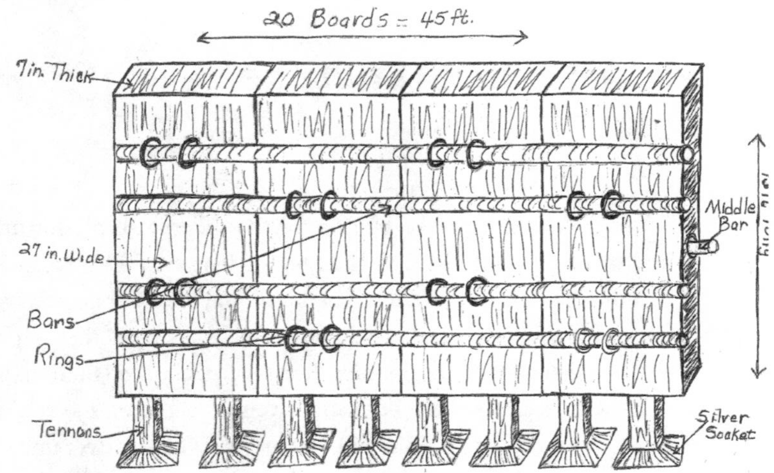

The Boards and Bars

<u>Building the habitation of God:</u> As we examine the structure of the Tabernacle, the "shadow" of ONE NEW MAN emerges. The structure of the Tabernacle refers to the boards, the foundation sockets, and the bars. You will see the body of believers, Jew and Gentile, united with Yeshua in the boards, the price of redemption for all of humanity in the silver sockets, and the stabilizing power of the Holy Spirit in the bars. The method used to assemble the Tabernacle structure demonstrates how Yeshua has reconnected all believers to Himself and to each other through the price He paid for the redemption of the human race.

The boards: The boards of the Tabernacle surround the Holy things; the furnishings that were either pure gold or covered with pure gold. Gold is symbolic of deity and is descriptive of God the Father, God the Son and God the Holy Spirit. Each board was *ten* cubits long, (approximately fifteen feet), one and a half cubits wide, (twenty-seven inches), and was approximately seven inches thick. When erected, the structure stood fifteen feet wide, forty-five feet long and fifteen feet high. There were twenty boards on each side. Each side connected to a corner board that united with six boards to form the back wall. The back wall was comprised of eight boards. The finished structure consisted of forty-eight boards. The boards reveal God's plan to unite Jew and Gentile. United through the blood of Yeshua they become ONE NEW MAN (Eph. 2:15). Number Twenty is representative of a double portion of man's completeness. The twenty boards on either side of the Tabernacle are "Shadows" of all those who have accepted Yeshua as the Messiah, and all those who died waiting for Yeshua the Messiah. Yeshua came for the Jew first and then the Gentile. The term "Jew" designates God's chosen people and "Gentile" represents the rest of humanity.

To make boards, a tree must be cut down, severed from its earth-bound roots and stripped of all its branches.[11] In order for Yeshua to become the ROOT of Jesse, the BRANCH that came to suffer and build the house of God, He stripped himself of all dignity. He, much like the process of making boards, stepped down from His place of majesty and submitted to His Father's will. "And in that day there shall be a root of Jesse, which shall stand for an ensign of the people; to it shall the Gentiles seek: and his rest shall be glorious" (Isa. 11:10). "I will bring forth my servant the BRANCH" (Zech. 3:8). "Thus speaketh the LORD of hosts, saying, Behold the man whose name is The BRANCH; and he shall grow up out of his place, and he *shall build the temple of the LORD*" (Zech. 6:12; my emphasis).

How do believers become boards in the household of God? Our primary focus must be this: It is Gods' building plan not ours just as was the Tabernacle. God gives the instructions and we follow. "Except the LORD build the house, they labour in vain that build it: except the LORD keep the city, the watchman waketh but in vain" (Ps. 127:1). We must fall at Messiah's feet with a submitted will and allow Him to cut away the stony heart that once was in control. God wants to transform us from SIN-MINDEDNESS to GOD-MINDEDNESS by replacing our stony heart with one that He controls; one that receives its life from Him (Ezek. 36:26-27). We must, in effect, remove the old man and put on the new. Our responsibility is to cut away those things that once held us in bondage. Things like deceitful lust and lying, because the new man is created after God in righteousness and true holiness (Eph.4:22-25). "In whom also ye are circumcised with the circumcision made without hands, in putting off the body of the sins of the flesh by the circumcision of Christ" (Col.2:11).

Circumcision is a covenant sign. Abraham circumcised the foreskin of his flesh as a reminder that he was in covenant with God. He cut himself in obedience, but he was not a participant in making the covenant. God alone did it all. We, on the other hand, cannot see the scar of our circumcised heart, but God can. Every time he looks at one of His children, He remembers His covenant promises. Just like Abraham, we do nothing except believe what God has already done. Although circumcision of the flesh continues today, becoming a new creature is what matters. "For in Christ Jesus neither circumcision availeth any thing, nor uncircumcision, but a new creature" (Gal. 6:15).

Believers are like the walls of the Tabernacle, in that God's presence dwells inside each individual believer. Our walls are continually before God (Isa. 49:16). The Great I AM chooses to live in us; we are the temple of the Holy Spirit (1 Cor. 6:19-20; 2 Cor. 6:16). The Holy Spirit dwells in every believer just as the "Shadow" of His presence ran through the center of each board of the Tabernacle. Although we cannot see Him, we know He is there. "To whom God would make known what is the riches of the glory of this mystery among the Gentiles; which is Christ in you, the hope of glory" (Col. 1:27).

God's plan to dwell inside man began long before the day of Pentecost, found in Acts chapters 1 and 2. He revealed His plan in many ways, one of them was through David in Second Samuel chapter 7. David desired to build a house for God, but man is not capable of building a place worthy of the GREAT I AM. Note: This was not God's idea. Although God honored David's desire by allowing David's son, Solomon, to build a great temple, it was never God's desire to remain within any stationary structure. God is Omnipresent. From the time of Adam, God's desire was to walk among His people and teach them His ways. The words of God to David reveal His plan to dwell inside regenerated man through Yeshua. "Also the LORD telleth thee that *he will make thee an house*" (2 Sam 7:11b; my emphasis) Through the linage of David, came the birth of God's Son (Mat. 1:1). The fullness of God indwelt Yeshua (Col. 2:9). Yeshua was the son of Abraham ushering in the fullness of God's covenant, and He was the son of David providing the way for the indwelling presence of the Spirit of God to come to all believers.

The boards of the Tabernacle are a shadow of the body of Messiah. God's plan for reconciliation is not to create two families. On the contrary, through Yeshua all men become a new creation, forming ONE NEW MAN. One example of God's plan to reunite all men into ONE family is found in Ezekiel when **Judah** and **Joseph** are ***united*** as one <u>*stick.*</u>

"The word of the LORD came again unto me, saying, Moreover, thou son of man, take thee one stick, and write upon it, For Judah, and for the children of Israel his companions: then take another stick, and write upon it, For Joseph, the stick of Ephraim, and for all the house of Israel his companions: "*And join them one to another into one stick; and they shall become one in thine hand*" (Ezek. 37:15-17; my emphasis). Judah represents all of Israel, and Joseph (through Ephraim and Manasseh, the half-breeds) represents all of the other nations. The Apostle Paul, when speaking to Jewish believers in Messiah, included the Gentile believers noting that we are all ONE IN HIM. "That ye may with one mind and one mouth glorify God, even the Father of our Lord Jesus Christ. Wherefore receive ye one another, as Christ also received us to the glory of God. Now I say that Jesus Christ was a minister of the circumcision for the truth of God, to confirm the promises made unto the fathers: And that the Gentiles might glorify God for his mercy; as it is written, For this cause I will confess to thee among the Gentiles, and sing unto thy name. And again he saith, Rejoice, ye Gentiles, with his people. And again, Esaias saith, There shall be a root of Jesse, and he that shall rise to reign over the Gentiles; in him shall the Gentiles trust. Now the God of hope fill you with all joy and peace in believing, that ye may abound in hope, through the power of the Holy Ghost" (Rom. 15:6-13).

God's plan becomes even clearer when he says that the blood of Yeshua has broken down the middle wall that divided the Jew and the Gentile to make of the two, ONE NEW MAN (Eph. 2:11-16).

We are a work in progress. We are being built into the household of God. Messiah is the corner stone, "*In whom all the building fitly framed together groweth unto an holy temple in the Lord: In whom ye also are builded together for an habitation of God through the Spirit*" (Eph. 2:18-22; my emphasis).

The boards of the Tabernacle fit perfectly together, so that no one on the outside could see through them to the mystery of God hidden inside. Only the ones called of God could enter inside and see His priceless treasure. The Body of Messiah fits tightly together like the boards of the Tabernacle. Yeshua knits our hearts together IN LOVE, that together we can understand the mystery of God the Father, and of Messiah; in whom are hid all the treasures of wisdom and knowledge (Col. 2:2-3). We are members of His body, of His flesh, and of His bones (Eph. 5:20). We need each other else we are incomplete. "But speaking the truth in love, may grow up into him in all things, which is the head, even Christ: From whom the whole body fitly joined together and compacted by that which every joint supplieth, according to the effectual working in the measure of every part, maketh increase of the body unto the edifying of itself in love" (Eph. 4:15-16).

Each board was 10 cubits tall (the number of completeness), one and a half cubits wide (27 inches) and 7 inches thick. Each board was sealed in gold foreshadowing the complete perfection that comes through Messiah. Apart From Him, no man is complete. The Ministry gifts are given to help each member of His body grow into the fullness of Messiah, "until we all come in the unity of faith, and the knowledge of the SON OF GOD, unto a perfect man unto the measure of the stature of the fullness of Messiah"(Eph. 4:4-8; 11-13; my emphasis). Why? "That we may stand perfect and complete in all the will of God" (Col. 4:12b).

Yeshua completed every responsibility toward God and man; saving both the Jew and the Gentile, and thus fulfilling the "Shadow" of DUAL COMPLETENESS documented in the boards. The twenty boards that formed each side of the Tabernacle reveals the complexity of God's' Grace and His love for the world. If we multiply five (the number of God's Grace) times four (the number for the earth) it equals twenty. Six boards formed the backside of the Tabernacle and two corner boards coupled the back and the sides together. Six (the number for man) plus two (the number for power, fellowship, and unity) equals eight (the number of a new beginning). The number of boards and the manner in which they were connected reveal the Father's plan of reconciliation. Jew and Gentile united by the Man Yeshua become ONE NEW MAN. "Therefore if any man be in Christ, he is a new creature: old things are passed away; *behold, all things are become new"* (2 Cor. 5:17; my emphasis).

The two revelations found within the walls of the Tabernacle are, Yeshua, the incarnate Son of God, and the body of believers. Both are the habitation of God.

There was a time when I had a judgmental spirit concerning the Jewish people. I ignorantly blamed them for Yeshua's death, and could not understand why they refuse to acknowledge Him as the Messiah. I also had a jealous spirit because they are Gods' chosen people. I pray you do not feel this way, but if you do, we have a forgiving God. Nevertheless, as I did, you must repent. Do you realize that God blinded the people He loved for a season so that we (the Gentiles) might have access to God's salvation? (Rom. 11-25-28). If Israel had recognized Yeshua and accepted Him as the Messiah, we (the Gentiles) would still be lost without hope (Eph. 2:12, 13).

God gave the Tabernacle and its ceremonies to Israel as a way to reveal Himself to them and through them, to the world. God chose Israel because they were fewer in number than any other people (Deut. 7:7). Through their weakness He revealed His strength. Their traditions preserved the written Word. Their blindness gives hope to the gentiles; therefore, we must show them mercy by taking their Messiah to them. "I say then, Have they stumbled that they should fall? God forbid: *but rather through their fall salvation is come unto the Gentiles,* for to provoke them to jealousy. *Now if the fall of them be the riches of the world, and the diminishing of them the riches of the Gentiles; how much more their fullness?* For if the casting away of them be the reconciling of the world, what shall the receiving of them be, but life from the dead? *For as ye in times past have not believed God, yet have now obtained mercy through their unbelief: Even so have these also now not believed, that through your mercy they also may obtain mercy. For God hath concluded them all in unbelief, that he might have mercy upon all"* (Rom.11: 11-12, 15; 30-32; my emphasis).

Each board was sealed in gold. Gold represents deity and in this case, it signifies the presence of the Holy Spirit. Believers, as members of the household of God, are sealed by the Holy Spirit. "Who hath also *sealed* us, and given the earnest of the Spirit in our hearts"

(2 Cor. 1:22; my emphasis). "In whom ye also trusted, after that ye heard the word of truth, the gospel of your salvation: in whom also after that ye believed, ye were *sealed* with that Holy Spirit of promise," And grieve not the Holy Spirit of God, whereby ye are sealed unto the day of redemption (Eph. 1:13: 4:30; my emphasis).

The boards of the Tabernacle clearly reveal the body of Messiah, Jew and Gentile united to become the dwelling place of God. ONE NEW MAN

The *sockets*: The foundation of the Tabernacle was silver. Each board was held in place by two silver sockets that weighed approximately one hundred pounds each.[12] The silver used to make the sockets came from the "Atonement Money". Atonement money was the price required to redeem the soul of men twenty years old and above. Every man paid the same price, one-half a shekel (Ex. 30:11-16).

There is a great revelation within the silver sockets of the Tabernacle. The Lord allowed me to see the provision of His love for all humanity through the numbers associated with the sockets. I pray that I am able to put it into words so that everyone will see and understand what a amazing God we serve.

One shekel paid the atonement money for two men. It takes 3,000 shekels to make one talent. 3,000 shekels pays the ransom for 6,000 men. Each of the 48 boards of the Tabernacle stood in 2 talents of silver, or 6,000 shekels, which is the ransom price for 12,000 men.

THE EQUATION:

6,000 shekels = payment for 12,000 men, 12,000 x 48, (the number of boards) =576,000 When you divide 576,000 by 4 (the number of the earth), it equals 144,000, the number of all the tribes of the children of Israel that were sealed in Revelation chapter 7. Please keep in mind that the 144,000 symbolically represents <u>ALL</u> of the people of Israel (Rom. 11:26-27). The first 144,000 represents the price of redemption for one-quarter of all the people of the earth. The remaining silver was equal to three times 144,000. Three (3), denotes sufficiency, showing that God has provided the sufficient price of redemption for ALL the remaining three-quarters of the earth. IT IS GOD'S DESIRE THAT NONE BE LOST (Jn. 17:12). The silver foundation of the Tabernacle clearly foreshadows the price Yeshua paid for the redemption of the human race through His death. "For other foundation can no man lay that is laid, which is Yeshua the Messiah." (I Cor. 3:11). **HE IS OUR RANSOM** (Mt. 20:28). "I will ransom them from the power of the grave; I will redeem them from death" (Hos. 13:14a). *"For ye are bought with a price*: therefore glorify God in your body and in your spirit, which are God's" (1Cor. 6:20; my emphasis). God's provision was more than enough because He is a God of more than enough (Eph. 3:20-21).

When Moses counted the men twenty years old and up, there were 603,550. Ninety-six talents of silver formed the foundation of the Tabernacle revealing the price of redemption for all people. Four talents remained to support the pillars of the Veil. One thousand seven hundred seventy-five shekels were used to make the silver utensils, the crowns on the pillars, and the hooks. Later you will see how the pillars of the Veil standing in their silver sockets foreshadow the redeemed entering into the presence of God for eternity. The remaining silver items are equally relevant (Ex. 38:25-28).

> **The *bars*:** "And thou shalt make bars of shittim wood; five for the boards of the one side of the tabernacle, And five bars for the boards of the other side of the tabernacle, and five bars for the boards of the side of the tabernacle, for the two sides westward. And the middle bar in the midst of the boards shall reach from end to end. And thou shalt overlay the boards with gold, and make their rings of gold for places for the bars: and thou shalt overlay the bars with gold" (Ex.26:26-29).

Five wooden bars overlaid with gold held the boards of the Tabernacle together. Gold rings were fastened on the outside of the boards to hold four of the bars in place. A hole was bored through the center of each board to accommodate the fifth bar. The fifth bar (the middle bar) was concealed inside the boards. The fifth bar, is a "Shadow' of the Holy Spirit; it acted as the stabilizer for the forty-eight boards.

The boards, as previously explained, are "Shadows' of redeemed man. Since the fall of Adam, every human being has an emptiness that can only be filled by the presence of the Lord. All men are like the boards of the Tabernacle; without the stabilizing presence of the Lord, they soon collapse. The Holy Spirit, like the middle bar, is not visible to the natural eye, but His mighty presence holds the household of the Son of God together with His love. "Messiah in you the hope of glory" (Col. 1:27).

I hope you are able to see the beauty of the Tabernacle in the revelation of its structure. It presents the "shadow" of ONE NEW MAN. Each new creation stands upright in the price paid for their redemption (silver), sealed by the Holy Spirit (gold) and held together by the love of God (the bars). The fullness of the Holy Trinity is present, Yeshua paid the price, the Holy Spirit seals the future, and the Father's love holds THE NEW MAN together. His desire is that none be lost. "The Lord is not slack concerning his promise, as some men count slackness; but is long-suffering to us-ward, not willing that any should perish, but that ALL should come to repentance" (2 Pet. 3:9).

SUMMARY

THE STRUCTURE: *The body of Messiah. The "shadow" of Jew and Gentile united in Messiah to become ONE NEW MAN.*

THE BOARDS: *Believers sealed by the Holy Spirit; each one is a member of the body of Messiah, the household of God.*

6 boards form the back wall of the Tabernacle. *The Man Yeshua*

+2 corner boards *the power of reconciliation*

8 boards complete the back side of the Tabernacle. *A NEW BEGINNING*

THE BARS: *the stabilizing power of God's love and grace. The middle bar is a "shadow" of the indwelling presence of the Holy Spirit.*

THE SILVER SOCKETS: *The price required for the redemption of the human race.*

CHAPTER 10

The Veil, Pillars and the Silver Sockets

"And thou shalt make a veil of blue, and purple, and scarlet, and fine twined linen of cunning work: with cherubim shall it be made: And thou shalt hang it upon four pillars of shittim wood overlaid with gold: their hooks shall be of gold, upon the four sockets of silver. And thou shalt hang up the veil under the taches, that thou mayest bring in thither within the veil the ark of the testimony: and the veil shall divide unto you between the holy place and the most holy" (Ex. 26:31-33 and Ex. 36:35-36).

The Veil

The Veil: The Veil of the Tabernacle is the "Shadow" of the body that was prepared for Messiah before He was born. "Wherefore when he cometh into the world, he saith, Sacrifice and offering thou wouldest not, but a body hast thou prepared me" (Heb. 10:5). "By a new and living way, which he hath consecrated for us, through the veil, that is to say, his flesh" (Heb. 10:20).

The different colors in the Veil hold the mystery of the gospel message. *Blue* conveys Yeshua's heavenly position, power, and authority. *White* represents the pure holiness of His life. *Red* points to Him as the suffering servant and also to the blood He shed. *Purple* presents Him as the royal one who will return as the KING of KINGS and LORD of LORDS.

Once, while presenting the secrets of the Tabernacle to a group of ladies, one of the ladies in the group shared a beautiful revelation in the colors. She noted that the colors used in the Tabernacle are always in the same order, blue, purple and scarlet. It is the blood of Yeshua (scarlet) that reunites fallen man with his heavenly Father (blue) to produce a new creation. His redeemed children become a royal priesthood (purple), a holy nation with His power and authority, or in other words, blue and red make purple. "Therefore if any man be in Christ, he is a new creature: old things are passed away; behold, all things are become new" (2 Cor. 5:17). But ye are a chosen generation, a royal priesthood, an holy nation, a peculiar people; that ye should show forth the praises of him who hath called you out of darkness into his marvelous light" (1 Pet.2:9).

The Veil was the only thing that separated the priests from the presence of God. It is a metaphor for the Man Yeshua who stands between God and men. "For there is one God, and one mediator between God and men, the MAN Messiah Yeshua (1 Tim. 2:5; my emphasis). The Veil was the only way into the throne room of God and accessible exclusively to the high priest once a year on the Day of Atonement (Lev. 16:2, 34; Heb. 9:6-8).

Yeshua is both the Veil (the LIFE) and the Great High Priest who intercedes for those who believe. Yeshua said, "*And I give unto them eternal life*; and they shall never perish, neither shall any man pluck them out of my hand' (Jn. 10:28; my emphasis). "*But Christ being come an high priest of good things to come*, by a greater and more perfect tabernacle, not made with hands, that is to say, not of this building; Neither by the blood of goats and calves, but by his own blood he entered in once into the holy place, having obtained eternal redemption for us" (Heb. 9:11-12; my emphasis)

God anointed Aholiab with extraordinary ability to embroider the image of cherubim on the Veil (Ex. 38:23). The image of cherubim was also on the white linen curtain that was directly above the holy things. The sight of cherubim reminded the priests of the holiness of God; angels accompany Him wherever He is. The presence of angels on the Veil gives credence to the fact that the fullness of God dwelt behind the flesh of Yeshua. "For in him dwelleth all the fullness of the Godhead bodily" (Col. 2:9, Jn.1:14).

The Ark of the Covenant with its Mercy Seat represents God's throne, and the items placed inside of it reveal the fullness of His being. He is the Word (the *Tablets of Stone*), the Living Bread (the pot of *Manna*), and the Resurrected One (*Aaron's rod* that bloomed). Each item foreshadowed one of the members of the Holy Trinity. God spoke the Word, the Son became the Life-giving Bread, and the Resurrecting power of the Holy Spirit raised Yeshua's dead body from the grave. Death could not keep Him in the grave. He conquered death, defeated the grips of hell itself, and rose from the grave to everlasting life. Yeshua is all God and all man. The Veil of the Tabernacle concealed the fullness of the Son in the Father, just as the veil of Yeshua's flesh concealed the fullness of the Father in the Son. "God was in Messiah, reconciling the world to Himself" (2 Cor. 5:19). "Who is the image of the invisible God, the firstborn of every creature" (Col. 1:15).

The Veil hung on four wooden pillars that were overlaid with gold. Gold hooks pierced through the Veil to hold it secure, and silver sockets supported the weight of the Veil. Yeshua, like the Veil, hung suspended in the air. His body, pierced with four nail holes, like the Veil of the Tabernacle, hung between the wrath of God and sinful man. At the same time of Yeshua's death, the veil in the temple in Jerusalem was ripped from the top to the bottom. This in itself was a miracle because tradition teaches that the temple veil was so thick that teams of oxen could not tear it. Some theologians believe that the Veil was twelve inches thick, however, this cannot be verified, and the Bible does not say. It is what the Veil symbolizes that matters.

It has been and still is taught that God ripped the veil to reveal His presence above the Ark and to give man access to His throne. Although symbolically this is partially true, history has proven that at the time of Yeshua's death, the Ark of the Covenant was not in the temple. It had been removed for safe-keeping. It remains hidden to this day. God ripped the veil to expose the hypocrisy of the religious leaders and of those preforming priestly functions. God ripped open the Veil to show the world that He was not in the temple, He was on the CROSS. It also made the way for the believers to approach God through the torn body of His Son. Yeshua's death provided a new and living way to the Father (Heb. 10:20). He is the Way, the Truth, and the Life and the only way to approach God (Jn. 14:6). Through Yeshua, believers have access to the throne of God (Heb. 4:16).

***The pillars*:** A pillar is the support column. One of the "Shadows" provided by the gold covered pillars is the enabling power and strength of the Holy Spirit. He is the person of the Holy Trinity that empowered Yeshua to face the cross with joy (Heb. 12:2). The same Spirit that gave Yeshua the strength to endure the cross dwells within every believer.

The second "Shadow" found in the pillars of the Veil is that of God's children. Each of the four pillars represents one of the four corners of the earth. Each pillar is sealed with gold and each one is standing upright in a silver socket. The four pillars are symbolic of the children of God who were gathered from the four corners of the earth to appear before the Lord. They are representative of those entering into everlasting life.

The gold sealed boards in chapter nine provided a shadow of Jew and Gentile connected through Yeshua and becoming One New Man. Now we will compare the pillars of the Veil to the boards to determine how the pillars relate to the believers. The believer's position before God becomes clear when you consider the difference between a board and a pillar.

A board is a flat piece of wood cut for a specific purpose, and a pillar is, an upright, slender structure used as a building support or as a monument. The boards of the Tabernacle are "Shadows" of the members of the household of Messiah. Each one has a specific purpose or calling to fulfill. The pillars, on the other hand, represent those who have completed their calling, those united in faith and strength, those who have overcome. The Holy Spirit is the one who seals both with His enabling power, represented by the pure gold overlay. He is the down payment, the earnest money, or in effect the engagement ring of the bride of Messiah. The Holy Spirit is the promise of God's love and that He will return for ALL who bear His engagement ring. "In whom ye trusted, after that ye heard the word of truth, the gospel of your salvation: in whom also after that ye believed, ye were *SEALED* with that Holy Spirit of promise, which is the earnest of our inheritance until the redemption of the purchased possession, unto the praise of his glory" (Eph. 1:13-14; my emphasis).

The Holy Spirit came in the name of Yeshua (Jn. 14:26). A day is coming when believers will wear the name of Yeshua and become pillars in the temple of God. Yeshua, the Lamb of God, will consummate His marriage and give those who overcome

His new name (Rev. 3:12). The same Spirit that empowered Yeshua empowers us to endure until that day comes.

The pillars of the Veil represent those who overcome, standing before God ready to enter into His presence forever. There are no crowns atop the pillars of the Veil; they are at the feet of Messiah. The Bride of Messiah wears the seal of His covenant on her forehead.

"And they shall see his face; and his name shall be in their foreheads" (Rev. 22:4). She hears the voice of her Bridegroom say: "Well done, thou good and faithful servant" (Mt. 25:21). The Veil no longer separates man from his Creator. Man and the God are united forever.

The silver sockets: The silver used to make the sockets for the Veil was a product of God's abundant supply. The silver foundation of the Tabernacle reveals the price paid for the redemption of the human race. The silver foundation of the pillars of the Veil reveals the abundance of God's wealth to redeem Yeshua, His firstborn Son. God required the redemption of every firstborn male, animal or human (Ex. 13:12-15). **"All the firstborn of thy sons thou shalt redeem"** (Ex. 34:20b). "But God will redeem my soul from the power of the grave: for he shall receive me. Selah" (Ps. 49:15).

Silver also reveals the insignificant value ungodly men put on the life of Yeshua. The prophet Zechariah prophesied concerning the price of Yeshua's betrayal. "So they weighed for my price thirty pieces of silver" (Zech. 11:12). Judas Iscariot, the one who betrayed Yeshua, received thirty pieces of silver fulfilling Zechariah's prophecy. "Then one of the twelve, called Judas Iscariot, went unto the chief priests, And said unto them, What will ye give me, and I will deliver him unto you? And they covenanted with him for thirty pieces of silver" (Mt.26:14-15).

The final message within the Veil is that of the Risen Redeemer. The Bible speaks of the day when all of heaven is silent as Yeshua stands to open the seal of judgment. "And when he had opened the seventh seal, *there was silence in heaven about the space of half an hour"* (Rev. 8:1; my emphasis). *"Be silent, O all flesh, before the LORD: for he is raised up out of his holy habitation."* (Zech. 2:13)

SUMMARY

THROUGH THE VEIL IS ETERNAL LIFE

CHAPTER 11

The Door, Pillars, Crowns, Hooks, and Sockets

"And thou shalt make a hanging for the door of the tent, of blue, and purple, and scarlet, and fine twined linen, wrought with needlework. And thou shalt make for the hanging five pillars of shittim wood, and overlay them with gold, and their hooks shall be of gold: and thou shalt cast five sockets of brass for them (Ex. 26:36-37). And the five pillars of it with their hooks: and he overlaid their chapiters and their fillets with gold: but their five sockets were of brass (Ex. 36:38).

The Door

Our journey through the Tabernacle has brought us to the Door, the only entrance into the Holy Place. From God's perspective, He stands at the Door looking toward the outer courtyard. Man, on the other hand, is outside in the courtyard making his way to the Door.

Inside the Tabernacle are two chambers, the Holy Place and the Holy of Holies. The Door is the screen that separated the outer court from the Holy Place. Behind the Door are the Golden Candlestick, the Table of Showbread and the Golden Altar of Incense. These three items reveal more of the relationship between God and man. *First:* God gave Aaron and his sons the privilege of sharing in the Holy offerings. Fellowship between God and humanity was experienced as the priest stood at the Table of Showbread eating the bread and drinking the wine of the Holy offerings; the portions that foreshadowed the body and the blood of Yeshua. *Second:* The Candlestick is the "Shadow" of the Word of God. The light from the Candlestick foreshadows the illuminating power of the Holy Spirit to clarify the Word of God. He gives life to the WORD. Every morning and evening the priests spent time before the Candlestick adding fresh oil and trimming the wicks. Tending the lamps foretold how to receive new revelations from the Word of God. We, like the priest, must spend time in the Word for the Holy Spirit to bring it to life. *Third:* The priests prayed at the Altar of Incense. Prayer is the way to intimacy with the Lord.

The Holy Place offered a quiet peaceful room where the priest and their Creator could share the intimacy of a relationship. The opposite was true of the outer court; it was a busy place. The outer court is where the people brought their sacrifices. The noise of a multitude of voices along with the bleating and mooing of the animals created an atmosphere of chaos. But just past the outer court was the Door. Yeshua said, "I am the door: by me if any man enter in, he shall be saved, and shall go in and out, and find pasture" (Jn. 10:9). God the Father is waiting on the other side of the Door for you to enter the Holy

Place so that he can teach you how to know Him. To experience intimacy, one must be willing to be exposed, nothing hidden, it means, in—to—me—see.

In the previous chapter, we explored the multi facetted aspects of the Veil. Now we will do the same with the door.

The Door, like the Veil, was made by weaving blue, purple, scarlet and fine linen threads. Absent from the instructions for the Door and the Veil was the measurements. We know however, since they served as screens, they had to be the same height and width of the building. Although both exhibit similarities, there are several differences. Missing from the Door were the cherubim. The Door hung on five pillars; the Veil had four. Each pillar had a golden crown and a golden hook; the Veil did not have crowns. The foundation for the pillars of the Door was brass; the pillars of the Veil stood in silver.

The most obvious difference between the Door and the Veil was the absence of cherubim. The absence of God's warrior angels points to the willing surrender of Yeshua, to die on the Cross of Calvary. Yeshua chose to separate Himself from heavens protection. The night of His arrest, in an effort to protect Yeshua, Peter cut off the ear of the high priests' servant. Yeshua said to Peter, "Thinkest thou that I cannot now pray to my Father, and he shall presently give me more than twelve legions of angels? But how then shall the scriptures be fulfilled, that thus it must be" (Mt. 26:53-54; Isa. 53:7)? The writer of Hebrews explains it this way, "But we see Yeshua, who was made a little lower than the angels for the suffering of death, crowned with glory and honor; that he by the grace of God should taste death for every man." (Heb. 2:9). No man took His life, He gave it that we might live.

In order to see the fullness of the "Shadow" of Yeshua in the DOOR, we will look for other scriptures that agree with this statement. Yeshua said, "I am the DOOR OF THE SHEEP" (Jn. 10:7: my emphasis). The Greek word translated door is *thuroros*, which came from the root word *thura*. Strong's Exhaustive

Concordance of the Bible defines *thuroros* as a watcher, a gatewarden and *thura* as a portal or entrance. Yeshua is both; He is the only way in and the one who protects those who enter. In the Old Testament, we find another "Shadow". Noah and his family entered into the Ark and God shut them in (Gen. 17:16). The Ark foreshadowed the place of Salvation and like the Tabernacle, there was only one-way in. "And the door of the ark shalt thou set in the side thereof" (Gen. 6:16). According to Strong's Exhaustive Concordance of the Bible, the Hebrew word translated Door is *pethach*. The definition of *pethach* is entranceway, begin, plough, carve, let go free. In this passage, the door is both the way and the means to Salvation, a beautiful and explicit "Shadow" of Yeshua. "Neither is there salvation in any other: for there is none other name under heaven given among men, whereby we must be saved" (Acts 4:12).

Yeshua is the DOOR and the keeper of it. God designed the chamber behind the door for intimacy. How can we develop the intimate relationship God intends for us? Intimacy is a product of knowledge; we must know Him. He used the furnishings inside the Tabernacle to reveal the fullness of His being. To know God, we must know what the Bible says about Him; and trust the Holy Spirit to give life to the written Word. We must learn the benefit of communicating. Communication is the key to knowing someone, so we need to spend time in prayer. Prayer is a two way street; listening is as important as speaking. The cost of discipleship is no small thing; it takes time and effort on our part. If we want to know Him, we must do as John said, "He must increase and I must decrease" (Jn. 3:30). We must die to self that He might live through us. Not all believers are willing to pay the price of discipleship. They live in what is referred to as cheap grace. They have protection from Hell's fire but they have not fallen in love with the one who saved them; all they have is fire insurance. It is sad to say, but many believers fall into this category. They prefer to remain outside the Door in the courtyard, doing busy work, instead of trusting God enough to enter into His quite place. As a result, they never grow up, they remain babies. Yeshua desires that we follow Him into a deeper relationship, one of supernatural power, wisdom and knowledge. To do that, we must depend solely on Him. We, the believers, are the sheep in Yeshua's fold. Yeshua identified Himself as the DOOR of the sheep and the GOOD SHEPHERD. He said, "Verily, verily, I say unto you, I am the door of the sheep. I am the door: by me if any man enters in, he shall be saved, and shall go in and out, and find pasture. I am the good shepherd; the good shepherd giveth his life for the sheep" (Jn. 10:7, 9, 11). Yeshua said, "But he that entereth in by the door is the shepherd of the sheep. To him the porter openeth; and the sheep hear his voice: and he calleth his own sheep by name, and leadeth them out. And when he putteth forth his own sheep, he goeth before them, and the sheep follow him: for they know his voice. And a stranger will they not follow, but will flee from him: for they know not the voice of strangers" (Jn. 10:2-5).

While a guest on a farm in Poland, I saw this principal in action. The keeper of the sheep led them out to pasture every morning. While they grazed, several of the visitors called to them but they did not respond. When the time of feeding ended, the shepherd came and called her sheep. I was amazed. They immediately ran to meet her and followed her wherever she went. Sometimes, one or two would wander off and she left the others and went to them calling them by name back into the fold. Then I remembered the words of Lord who said, "What man of you, having an hundred sheep, if he lose one of them, doth not leave the ninety and nine in the wilderness, and go after that which is lost, until he find it? And when he hath found it, he layeth it on his shoulders, rejoicing. And when he cometh home, he calleth together his friends and neighbors, saying unto them, Rejoice with me; for I have found my sheep which was lost. I say unto you, that likewise joy shall be in heaven over one sinner that repenteth, more than over ninety and nine just persons, which need no repentance" (Lk. 15:4-7). Often in our walk as believers, we stray away and when we do, Yeshua brings us back into His fold. He calls us by name and all heaven rejoices when we repent.

The Door is also representative of the truth. Yeshua is TRUTH, He said, "And ye shall know the truth, and the truth shall *make you free*!" and "If the Son therefore shall *make* you free, ye shall be free indeed" (Jn. 8:32, 36; my emphasis). Please note, He said the Truth we KNOW makes us free. To make is a process and aside from Him, there is no freedom. Truth is revealed little by little, line upon line, precept upon precept, here a little and there a little. When you know Him and the power of His might, there is nothing lacking. Intimacy produces Spiritual freedom from which comes healing, deliverance, salvation, prosperity, faith, discerning of spirits, the ability to speak other languages, and interpret them, along with the working of miracles. If you are outside the Door and you want to enter, but you fear being ostracized by those who trust in the traditions of men, FEAR NOT! Because He will keep you if you obey His voice, and follow Him. He said," While I was with them in the world, I kept them in thy name: those that thou gavest me I have kept, and none of them is lost, but the son of perdition; that the scripture might be fulfilled" (Jn. 17:23).

The Brass Sockets: Brass as you recall, is symbolic of judgment. The brass sockets of the Door portray two judgments, the judgment suffered by Yeshua and the final judgment of the believer. God poured His wrath on Yeshua for all humanity. The Judgment Seat of Messiah is the place of judgment for every believer. For further clarity, we must see the relationship between the pillars and the sockets.

The five pillars: The pillars of the Door, like the pillars of the Veil, were made of wood overlaid with gold. The wood is symbolic of unsaved natural man; the gold overlay reveals a change. Salvation changes the natural man into the righteousness of God. "For he hath made him to be sin for us, who knew no sin; that we might be made the righteousness of God in him" (2 Cor. 5:21). Number 5(the number of the pillars) reveals the unmerited favor of God; it is by His Grace that we are saved (Eph. 2:8, 9). The old man dies, and a new one is born. The gold covered pillars are representative of the *new man*. The new man is standing in five brass sockets; he is at the judgment seat of Messiah. There, Yeshua judges every work, good or bad. Good works receive a reward; everything else is burned with fire (1 Cor. 3:11-15). After being judged, the believers enter into the kingdom God has prepared for them (Mt. 25:31-34).

Yeshua is the judge of ALL men and the Bible speaks of two judgments. The Judgment Seat of Messiah is one of them and the White Throne Judgment is the other (Jn. 5:22; Rom.14:10; 2 Cor. 5:10; Rev. 20:11-15). The White Throne Judgment is for those who refuse to accept Yeshua as the Messiah (Rev. 20: 11-15). All who are not found in the Book of Life will burn in the lake of fire for eternity.

The Five Gold Hooks: Gold is symbolic of deity. Each pillar had a gold hook that pierced and secured the hanging of the Door. A "Shadow" of Yeshua's suffering, while on the cross, is revealed through the five hooks. He experienced indescribable pain as His body was pierced causing five puncture wounds, His hands, His feet, and His side. "They pierced my hands and my feet" (Ps 22:16). "And they shall look upon me whom they have pierced, and they shall mourn for him, as one mourneth for his only son, and shall be in bitterness for him, as one that is in bitterness for his firstborn" (Zech. 12:10). "But one of the soldiers with a spear pierced his side, and forthwith came there out blood and water. And again another scripture saith, they shall look on him whom they pierced" (Jn. 19:34, 37).

The fifth hook and the fifth puncture wound in Yeshua's body provide a "Shadow" of the birth of Yeshua's bride. God took Adam's bride from his side (Gen. 2:21-22), foreshadowing how the Bride of, **the last Adam**, YESHUA, would come (1 Cor. 15:45).

Blood and water are always present at a birth. Blood and water gushed from Yeshua's side revealing that something was being born. From that day forward the community of believers, called the church, began.

Every believer is responsible for sharing the message of the Door. Yeshua is the DOOR and He is the TRUTH; He is the only way into the place of intimacy. He has secured the believer's relationship with the Father, but how close and intimate that relationship is remains with YOU. THE CHOICE IS YOURS. "Choose you this day whom ye will serve; but as for me and my house, we will serve the LORD" (Josh. 25:15).

The Golden Crowns: A Golden crown was on the top of each of the five pillars. Each of the five crowns represents a reward for good works (Mt. 25:21). The Bible chronicles each; they are the crown of joy, the crown of righteousness, the crown of life, the crown of glory, and the incorruptible crown.

1) <u>The Crown of Joy</u> (1 Thess. 2:19): This crown speaks of the joy that comes in seeing people born into the kingdom of God. To receive this crown you must have a heart for the lost.
2) <u>The Crown of Righteousness</u> (2 Tim. 4:8): This crown speaks of keeping in right relationship with God by doing what He commands. Yeshua said those who love Him, keep His commandments (Jn. 14:15-26). He also said that if we keep His commandments, as He kept the Father's, we will abide in love (Jn. 15:10). This crown belongs to those who love Him enough to do His word.

<u>WHAT DID GOD COMMAND MEN TO DO?</u>

He said, "Hear O Israel: The Lord our God is one Lord: and thou shalt love the Lord thy God with all thine heart, and with all thy soul, and with all thy might. And these words, with I command thee this day, shall be in thine heart: And thou shall teach them

> diligently unto thy children, and shalt talk of them when thou sittest in thine house, and when thou walkest by the way, and when thou liest down, and when thou risest up. And thou shalt bind them for a sign upon thine hand, and they shall be as frontlets between thine eyes. And thou shalt write them upon the post of thy house, and on thy gates. And thou shalt love thy neighbor as thy self: I AM THE LORD" (Deut. 6:4-9; Lev. 19:18b; my emphasis).

Yeshua quoted part of this passage when he answered the question, which is the great commandment in the law? He said, *"Thou shalt love the Lord thy God with all thy heart, with all thy soul, and with all thy mind.* This is the first great commandment. And the second is like unto it, *Thou shalt love thy neighbor as thyself.* On these two commandments hang all the law and the prophets" (Mt. 22:37-40; my emphasis). Yeshua added one commandment to these, He said, "A new commandment I give unto you, That ye love one another; as I have loved you, that ye also love one another. By this shall all men know that ye are my disciples, if ye have love one to another" (Jn. 13:34-35). Yeshua requires that we become doers of His Word not just hearers, because hearing the Word does not reveal the love that comes from obeying the Word. Obedience produces Agape (Gods' unconditional love) which works like a magnet drawing men to Yeshua.

3) <u>The Crown of Life</u> (Ja. 1:12): This crown represents the power and authority Yeshua gives to those who love Him. Intimacy gives birth to strength and endurance. It produces the power needed to overcome the fiery trials and temptations of life and remain faithful.
4) <u>The Crown of Glory (1 Pet. 5:4):</u> This crown belongs to pastors, those who are willing to feed the flock--those who are not serving out of obligation but rather with a willing heart, not seeking wealth and riches. Instead, they are looking for the reward that comes from seeing

the eyes of one who has never understood the love of God opened, so that he might become a productive member of the household of God. This crown also belongs to Yeshua. He is the GOOD Shepherd and He alone is deserving of glory.

5) <u>The Incorruptible Crown</u> (1 Cor. 9:25): The incorruptible crown is a crown given to those who participate in the spiritual race. The unsaved cannot participate in this race. Only those who exercise their faith and keep their souls, minds and bodies in submission to the counsel of the Word of God can expect to finish the race and receive this crown. ***The depth of one's faith is measured by his obedience to the WORD OF GOD.***

The crowns are not the means of ones eternal salvation; they are treasures given by the Lord to those who serve Him. They are not to keep, but to cast at Yeshua's feet. Yeshua is the King of Kings; John saw Him and described His appearance. "And I saw heaven opened, and behold a white horse; and he that sat upon him was called Faithful and True, and in righteousness he doth judge and make war. His eyes were as a flame of fire, and *on his head were many crowns*; and he had a name written, that no man knew, but He Himself. And He was clothed with a vesture dipped in blood: and His name is called the Word of God. And the armies which were in heaven followed Him upon white horses, clothed in fine linen, white and clean" (Rev. 19:11-16; my emphasis). I am convinced that the crowns Yeshua has on are the ones that were cast at His feet, because they represent His completed work in the earth. He is coming back as the King of Kings to make war on unbelief. Yeshua fulfills every aspect of the Tabernacle Door.

SUMMARY

The Door: *Yeshua is the Door and the Truth*
The 5 Pillars: *Believers sealed by the Spirit of God, His perfect Grace.*
The Crowns: *We have been crowned with all that he is, and one day we will cast the crowns at his feet, and see him wearing them when he returns as the King of Glory.*
The Hooks and Rods: *His work is held secure because of who he is.*
The Sockets of Brass: *He stood in judgment for us, and he will judge our works.*

CHAPTER 12

The Brazen Altar

"And thou shalt make an altar of shittim wood, five cubits long, and five cubits broad; the altar shall be foursquare: and the height thereof shall be three cubits. And thou shalt make horns of it upon the four corners thereof: his horns shall be of the same: and thou shalt overlay it with brass. And thou shalt make his pans to receive his ashes, and his shovels, and his basins, and his flesh hooks, and his fire pans: all the vessels thereof thou shalt make of brass. And thou shalt make for it a grate of network of brass; and upon the net shalt thou make four brazen rings in the four corners thereof. And thou shalt put it under the compass of the altar beneath that the net may be even to the midst of the altar. And thou shalt make staves for the altar, staves of shittim wood, and overlay them with brass. And the staves shall be put into the rings, and the staves shall be upon the two sides of the altar, to bear it. Hollow with boards shalt thou make it: as it was showed thee in the mount, so shall they make it (Ex. 27:1-8).

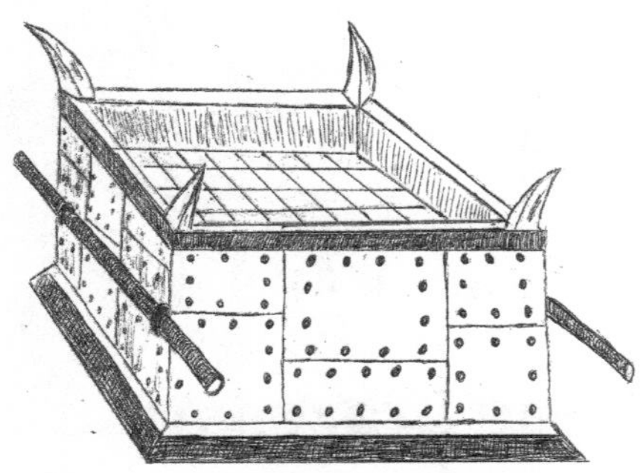

The Brazen Altar

We have left the protective coverings of the Tabernacle and arrived at the Brazen Altar, the place of death. The *Brazen Altar* is the first thing you see as you enter into the courtyard. It was the largest of all the furnishings. It measured five cubits square and three cubits high, and had a horn on each corner. Unlike the furnishings inside the Tabernacle that were overlaid with gold, the Altar was covered with brass. It was made for one purpose, to burn the sacrificial offerings. As we look at the different features of the Altar, Yeshua's sacrificial death will become evident, for the "Shadow" found in the Brazen Altar is that of Calvary.

The wood of the altar, like the wood in the other furnishings, relates to the man Yeshua, or His humanity. As a man, He experienced the same things as other men, but without sin. He chose to take on the form of a man, "to minister, and to give his life a ransom for many" (Mk. 10:45). "For verily he took not on him the nature of angels; but he took on him the seed of Abraham. Wherefore in all things it behooved him to be made like unto his brethren, that he might be a merciful and faithful high priest in things pertaining to God, to make reconciliation for the sins of the people" (Heb. 2:16, 17).

The brass that covered the altar was made from two hundred and fifty brass censers. It was put there to remind the people that all sin must be judged. Censers were used for burning incense. Following is a brief synopsis of how the brass censers came to be used to cover the Brazen Altar.

Korah was a Levite; a member of the family that was set apart from the other sons of Israel to serve God. But, he was not a member of Aaron's family. Aaron and his sons were the only ones authorized to offer incense before God. Korah, along with other men, rebelled against God's choice of the High Priest. They took censers and burned incense before the Lord. Their rebellion resulted in immediate judgment. God destroyed all two hundred and fifty men and everything that was associated with them including their families and their livestock. God sent fire from heaven that burned up the two hundred and fifty men, and then the earth opened up and swallowed everything that belonged to them. Please read the entire account of this event in Numbers 16. Following the death of Korah and the two hundred and fifty men, "Eleazar the priest took the brazen censers, wherewith they that burnt had offered; and they were made broad plates for a covering of the altar: To be a memorial unto the children of Israel, *that no stranger, **which is not of the seed of Aaron***, come near to offer incense before the Lord; that he be not as Korah, and as his company: as the Lord said to him by Moses" (Nu. 16:39-40; my emphasis).

The Brazen Altar was the place of death; a place where the innocent suffered the fire of God's judgment. The brass plates represent sin, and nailing them to the wooden frame of the Altar narrows the path to the Cross of Calvary. The Bible teaches that Yeshua was made to be sin for us so that we could become the righteousness of God (2 Cor. 5:21). Yeshua was innocent of ALL sin, yet He was nailed to a wooden cross to suffer the wrath of God's judgment for all men (1 Pet. 3:18). God required a blood sacrifice for the remission of sin (Lev. 17:11; Heb. 9:22). The blood of many animals was poured on the Brazen Altar, but *THERE IS NO SUBSTITUTE FOR THE BLOOD OF YESHUA*. He is the only one qualified to provide justification for the human race (Heb. 9:11-14).

The Brazen Altar's immense size and design shows the infinite power of God's love and grace. Its measurements reveal the unity of the Holy Trinity. Every member of the Holy Trinity was present at Calvary. The Brazen Altar was *five cubits* square (seven and a half feet) and *three cubits* tall (four and a half feet). Five is the number identified with the Grace of God, and four is the number for the earth; all four of its sides are equal, showing man that God's grace is the same for everyone. "For all have sinned, and come short of the glory of God; being justified freely by his GRACE through the redemption that is in Messiah Yeshua" (Rom. 3:23-24; my emphasis). Three is the number identified with the Holy Trinity, God the Father, God the Son and God the Holy Spirit. The number three points to the single-minded purpose of the Holy Trinity; they all took part in the final sacrifice for sin. "Messiah (the **Son**) through the (eternal **Spirit**) offered himself without spot to God (the **Father**)" (Heb. 9:14; my emphasis).

The Brazen Altar was an awesome sight as one entered into the courtyard. The smoke from the burning flesh filled the air and its *four horns* glistened in the light of the sun. Four, the number for the earth, in relation to the Brazen Altar, reveals the uncompromised love of God, for He is no respecter of persons (Acts 10:34). Horns are symbols of power. The horns of the brazen altar reveal the power of God to save ALL who will accept His sacrifice. Yeshua said, "And as Moses lifted up the serpent in the wilderness, even so must the Son of man be lifted up: that whosoever believeth in him should not perish, but have eternal life. For God so loved the world, that he gave his only begotten Son, that whosoever believeth in him should not perish, but have everlasting life. For God sent not his Son into the world to condemn the world; but that the world through him might be saved" (Jn. 3:14-17).

Brass netting was used to make the grate; it had to be strong enough to support the weight of the sacrifice and durable enough to withstand the heat of the fire. The grate was positioned in the center of the Altar and held in place with four brass rings that attached underneath the rim. The placement of the grate made it the same height as the Ark of the Covenant and the Table of Showbread, 27" or (2+7=9). Nine is the self-repeating number that identifies the eternal character of God who never changes. We have already established that the Ark of the Covenant and the Table of Showbread are "Shadows" of the Son in the Father and the Father in the Son. Through the height of the grate, (27") we have the "Shadow" of the perpetual character of God. The height of the grate reveals that God in the person of Yeshua is the sacrifice for all sin.

The ashes from the offerings were caught in brass pans as they fell through the netting and the blood was poured out at the foot of the Altar. Yeshua's blood, like the blood of the Tabernacle offerings, ran down the Altar of the Cross and spilled onto the ground. His blood fulfilled the words of God concerning atonement. "For the life of the flesh is in the blood: and I have given it to you upon the altar to make atonement for your souls: for it is the blood that maketh an atonement for the soul" (Lev. 17:11). John recognized Yeshua as God's sacrifice when He said, "Behold the Lamb of God, which taketh away the sin of the world." (Jn. 1:29).

The purpose of the Brazen Altar along with the sacrifices and the offerings was to point to the FINAL sin sacrifice, Yeshua. His altar was the cross. The writer of Hebrews, speaking of Yeshua, said, "in the end of the world hath he appeared to put away sin by the sacrifice of himself" (Heb. 9:26). The Altar and the sacrifice is what brought hope to humanity.

When the sin offering was placed on the Altar for the first time, God sent fire from heaven and consumed the entire sacrifice (Lev. 9:24). The Bible tells us that God is a consuming fire (Deut. 4:24, Heb. 12:29). Yeshua's sacrifice was a sweet savor to the Father just like the smoke that rose up from the Altar as the innocent sacrifice burned, "Messiah also hath loved us, and hath given himself for us an offering and a sacrifice to God for a sweet smelling savor." (Eph. 5:2).

Because of Calvary, forgiveness of sin and fellowship with God are freely offered to all.

Yeshua on the Cross (by Christa Shore)

SUMMARY

The Altar: *the place of sacrifice and offering, the cross.*
The Brass Plates: *our sin nailed to the cross of Yeshua.*
The 4 Horns: *His far-reaching power to save.*
The Size: 5 cubits square = *God's grace is the same for all the earth.*

3 cubits high = *every member of the Holy Trinity was involved at Calvary.*

CHAPTER 13

The Outer Court

The pillars, the hangings, the sockets, the hooks, the fillets, the pins, and the gate

"And thou shalt make the court of the tabernacle: for the south side southward there shall be hangings for the court of fine twined linen of a hundred cubits long for one side; and the twenty pillars thereof and their twenty sockets shall be of brass; the hooks of the pillars and their fillets shall be of silver. And likewise for the north side in length there shall be hangings of a hundred cubits long, and his twenty pillars and their twenty sockets of brass; the hooks of the pillars and their fillets of silver. And for the breadth of the court on the west side shall be hangings of fifty cubits: their pillars ten, and their sockets ten. And the breadth of the court on the east side eastward shall be fifty cubits. The hangings of the one side of the gate shall be fifteen cubits: their pillars three and their sockets three. And on the other side shall be hangings fifteen cubits: their pillars three, and their sockets three. And for the gate of the court shall be a hanging of twenty cubits, of blue, and purple, and scarlet, and fine twined linen, wrought with needlework: and their pillars shall be four, and their sockets four. All the pillars round about the court shall be filleted with silver; their hooks shall be of silver, and their sockets of brass. The length of the court shall be a hundred cubits and the breadth fifty everywhere, and the height five cubits of fine twined linen, and their sockets of brass.

> All the vessels of the tabernacle in all the service thereof, and all the pins thereof, and all the pins of the court, shall be of brass (Ex. 27:9-19, 38:9-20).

As the journey through the Tabernacle continues, the details of God's Master plan become even more evident. An in-depth look at the outer court will reveal God's love for both the lost and the saved.

We get our first glimpse of God's love in the measurements used to describe the perimeter of the outer court; it was *three hundred cubits.* The hanging of the fence was *five cubits high.* Remember, number five identifies the grace of God, and we see His grace through each number describing the outer court; each is divisible by five. The fence was *one hundred cubits* long on both the north and the south sides. The west end was *fifty cubits*, and on the east, the Gate was *twenty cubits* with *fifteen cubits* of fence on either side.

If we multiply the sum of the perimeter by the height (5 x 300 = 1500), which is believed to be the number of years from the first Passover to the birth of Yeshua, our Passover Lamb (Jn. 1:29).[13] Therefore, as you can see, through the perimeter measurements alone God is beginning to reveal His love.

The *pillars* of the court are different from all the other pillars of the Tabernacle; they contained no wood, they were solid brass. As we have seen, brass represents judgment, and in this case, because wood was not present the human element is missing. I believe the absence of wood reveals the magnitude of God's wrath towards sin (Nu. 21:9). Sixty brass pillars supported by sockets of brass surrounded the outer courtyard. The sixty pillars contain a two-fold revelation, if we use the equation 6 x 10 to arrive at *sixty.* First, *number six* is usually associated with man. Six, in this equation, identifies Yeshua, the MAN, who took the full brunt of God's wrath and judgment for all humanity (Jn. 3; 16-17). Second, *number ten* is symbolic of two things, man's completeness and God's handwritten promises (the Ten Commandments). Number ten, in this equation, reveals the state of the human soul; he has broken every law of God. It represents the totality of his sin. Therefore, the sixty brass pillars reveal the severity of the judgment Yeshua received in man's place. God is just, and through the pillars and the sockets of the fence, the "Shadow" of His just judgment is revealed. Behind the pillars was the Tabernacle where the presence of God dwelt, showing man that on the other side of judgment is the habitation of God. "Justice and judgment are the habitation of thy throne" (Ps. 89:14).

There are different kinds of judgment. There is God's judgment, self-judgment and the final judgment (1 Cor. 11:31-32). God is faithful; He declared that sin must be judged. Before a man could enter into the outer court, he had to bring an offering to God, one to take his place on the altar of death, foreshadowing Yeshua's death. If you fail to judge yourself and repent, you are destined to experience the complete wrath of God's judgment (Rom. 14:10-11). God has made the way for you to escape the severity of His judgment. You can be forgiven through the experience of Calvary, by accepting Yeshua as the Messiah. He suffered the judgment for your sin, therefore, you will not be judged anymore concerning sin. The motives behind your works and good deeds, after accepting Yeshua, will be judged (2 Cor. 5:10).

The *fillets* and *hooks* of the outer court were made of silver. Silver was the medium of exchange chosen by God as payment for redemption. Fillet is the name used for the cross bar that separated the pillars. The solid brass pillars were spaced evenly <u>five</u> cubits apart (God's grace). The fillets were joined to the pillars by the silver hooks. The white linen fence hung from the fillets. The silver fillets and hooks point to the atoning redemptive power found in Yeshua's death and resurrection. The fillets separated the brass pillars (judgment) like the atoning power of Yeshua's sacrifice held back the judgment of God from humanity.

The fence was made from pure white linen providing a "Shadow" of the perfect righteousness of Yeshua. His righteousness restores peace between man and God. "Mercy and truth are met together; righteousness and peace have kissed each other" (Ps. 85:10). "And the work of righteousness shall be peace; and the effect of righteousness quietness and assurance forever" (Isa. 32:17).

Each pillar was topped with a silver crown called a capital, and through them we have a "Shadow" of the crowns of God's loving-kindness and tender mercies that come through redemption (Ps. 103:4).

The *hanging* of the court (the fence) was made from the same fine linen as the first curtain of the Tabernacle. Both of them contained the same amount of linen, 280 cubits. The first covering consisted of 10 strips that were 28 cubits long, 10 x 28 = 280 cubits, and the hanging of the fence was of 100 cubits on the north side, 100 cubits on the south side, 50 cubits on the west end, 15 cubits on the south side of the gate and, 15 cubits on the north side of the gate for a total of 280 cubits. The measurements had to be identical to present an accurate portrait of the righteousness of God, because it never changes. The first curtain is representative of the righteousness that covered Yeshua. Directly underneath it were the Holy furnishings, which previously were determined to reveal various attributes of His character. The hanging for the fence presents the "Shadow" of the believer's covering of righteousness (Isa.1:18; 61:10; 2 Cor. 5:21; Rev. 3:5). Remember, in a blood covenant those making the covenant exchange robes; Yeshua exchanged His robe of righteous for humanity's robe of sin. The believer receives the garment of salvation, Yeshua's robe of righteousness (Isa. 61:10). The hanging of the outer court fence was seven and one half feet high, taller than the average man. The Gate was the only entrance into the outer court. Those inside the fence were hidden in a place of safety, foreshadowing the place of the redeemed. For we are dead and our lives are hidden with Messiah in God (Col. 3:3). "He that dwelleth in the secret place of the Most High shall abide under the shadow of the Almighty." (Ps. 91:1). Messiah is the secret place of the Most High! Therefore, the **280** cubits used to make the first curtain and the outer court fence present two revelations. First, God's Righteousness (Yeshua) protects and shields His own until they enter with Him into the Eternal Promised Land. Second, God's righteousness is big enough to cover ALL mankind.

Early one morning the Lord woke me and began to show me how the numbers **40** and **70** relate to the purpose of both the first covering and the hanging of the fence. If you divide 280 by **7**, ***God's perfect number***, the answer is **40**, ***the number for testing and also the number of years His children were protected by His righteous presence as they journeyed in the wilderness***. If you divide 280 by **4, *the number of the earth,*** the answer is **70, *which is the number of Israel's children that entered into Egypt with him when they were reunited with Joseph.*** Seventy went in and over one million came out. 70 is also the number of known nations at the time of God's appearance on Mt. Sinai.

> According to Rabbi Joseph Hertz's writings:
>
> "The Revelation at Sinai, it was taught, was given in desert territory, which belongs to no one nation exclusively; and it was heard not by Israel alone, but by the inhabitants of all the earth. The Divine voice divided itself into the seventy tongues then spoken on earth, so that all the children of men might understand its world-embracing and man-redeeming message."[14]

Rabbi Moshe Weissman confirms Hertz's statements in his book.

> "When G-d gave the Torah on Sinai, He displayed untold marvels to Israel with His Voice. What happened? G-d spoke and the voice

> reverberated throughout the world. It says, And all the people witnessed the thunderings (Ex. 18, 15). Note that it does not say "the thunder," but "the thunderings"; wherefore, R. Johanan said that G-d's Voice, as it was uttered, split up into seventy voices, in seventy languages, so that all the nations should understand. When each nation heard the Voice in their own Vernacular, their souls departed [i.e. they were in fear], save Israel, who heard but who Were not hurt...

Exodus Rabbah 5.9

> On the Occasion of Matan Torah (the giving of the Torah), the Bnai Yisrael (the children of Israel) Not only heard Hashem's (the L-rd's) Voice but actually saw the sound waves as they emerged from Hashem's (the L-rd's) mouth. They visualized them as a fiery substance. Each commandment that left Hashem's (the L-rd's) mouth traveled around the entire Camp and then came back to every Jew individually, asking him, "Do you accept upon yourself this Commandment with all halachot (Jewish law) pertaining to it?" Every Jew answered, "Yes", after each Commandment. Finally, the fiery substance which they saw, engraved itself on the luchot (tablets).[15]

Twisted linen Cords were used to hold the pillars of the outer court upright. To do that, the tension had to be equal on both sides. Twisting the linen made the cords stronger. The cords had to be strong enough to support the weight of the fence. Isaiah chapter 40 uses the principle of twisting to explain how spiritual strength is produced. "But they that WAIT upon the Lord shall renew their strength; they shall mount up with wings as eagles; they shall run, and not be weary; and they shall walk, and not faint" (Isa. 40:31; my emphasis). The Hebrew word translated wait is **qavah,** pronounced *(kaw-vaw),* qavah means to bind together as in twisting; in other words, our strength comes from being wrapped up and tangled up with God.

The twisted linen cords provide a "Shadow" of the power of God's love. They fastened to the hooks and to the brass nails, inside and outside of the courtyard, to provide support for the fence. What a beautiful picture of God's love for the lost as well as the saved.

"But God commendeth his love toward us, in that, while we were yet sinners, Christ died for us" (Rom.5:8). To those on the outside, God's love beckons saying, "Come unto me, all ye that labor, and are heavy laden, and I will give you rest" and "I am the Way, the Truth, and the Life: no man cometh unto the Father, but by me" (Mt. 11:28, 14:6). The price for your soul has been paid, and His gift of love is free (Jn. 3:16). All who accept His gift can come inside the courtyard. To those who have entered, the message of the cords is this, stay in Him (Jn. 15:7). His cords of love hold secure the price paid for your sin (1 Cor. 6:20). You are surrounded with His righteousness. You are hidden in Him. "Thou art my hiding place; thou shalt preserve me from trouble; thou shalt compass me about with songs of deliverance" (Ps. 32:7). When the devil looks at you, he sees nothing but the righteousness of God, and if he steps back to get a better look, he will see the Tabernacle, the very presence of God Himself.

Brass *pins or nails* were used to anchor the cords. The "Shadow" revealed in the brass nails is the power of God's righteous judgment to anchor the cords of His love. When the desert wind blew, the nails held everything secure, unmoved. "The judgments of the Lord are true and righteous altogether" (Ps. 19:9b). His decision to love is unyielding, as were the nails that held the cords in place. He chose to love man. That love was so strong that God gave the life of His only begotten Son to be judged in man's stead. God's love is not based on how good or how bad you are. His love was so strong that Messiah died for us while we were still sinners. "For Messiah also hath once suffered for sins, the just for the unjust, that he might bring us to God, being put to death in the flesh, but quickened by the Spirit." (1 Pet. 3:18).

B. R. Hicks wrote about houses that were built during the time of the children of Israel. The builder installed long nails into the walls during construction. The nails were used for hanging curtains, utensils, etc. They were often used in palaces, found mostly in the armory. Kings used them to hang their weapons of warfare[16]. The book of Isaiah records the prophecy of the Sure Nail. God told King Shebna a day would come when he would be removed from power, and his power would be given to another. The description of his replacement is one of Yeshua. The name of the man who would replace Shebna was *Eliakim*, which means ***God will establish***, and his father's name *Hilkiah*, means ***Jehovah is my portion***. What a beautiful description of Yeshua. The scripture goes on to say that Shebna's replacement is a sure NAIL, a glorious throne to his father's house, government was committed into his hands, he held the key to the house of David so he will open and none can shut, and he will shut and none will open. On him all the glory of the father's house was hung (Isa. 22:15-25). Yeshua spoke the same words when He said of Himself, "These things saith he that is holy, he that is true, he that hath *the Key of David, He that openeth, and no man shutteth, and shutteth, and no man openeth*" (Rev. 3:7; my emphasis).

Yeshua is the NAIL and the GRACE of God. "And now for a little space GRACE hath been showed from the Lord our God, to leave us a remnant to escape, and to give us a NAIL in his holy place, that our God may lighten our eyes and give us a little reviving in our bondage" (Ezra 9:8; my emphasis).

The nail is where the entire armor of the King's house was hung. Yeshua is that nail in the household of the Father. The armor of God is available to every believer. God's armor, described in Ephesians 6:10-17, is descriptive of Yeshua; or rather they describe His attributes. So, when you put on God's armor, you are putting on Yeshua Himself. Remember, the Lord goes before you and the God of Israel is your rearward (Isa. 52:12). You are protected on all sides!

The Gate (by Christa Shore)

Our journey has brought us to the gate. The Gate is also a "Shadow" of Yeshua. The *gate* was not attached to the fence. A space of five cubits on either side of the Gate separated it from the fence. The Gate hung on four pillars and like the Door and the Veil, was white linen intertwined with blue purple and scarlet thread. God did not give a measurement for the Door or the Veil, but since they acted as screens, they were the same height and width as the Tabernacle, fifteen feet high and fifteen feet wide. That means they were (10) ten cubits high and (10) cubits wide. There are "Shadows" of Yeshua in both of them. Now, we see God giving specific measurements for the Gate; it was thirty feet wide and seven and a half feet high, or twice as wide and half as high as the Door and the Veil. This puzzled me; so, I asked the Lord how the gate could be a "Shadow" of Yeshua if its measurement was so different from the Door and the Veil. He is always faithful. ***He said to me, the gate was the only way to get to the brazen altar where the sacrifice was offered. He told me to divide the gate in half, and stand the two pieces upright and side-by-side, and I would see that they are the same size as the Door and the Veil. He said the only way He could become the offering for me was to lay down His life so that I could come in. <u>The Gate is a picture of Yeshua prostrate in death that we might live</u>. PRAISE HIS HOLY NAME!***

There is something else to see concerning the combined measurements of the Gate, the Door, and the Veil. Each hanging measured **100** square cubits; so, their combined measurement was **300**, which is the same number found in the perimeter measurement of the outer courtyard.

Yeshua is the Gate, **<u>THE WAY</u>**. God has made it very clear that the only way to get to Him is through His Son, Yeshua (Jn. 14:6). **He is the covering that surrounds ALL men and the only way to the Father.**

SUMMARY

THE BRASS PILLARS AND SOCKETS: *justice and judgment*
SILVER FILLETS AND HOOKS: *mercy and redemption*
TWISTED LINEN CORDS: *the strong pure love of God (AGAPE)*
BRASS NAILS: *the judgment He bore secured everything*
THE WHITE LINEN HANGING: *His righteousness, our garment of salvation and wedding dress.*
THE GATE: *His willing death MADE THE WAY*

CHAPTER 14

The Priesthood and Their Duties

(Exodus 28, Numbers 3 & 4)

"And the LORD spake unto Moses, saying, And I, behold, I have taken the Levites from among the children of Israel instead of all the firstborn that openeth the matrix among the children of Israel: therefore the Levites shall be mine; Because all the firstborn are mine; for on the day that I smote all the firstborn in the land of Egypt I hallowed unto me all the firstborn in Israel, both man and beast: mine shall they be: I am the LORD" (Nu. 3:11-13).

And take thou unto thee Aaron thy brother, and his sons with him, from among the children of Israel, that he may minister unto me in the priest's office, even Aaron, Nadab and Abihu, Eleazar and Ithamar, Aaron's sons (Ex. 28:1).

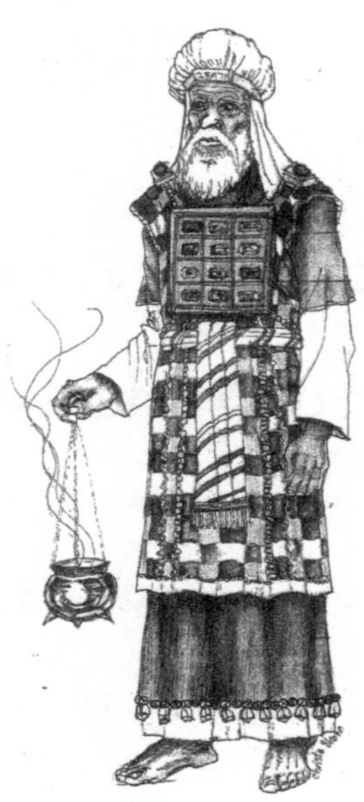

The High Priest (by Christa Shore)

Jacob, "Israel", had twelve sons; his sons are referred to as the twelve tribes of Israel. One tribe out of the twelve was chosen by God to serve Him, the tribe of Levi. From Levi the Lord chose one family to enter the priesthood, the family of Aaron. God chose the tribe of Levi to serve Him for two specific reasons. First, the Levites were set apart unto God; they became the substitute for all of the firstborn of the children of Israel (Nu. 3:11-13). Second, through them, God established the pattern for the relationship that all men would share with Him, as members of His family.

The High Priest was the only man who was permitted to approach God, and then, only once each year on the Day of Atonement. God interacted with the people through the high priest. The high priest was God's representative to the people and the people's advocate before God. Through him, God taught the people His ways and through him the people brought their petitions to God.

Yeshua, the Great High Priest, like the high priest of the Tabernacle, operates the same way. He came to show man the heart of the Father, so that we might ***know*** Him. As our High Priest, He stands before the Father's throne interceding for all who believe (Heb. 7:25). Yeshua is the High Priest and mediator between God and men and because He ever lives, so does our relationship with the Father (Heb. 7:23-24; 1 Tim. 2:5).

The duties of the priests were to assist the high priest with the things of God.

Our relationship with Yeshua is, in many ways, like the priests of old. We are workers together with Him accomplishing God's will in the earth (2 Cor. 6:1). The believer's job is to let the indwelling presence of Yeshua draw others to the saving knowledge of who He is. The believer's relationship with Yeshua is more than being a member of His royal priesthood. We are the children of God, members of His family. Each of us is assigned a position of ministry; first to Him, and then to each other. United, Jew and Gentile "believers" have become like the tribe of Levi; in Yeshua we have become one family unit, one new man. "But to us there is but one God, the Father, of whom are all things, and we in him; and one Lord *Yeshua the Messiah*, by whom are all things, and we by him" (1 Cor. 8:6; my emphasis).

Not all of the Levites entered into the high priestly line. Five of Levi's decedents were called by God to fill the office of high priest. They were Aaron and his four sons, Nadab, Abihu, Eleazar, and Ithamar. Aaron was the first high priest. Upon his death, one of his sons would fill the high priest office. Aaron and his sons were given the responsibility of serving as the intermediaries between God and the people (Nu. 3:9).

Once again God reveals His grace through the number five. Five men entered into the priestly line. They were gifts from God to the people of Israel. They were anointed by God with everything needed to serve in the priest office. Today, believers are servants, and like the priests of the Tabernacle, we are equipped to serve the people of God. We, "the church" are furnished with five ministry gifts, apostles, prophets, evangelists, pastors, and teachers. The duties of Aaron and his four sons and the *five* ministry gifts are alike; they both work toward the common goal described in Ephesians. "And he gave some, apostles; and some, prophets; and some, evangelists; and some, pastors and teachers; *For the perfecting of the saints, for the work of the ministry, for the edifying of the body of Christ:* Till we all come in the unity of the faith, and of the knowledge of the Son of God, unto a perfect man, unto the measure of the stature of the fullness of Christ" (Eph. 4: 11-13; my emphasis).

God revealed His grace when He set these five men apart, out of the two thousand plus children of Levi, just as He does when He calls believers and places them in the *five* ministry offices. God anoints believers with the ability to serve and teach His children that His grace is what brings man back into a right relationship with their Creator.

The priests entered into God's service at the age of thirty and finished at fifty. Yeshua's ministry began at age thirty fulfilling the law concerning the priesthood. Since Yeshua's Priesthood is eternal, His term as High Priest will never end.

Nine of Levi's sons were a part of either the ministry or care of the Tabernacle--Moses, Aaron, Nadab, Abihu, Eleazar, Ithamar, Gershon, Kohath, and Merari. Together they provide a "Shadow" of the body of Messiah operating in the *nine* gifts of the Spirit. Although each man was different and had different tasks to perform, they operated in one accord, performing their task as one single unit.

The body of Messiah operates the same way through the word of wisdom, the word of knowledge, faith, gifts of healing, working of miracles, prophecy, discerning of spirits, divers kinds of tongues, and the interpretation of tongues. (1 Cor. 12:8-10). Although there are nine different gifts, they all come from the same Spirit and work together as one body. "Now there are diversities of gifts, but the same Spirit. And there are differences of administrations, but the same Lord. And there are diversities of operations, but it is the same God which worketh all in all. But the manifestation of the Spirit is given to every man to profit withal. But all these worketh that one and the selfsame Spirit, dividing to every man severally as he will For as the body is one, and hath many members, and all the members of that one body, being many, are one body: so also is Christ. For by one Spirit are we all baptized into one body, whether we be Jews or Gentiles, whether we be bond or free; and have been all made to drink into one Spirit" (1 Cor. 12:4-7, 11-13) . The mysteries of the riches of God are revealed through His Spirit. It takes all of the Spiritual gifts working as one body, to fully understand that mystery. We need each other!

God gave an example of how the different Ministry and Spiritual gifts work together through the duties of the Levites and the priests. Aaron appointed heads of each family and held them accountable for the duties of their clan. He called each man by name and assigned each one a specific task. Eleazar was responsible for the oversight of the Tabernacle under the direction of his father, Aaron, and Moses. He also had charge of the oil for the light, the sweet incense, the daily meat offering, and the anointing oil (Nu. 4:16). Kohath's clan had charge of the most holy things (Nu. 4:2-15). Aaron called Elizaphan to be the head of Kohath's family (Nu. 3:30). The Kohathites could not approach the Most Holy things until Aaron and his sons prepared them for travel (Nu. 4:20). The Most Holy things were the Veil, the Ark of the Covenant, the Table and the Showbread along with the utensils of service, the Golden Candlestick, the Golden Altar of Incense, and the Brazen Altar with all the utensils. Aaron appointed Eliasaph the head of Gershon's clan and made the Gershonites responsible for the inner and outer coverings, the hanging for the door and the gate, the hanging for the outer court, the brazen altar and its tools, and the maintenance of them (Nu. 3: 24; 4: 22-28). He chose Zuriel to be the head of Merari's clan and gave them charge over the boards, the bars, the pillars, the sockets, the pillars of the court, their sockets, the nails, and the cords (Nu. 3: 35-36; 4:29-33). Ithamar, Aaron's son, was assigned the oversight of the duties of Gershon and Merari (Nu. 4:28, 33). If any of the Levites failed to do their appointed jobs, or tried to operate in the service assigned to another man, his actions affected the whole body.

Nadab and Abihu are examples of how the impulsive actions of men interfere with God's plans. They allowed their emotions to rule when they offered a sacrifice of strange fire. The consequence of their actions resulted in death and delayed God's plan for His people (Lev. 10:1-7). We, "the believers", need to learn by their example. Often, people want to compare their place in the body of Messiah to another's. We need to be content with our assigned place, because there is no position that is more important than another (1 Cor. 7:20). It takes every member of the body working together under the direction of the Holy Spirit, to show the people of the world what an awesome God we serve.

As the children of Israel moved from place to place, the Tabernacle had to be dismantled. You might want to read Numbers chapters 4 and 10 before continuing.

God gave detailed instructions to Aaron and his sons concerning the type of coverings, the order of placement, and the colors used to cover the Holy things, *(the Ark of the Covenant, the Table of Showbread, the Golden Candlestick, the Golden Altar of Incense, and the Brazen Altar*). Through them, God continues to reveal "Shadows" of Yeshua the Messiah. The colors used reveal the following about Yeshua. A red cloth denotes *His blood*, a purple cloth signifies *His royalty*, a blue cloth stands for *His heavenly position*, and *the enabling power of the Holy Spirit,* the badgers' skin is descriptive of *His flesh,* and the Veil *His righteousness.*

The Ark of the Covenant and the Mercy Seat present a "Shadow" of God's throne. The contents of the Ark reveal the fullness of His being. Before moving the Ark, Aaron covered it with the Veil, a badgers' skin, and a blue cloth. The Ark, the placement of the coverings and the colors is a revelation of the sinless Son of God that was wrapped in a flesh body, and anointed with heavenly power (Nu. 4:5-6; Jn. 1:14, 33; Col. 1:19; Heb. 10:5).

The Table was the place of fellowship. It is where the priests ate the Showbread and drank the wine offering. The Table and the Showbread were covered with a blue cloth, a red cloth, and a badgers' skin; revealing the heavenly position Yeshua obtained for man by shedding of His blood. Yeshua gave up His rightful place with the Father to become the man who shed His blood on the cross to give men everlasting life. His broken body is the Living Bread that sustains man's new life. Every time we share the communion cup and the bread we enter into a place of fellowship, and through Yeshua an everlasting relationship with the Father (Jn. 6:53-58).

Unlike the Ark of the Covenant and the Table of Showbread, which were covered with three coverings, the Candlestick was covered with only two, a blue cloth and badgers' skin. The solid gold Candlestick and the blue covering reveal Yeshua as the Son of God while the badgers' skin reveals Him as the Son of Man. The Candlestick prefigures Yeshua as the Light of the World and Light that lights every man (Jn. 1:9). His heavenly origin was concealed beneath the covering of His flesh, but is now revealed through the redeemed, who have become a light in a dark and dying world (Mt. 5:14-16).

The Golden Altar was taller than the Table and the Ark. It is where the priests prayed and burned incense before the Lord. Its elevated height points to the exalted name of the Son of God. The Golden Alter was covered with a blue cloth and badgers' skin, showing the heavenly authority and power found in the name of Yeshua. The name Yeshua means God is salvation; it is the name that is above everything that is named (Phil. 2:9-11, Acts 4:12, Eph. 3:15). Yeshua exchanges names with every individual who accepts Him as the Messiah. With His name comes all that His name possesses. Believers are admonished to pray with the authority found in His name. Yeshua said to ask anything in His name. "And whatsoever ye shall ask in my name, that will I do, that the Father may be glorified in the Son. If ye shall ask any thing in my name, I will do it" (Jn. 14:13-14).

The Brazen Altar was the place of death where all of the sacrificial animals were burned. It, along with all the instruments of service, was covered with a cloth of purple; next it was covered with a badger's skin. The Altar and its coverings present the person of God embodied in Yeshua; the one who sacrificed His life for all mankind and the cruel means by which He died (Jn. 10:11, 17-18). The purple cloth points to His return as the King of all Kings.

As you can see, if Aaron and his sons failed to follow God's instructions, the revelation of Yeshua would have been marred. We need to follow their example, and to do that, we must know what the Word of God says. The way to show the lost world the reflection of God's Son, is to be obedient to what He says.

The camp of Israel, it is estimated, covered twelve square miles. The twelve tribes camped in groups of three on the north, south, east and west sides of the Tabernacle. Each campsite had a leader and his banner represented the camp. The Levites and the priests camped next to the Tabernacle. The priests (Moses and Aaron's family) camped next to the tribe of Judah. Kohath camped next to the tribe of Reuben, Gershon camped next to the tribe of Ephraim, and Merari camped next to the tribe of Dan. The Tabernacle was always in the center of the camp. God was specific as to where each of the tribes pitched their camp in relation to the Tabernacle. He gave detailed instructions for breaking camp and in what order each camp moved. (Nu.2:1-34). Judah moved first, Reuben and the Levites with the Tabernacle structure moved second, Ephraim moved third and Dan moved last. A word study of the Hebrew names associated with each camp, the rank order of each camp and the preparation of the items they carried tell a portion of the gospel message. They portray different stages in the life of Yeshua.

Names are important to God. The Hebrew language cannot be translated word for word as other languages. Many times a word contains a complete thought and that is what you will see in the translation of the names associated with each camp as recorded in Numbers 2. The meanings of the names reveal that God's salvation plan included all men from the time of creation. Every name, every word, every detail recorded in the scriptures serve to reveal the LOVE of GOD to the world.

Before any of the camps moved, the Ark of the Covenant was prepared for travel by Aaron. As seen earlier, the Ark was covered first with the Veil, next the Badgers' skin, and finally a cloth of blue. The coverings are significant because of what they represent. For example, one had to pass through the Veil to enter into the presence of God. The badgers' skin is symbolic of the flesh body of Yeshua. The blue cloth reveals His heavenly origin. Inside the Ark were the items that prophesied the fullness of the God Head, God the Father, God the Son and God the Holy Spirit. They were the Golden pot of manna, Aaron's rod that budded, and the tablets of stone. In them are the "Shadows" of (God the Son, Yeshua) who is the Bread of Life, (God the Holy Spirit) who is the resurrecting power of God and (God the Father) who gave His people His hand written marriage covenant. When the Ark went before the people it was their assurance that God was with them. The Ark and its contents is representative of the presence of the Holy Trinity, who always work in unity. "And God said, Let us make man in our image, after our likeness" (Gen. 1:26a).

Judah moved out first: The meaning of each Hebrew name associated with Judah's camp is: Judah means – *praised of God,* Nahshon means- *worker of wonders,*

Amminadab –means *my people are many,* Zebulun means– *dwelling,*

Eliab means- *God is Father,* Helon means– *strong,* Issachar means- *man of hire,*
Nathaniel means – *God has given,* Zuar means- *small – little,* Levi means – *joined,*
Moses means – *drawn out,* Aaron means – *bright – shining*

As Judah's camp moved out, his banner waived in the desert breeze displaying a gold lion's head on a field of blue symbolic of the heavenly King, the blessed and praised Son of God. The meanings of the names mentioned in Judah's camp proclaimed:

The praised of God is a worker of wonders. His people are many, and God gave Him as a man of hire to serve, a small thing to confound the wise. He will dwell with His people, God is His Father, and He is strong. He joins with His people, to draw them out as a bright and shining light.

Moses and Aaron moved out with Judah's camp after preparing the MOST HOLY things for the Levites to carry. **Their preparations represent the time when Yeshua was with the Father, being prepared to come as a man.**

Immediately following Judah's camp the Levites (the sons of Gershon and of Merari) came with the Tabernacle structure, the curtains, coverings and the instruments of service (Nu. 25:26). The items they carried prophesied Yeshua's purpose as the Son of God and the Son of man.

Reuben's camp moved second: The men associated with Reuben's camp are:

Reuben means- *behold a son,* Elizur means – *God is a rock,*
Shedeur mesns – *caster forth of light,* Gad means – *good fortune,*
Eliasaph means – *God has added,* Simeon means – *hearing,*
Shelumiel means – *at peace with God,* Zurishaddai means- *the almighty is a rock.*

The symbol of a Man's head was Reuben's banner. **The symbolic meanings found in the names of the men in Reuben's camp and the items being carried by the Levites preceding and following them, tell the story of the birth of the precious Son of God and the work He accomplished as the Son of Man for all humanity.**

Behold a Son, the rock of God, is the caster forth of light. He hears the Father, and is at peace with Him. The Almighty is the rock. He brings good fortune drawing out men and changing them into the friends of God as he adds them to His family.

Following behind Reuben, the Kohathites set forth bearing the sanctuary (the Most Holy things). By the time they reach the camp sight, the Tabernacle will already be set up so that Moses and Aaron can put the Ark of the Covenant and the Most Holy things back inside the Tabernacle (Nu. 10:21) **Putting the Ark of the Covenant and all of the Holy things back inside the Tabernacle presents a "Shadow" of Yeshua reuniting to the Father and resuming His rightful position as the King of Kings and Lord of Lords.**

The third camp is Ephraim: The meaning of each Hebrew name associated with Ephraim's camp is: Ephraim means- *doubly fruitful,* Elishama means – *God has heard,* Ammihud means- *my kinsman is glorious,* Benjamin means- *son of the right hand,*

Abidan means- *the father is judge,* Gideoni means- *a cutting down,*
Manasseh means- *making to forget,* Gamaliel means- *God has rewarded,*
Pedahzur means- *The (Rock) God has redeemed.*

This camp moved out under the banner of Ephraim, which is the Ox head, the symbol of a servant. **The message found within the Hebrew names and items carried by the Levites**

revealed what Yeshua accomplished for man through His death and resurrection.

The people of God are doubly fruitful for God has heard the prayer of His Son. He is our kinsman, and He is glorious. God rewards His people by forgetting their sins. The Rock, the Son of His right hand (God), has redeemed. The Father has judged sin, cutting down from the vine those who are unfruitful.

The fourth camp is Dan: The men associated with Dan's camp are:

Dan means– *judge,* Ahiezer means – *brother is help,*
Ammishaddai means- *my kinsman is the Almighty,*
Naphtali means- *my wrestling/fight/struggling,* Ahira means – *my brother is evil,*
Enan means- *having fountains,* Asher means- *happy/joy,* Pagiel means- *God meets,*
Ocran means– *troubled.*

The last camp moved out under the banner of Dan, the eagle's head. **The symbolisms in the Hebrew names of these men tell of the Day of Judgment for both the redeemed and the lost.**

All will be judged, but my brother, (Yeshua) is my help. The Almighty is my kinsman and He is my joy. He has fought the enemy and defeated him. My brother (the brotherhood of man) is evil; his fountains overflow. God meets the troubled at the Great White Throne.

God planned the movement of the camps; His order is always perfect, He says, "To whom then will ye liken me, or shall I be equal? Saith the Holy One. Lift up your eyes on high, and behold who hath created these things, that bringeth out their host by number: he calleth them all by names by the greatness of his might, for that he is strong in power; not one faileth" (Isa. 40:25-26).

As you can see, names are important to God. He named Adam, he changed the name of Abram to Abraham, He also changed Jacob's name to Israel, He named John the Baptist, and of course, He named his Son, Yeshua. God knew the message carried in the names of the men associated with the Tabernacle would help us become more aware of the extent of His love. That revelation causes a longing to know Him. The Bible is full of gems waiting to be revealed if we will just take the time to see them.

Israel moved as one body with many members, the same way the body of Messiah should move. The revelation of Yeshua would have been flawed if one camp moved out at the wrong time, As members of the Body of Messiah, we each have an assigned place and it takes all the members moving as one to show the lost people of the world that man's only hope is in Messiah Yeshua. "Even the mystery which hath been hid from ages and from generations, but now is made manifest to his saints: To whom God would make known what is the riches of the glory of this mystery among the Gentiles; which is Messiah in you, the hope of glory" (Col. 1:26-27).

THE PRIESTLY GARMENTS: (Ex. 28:2-43)

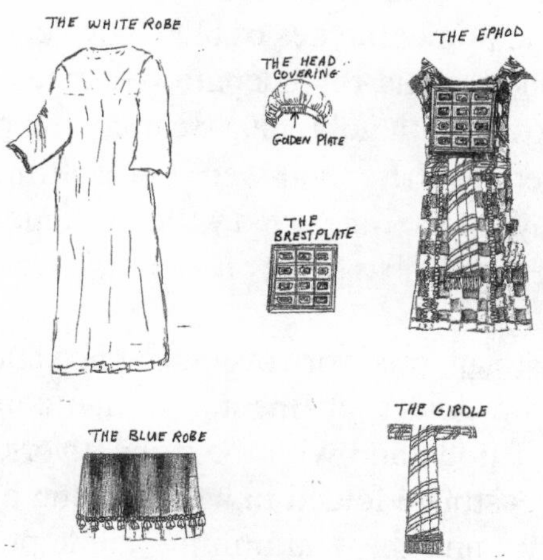

The Priestly Garments

The priests were required to wear special clothing when performing their duties in the Tabernacle. All of the priests had four garments in common.

(1.) Linen breeches, an undergarment that fit from the waist to the thigh.
(2.) A white linen embroidered coat that reached to the ankles (Ex. 28:39). The Hebrew word translated embroider is *shabats*, which means to make strong by interweaving (threads into squares). This is the only place in the Bible where this word was translated embroider, signifying the unique quality the coat represents.
(3.) A mitre or bonnet, a white linen head covering.
(4.) A girdle, a long linen belt or sash worn around the waist which contained colors of gold, blue, purple and scarlet.

The high priest wore additional garments of beauty and majesty:

(1.) A blue robe woven in one piece and reinforced at the neck, which made it difficult to rip. It most likely, hung just below the knees. Around its hem were sewn golden bells and pomegranates of blue, purple, and scarlet.
(2.) The ephod, a mid-thigh length vest made of white linen interwoven with gold, blue, scarlet, and purple. On the shoulders of the ephod were two settings of gold that held onyx stones engraved with the names of the twelve sons of Israel, six names on one shoulder and six on the other.
(3.) A breastplate was worn over the ephod and was fastened to it with golden chains and a blue cord. It was also made of linen and with the same colors as the ephod. The breastplate folded in half forming a pocket where the Urim and the Thummim were kept. It fit directly over the heart of the high priest and had twelve settings

of gold, three stones in each of its four rows. Each setting held a precious gemstone engraved with the name of one of the twelve sons of Israel. The Lord was specific as to the order and placement of each stone, most likely representing their birth order. "Aaron shall bear the judgment of the children of Israel upon his heart before the Lord continually" (Ex. 28:30).

(4.) The final garment worn only by the high priest is the golden plate. The golden plate was etched with the words *"Holiness to the Lord"* and attached to the head covering with a blue cord. The high priest was to wear the golden plate on his forehead always (Ex. 28:36-39).

You might be saying to yourself, "What has all of this to do with my life as a believer today?" I pray that you will be able to see as we look closer and examine the purpose for each garment. First, it is imperative to understand the position of Moses to Aaron and his sons. The Scripture says that Moses was to be like God to Aaron and his family. God said, speaking to Moses, "You will speak to him and put the words in his mouth; and I will be with your mouth and his, teaching you both what to do. Thus he will be your spokesman to the people, in effect; for you, he will be a mouth; and for him you will be like God" (Ex. 4:15-16). Moses spoke directly with God and then conveyed the will of God to Aaron and his sons. In turn, Aaron and his sons ministered to God on behalf of the entire family of Israel. Keeping this order in mind, we will now examine the order of dress for the priests.

White linen breeches

Each priest was responsible for putting this garment on himself. The breeches covered their bare flesh. It was the under garment; the foundation for the remaining items of clothing. Entering into the presence of God without the white linen breeches was instant death. Each man put the breeches on by bowing down and bending his knees. In doing so, they provide a portrait salvation. Every man must bow his knee to the Lord to receive the GIFT of SALVATION. **This garment is a "Shadow" of SALVATION.**

God provides the covering for sin, but each man was responsible for accepting His Gift. "**Salvation belongeth unto the LORD**: thy blessing is upon thy people. Selah (Ps. 3:8; my emphasis). "Wherefore, my beloved, as ye have always obeyed, not as in my presence only, but now much more in my absence, **work out your own salvation with fear and trembling**" (Phil. 2:12; my emphasis). The white linen breeches were just a covering for the priest; they needed to be replaced from time to time. The blood of Yeshua eradicates sin and covers those who have received the free GIFT of SALVATION with His righteousness, which never needs replacing. Sin is not just covered; it has been destroyed and forgotten (Rom. 11:27, Heb. 8:12).

Part of the ceremony of entering into the priesthood required a Mikveh, a washing or emersion, (used in Orthodox Judaism to this day for ritual purification). Please keep in mind what God declared about Moses's position in relation to Aaron and his sons. Moses, as God's representative, washed Aaron and his sons with water at the door of the Tabernacle (Ex. 40:12). "Not by works of righteousness which we have done, but according to his mercy he saved us, by the washing of regeneration, and renewing of the Holy Ghost;" (Titus 3:5). Washing with water is a "Shadow" of the cleansing power of the Word of God "That he might sanctify and cleanse it with the washing of water by the word," (Eph. 5:26). "Sanctify them through thy truth: thy word is truth. And for their sakes I sanctify myself, that they also might be sanctified through the truth" (Jn. 17:17, 19).

Moses waited until Aaron had put on the white linen breeches to dress him in the white linen coat. **The white linen coat** is symbolic of God's righteousness. HIS righteousness covers everyone who has been forgiven by the blood of the sin sacrifice. It is a perfect "Shadow" of what the Father does for redeemed man through Yeshua. "For he hath made him to be sin for us, who knew no sin; that we might be made the righteousness of God in him" (2 Cor. 5:21). "Therefore if any man be in Messiah, he is a new creature: old things are passed away; behold all things are become new" (2 Cor. 5:17). "I will greatly rejoice in the Lord, my soul shall be joyful in my God; for he hath clothed me with the garments of salvation, he hath covered me with the robe of righteousness." (Isa. 61:10). **Only God can clothe man in His pure righteousness.**

Once a year, on the Day of Atonement, the high priest carried the blood from the sin sacrifice before the Lord, for himself first and then the people. Before entering into the presence of the Lord, the high priest removed the garments of majesty and beauty and wore only the white linen garments and the golden plate. His dress represented the sinless adorning given to him by God (Lev.16:4). The high priest of the Tabernacle is the shadow of the Great High Priest, Yeshua the Messiah. Yeshua put aside His deity, majesty, and beauty and as *The Sinless Man,* carried His own blood into the heavenly Holy of Holies for the sin of the world. He took man's place on the cross and exchanged His pure white robe of righteousness for man's dirty, sin-ravaged, filthy rags.

So far we have seen Aaron washed with the pure water from the laver, receive salvation, and clothed in the righteousness of God. Next, he will be anointed with the enabling power of the Holy Spirit represented by the **blue robe**: Once again Moses, God's representative, put the blue robe on Aaron. The blue color of the robe is symbolic of its heavenly origin. The golden bells and pomegranates around the hem are "Shadows" of the gifts and the fruit of the Holy Spirit. His gifts are not the personal property of the one who has been anointed; they belong to the Lord. The Holy Spirit works through man to administer whatever gift is needed.

It was not necessary for Yeshua to follow Aaron's example, but He did in order to fulfill the complete law of the Father. He entered into the priestly ministry through a public washing or cleansing symbolic of repentance. Although he was not guilty of any sin, He was obedient to all that God had commanded and was baptized by John the Baptist in the Jordan River. Immediately, the Spirit of God descended from heaven as a dove and anointed Yeshua with power; the same power foreshadowed by the blue robe worn by the high priest of the Tabernacle (Mt. 3:16, Jn.1: 32). The Spirit lead Yeshua into the wilderness (one passage says that He was driven by the Spirit) to come face to face with all the temptations known to man, *the lust of the flesh, the lust of the eyes, and the pride of life* (Mk. 1:12-13, I Jn. 2:16). Yeshua had been without food or water for forty days and nights. *His flesh* was crying out for nourishment when the devil tempted Him to turn stones into bread. To most this might not seem to be a real temptation, but it is if you are familiar with the stones found all over the countryside in Jerusalem; they look like fresh baked bread. Perhaps that is why Yeshua used stones as an illustration when He told His followers about the soon coming gift of the Holy Spirit. He said, "If a son shall ask bread of any of you that is a father, will he give him a stone? If ye then, being evil, know how to give good gifts unto your children: how much more shall your heavenly Father give the Holy Spirit to them that ask him?" (Lk. 11:11, 13). His hunger was real and Satan counted on His weakened condition and the appearance of the stones to cause Him to fall, but He didn't (Mt. 4:4). The next temptation was the *pride of life*; Satan enticed Yeshua to jump from the pinnacle of the temple, because God had promised to send heaven's angels to protect Him, yet he remained faithful. (Ps. 91:11). At some point, all of God's children are faced with this type of temptation. As God's children and heirs to His promises, we often become puffed up with pride, which leads us into areas that should be off limits. Finally, Yeshua was tempted with the *lust of the eyes*. Satan forced Yeshua to look at all the kingdoms of the earth that once were His. Satan promised to give them back to Yeshua if He would bow down and worship him. Once again, Yeshua overcame by the Word of God. The Holy Spirit gave Yeshua the power needed to overcome every temptation (Mt. 4:1-11). The in-dwelling presence of Spirit of God is how redeemed man is able to be an overcomer; He is the promised gift from the Father (Jn. 14:16-17). Praise His name!

Forty days after His resurrection, Yeshua ascended into heaven (Acts. 1:3, 9-11). Ten days later, on the fiftieth day, in Hebrew *Shavuot*, which is also referred to as Pentecost, God fulfilled His promise and poured out the gift of the Holy Spirit (Acts 2). God revealed Himself to those waiting in the upper room as he did to the children of Israel at Mt. Sinai on the first Pentecost. He appeared as fire and a mighty rushing wind much like he did at Mt. Sinai on the fiftieth day after the children of Israel left the bondage of Egypt.

The Holy Spirit releases His fruit (the supernatural love of God) into the believer's life and displays His power through His gifts. Paul said if he had all the gifts of God manifested in his life without love, "I am become as sounding brass, or a tinkling cymbal" (1 Cor. 13:1). **The gift of God's love that comes through the gifts of the Spirit brings glory to God, not man.** "The love of God is shed abroad in our hearts by the Holy Ghost which is given to us" (Rom. 5:5). That is the message found in the design of the blue robe. The pomegranates that separated the golden bells are symbolic of the fruit of the Spirit (the Love of God); the golden bells are symbolic of the various gifts of the Spirit. God's design put fruit between the golden bells to cushion the sound. If the bells hit against each other the sound would be offensive, like the sounding brass and tinkling cymbals spoken of by Paul, but the pomegranates (the fruit) kept that from happening. People attempting to minister the gifts of the Spirit without the love of God are only making noise.

Paul revealed the hidden message found in the design of the blue robe when he wrote first about the gifts of the Spirit in chapter twelve of 1Corinthians. Next he wrote about the love of God, which is the Fruit of the Spirit, in chapter thirteen, and finally in chapter fourteen he wrote again concerning the gifts. Sandwiched between the gifts of the Spirit is the fruit of the Spirit, just like the blue robe of the high priest, a bell and a pomegranate, a bell and a pomegranate. **The blue robe is the "Shadow" of how the Holy Spirit administers His power and love.**

It has been taught that the high priest wore the blue robe inside the Holy of Holies. Some say that a rope was tied around the high priest ankle as a means to pull him out of the Holy of Holies should he die while serving in the presence of God. If the bells stopped ringing, it was assumed that he had died. This may have happened later as the people got further away from God's ways, but it was certainly not true of the priests of the Tabernacle. Chapter sixteen of the book of Leviticus is explicit in regard to what the high priest could wear on the Day of Atonement. The blue robe represented beauty and majesty. We have already established that Aaron's position as high priest foreshadowed that of Yeshua. Yeshua did not enter heaven as deity; He entered as a man (Heb. 10:12). Yeshua, like Aaron, was the representative of the people before God. Aaron removed everything that represented glory and majesty and entered into God's presence as a forgiven man to offer the blood of the sin sacrifice. After offering the blood, he left the Holy of Holies and resumed the position of God's representative to the people. He stopped in the Holy place and put back on the blue robe, which caused the bells to ring. When the people heard the bells ringing they knew that God had accepted their sacrifice. Their sins were forgiven for one more year.

Yeshua entered the heavenly Holy of Holies as a man, carrying His own blood, satisfying the Father's requirement for sin (Heb. 9:24-26). Then He picked up His heavenly blue robe and dropped Him to earth as He poured forth the promise of the Father. Yeshua clothed all of those waiting for the Father's gift with the Holy Spirit. The book of Acts describes that day as loud; "suddenly there came a sound from heaven as of a rushing mighty wind, and it filled all the house where they were sitting. And there appeared unto them cloven tongues like as of fire, and it sat upon each of them. And they were all filled with the Holy Spirit, and began to speak with other tongues, as the Spirit gave them utterance" (Acts 2:2-4). The sound coming from the upper room caused people to gather to find out what was happening. A very large crowd of people, who had come to Jerusalem to celebrate the feast of Shavuot, stood listing. There were, "Parthians, and Medes, and Elamites, and the dwellers in Mesopotamia, and in Judaea, and Cappadocia, in Pontus, and Asia, Phrygia, and Pamphylia, in Egypt, and in the parts of Libya about Cyrene, and strangers of Rome, Jews and proselytes, Cretes and Arabians, we do hear them speak in our tongues the wonderful works of God" (Acts 2:9-11). People who spoke different languages and dialects heard the message of salvation in their own language. Just as the ringing of the bells on the high priest's robe meant God had accepted the sin sacrifice, the people in the city of Jerusalem that day knew God was doing something great. They heard common uneducated men speaking in languages they had never been taught. The Spirit of God was being poured out on the believers in the upper room and they were proclaiming the multi-lingual message of salvation, which meant, God had accepted the blood of Yeshua, and sin had been removed forever. Yeshua's job was finished, and He was ringing the bells of redemption, beaconing all into the family of God. Three thousand people became believers that day replacing the three thousand that died at the first Pentecost (Acts 2:41, Ex. 32:28).

Next Moses put **the ephod** on Aaron. **The ephod** was made of linen interwoven with gold, blue, purple and scarlet. Four of the colors of the ephod are the same as those in the Veil, the Door, and the Gate with one exception, GOLD. Gold is the predominate color of the ephod. The colors express the glory and majesty of God. Gold represents His deity, blue His heavenly position, purple His royalty, scarlet symbolizes His blood, and fine linen represents His righteousness. The ephod was a vest worn over the blue robe to support the breastplate. On its shoulders were two onyx stones mounted in gold. The onyx stones were engraved with the names of the twelve sons of Israel. When Aaron wore the ephod, it revealed the awesome responsibility of the High Priest. The lives of God's children rested on Aaron's shoulders because he alone ministered on their behalf before the Lord. Aaron's reign and accountability to the children of God foreshadowed that of Yeshua, with one difference; his responsibility ended at his death. Yeshua's reign as High Priest will never end because He will never die. The weight of man's salvation solely rests on the shoulders of Yeshua (Heb. 7:21-24). "For unto us a child is born, unto us a son is given: and the government shall be upon **his shoulder**: and his name shall be called Wonderful, Counselor, The mighty God, The everlasting Father, The Prince of Peace. Of the increase of his government and peace there shall be no end, upon the throne of David, and upon his kingdom, to order it, and to establish it with judgment and with justice from henceforth even forever. The zeal of the Lord of hosts will perform this" (Isa. 9:6-7; my emphasis).

The Breastplate was the next article of clothing Moses put on Aaron. It was made with the same colors as the ephod and was worn directly over the heart. The Breastplate had twelve gold settings. Each setting secured a gemstone inscribed with a name of one of the twelve sons of Israel. Each stone represented one son and each one was different. The design of the Breastplate provides a "Shadow" of how God Himself individually designs His children and holds them secure in His hands.

The high priest wore the Breastplate, while he prayed at the Golden Altar and while he ate the Showbread. Through the High Priest, the children of Israel entered into the presence of God. **The design and position of the Breastplate reveals the love of God for His children; they are always on His heart.**

Yeshua, as the Great High Priest, continues to bear the names of Israel along with the names of all of God's children. He is ever interceding for man. A day is coming when He will write His new name on us, and we will wear His name forever in the presence of the Father (Rev. 3:12-13).

Aaron's dress was almost complete. Moses put the ornate girdle around his waist; the girdle held everything together. **The girdle was a "Shadow" of the strength and faithfulness of Yeshua; He holds all things together by the power of His Word** (Hebrews 1:3). Isaiah spoke of Yeshua when he said, "And righteousness shall be the GIRDLE of his loins, and faithfulness the GIRDLE of his reins." (Isa. 11:5; my emphasis). "And I will clothe him with thy robe, and strengthen him with thy GIRDLE, and I will commit thy government into his hands" (Isa. 22:21; my emphasis).

Next Moses put **the mitre** on Aaron's head. The Hebrew word that was translated mitre is *MITSNEPHETH*, which means an official turban of a king or priest. We have already determined that white linen symbolizes righteousness. The mitre is a "Shadow" of wrapping one's mind with the righteousness of God. Paul said, "Fulfill ye my joy, that ye be like-minded, having the same love, being of one accord, of one mind. Let this mind be in you, which was also in Messiah Yeshua" (Phil. 2:1, 5; my emphasis). The Word of God is the means to a renewed mind. "And be not conformed to this world: but be ye transformed by the renewing of your mind, that ye may prove what is that good, and acceptable, and perfect, will of God." (Rom. 12:2) As children of God, we need to diligently study His word, and allow Him to reprove, correct, and instruct us in His ways, the ways of righteousness (2 Tim. 2:15). The Word of God is able to make one wise. It leads to salvation through faith in Messiah Yeshua (2 Tim. 3:15-16). **Wearing the mitre was the outward evidence of submitting to the will of God, the God of Abraham, Isaac, and Jacob**.

The final article of the high priest garments was the golden plate engraved "Holiness to the Lord". God referred to it as the crown (Ex. 29:6). The Golden Plate is the "Shadow of Holiness. This was perhaps the most important item that the High Priest wore. It lay across his forehead at all times to remind him of the holiness of God. "For I am the LORD your God: ye shall therefore sanctify yourselves, and ye shall be holy; for I am holy" (Lev. 11:44). "Speak unto all the congregation of the children of Israel, and say unto them, Ye shall be holy: for I the LORD your God am holy" (Lev. 19:2). "Because it is written, Be ye holy; for I am holy" (1 Pet. 1:16). **The Golden Plate is the "Shadow" of Holiness.**

There is a prayer that is chanted every Sabbath by Orthodox and Messianic Jews alike. It is the *Shama*. It begins, *"Here O Israel: The Lord our God is One."* It is found in the Book of Deuteronomy (Deut. 6:4-9). If you read this passage of scripture, you will see that God is instructing His people to remember His good counsel (the *Torah*) so that things will go well with them when they enter into the Promised Land. The eighth verse is applicable to the Golden Plate, it says, "And thou shalt bind them for a sign upon thine hand, and they shall be as frontlets between thine eyes."

God calls each believer out of the darkness of sin into His marvelous light and makes them royal priests and kings as citizens of a holy nation (1 Pet. 2:9). Just as the priests of the Tabernacle, we must have an offering. We are told to offer our bodies as living sacrifices unto God (Rom. 12:1). We must die to self and live unto God. Animal sacrifices are no longer necessary because Yeshua's death fulfilled that requirement. We are to live as true children of God who have received eternal life through the sacrifice of God's own Son. He is the God of the living, not of the dead (Mt. 22:32).

Just as Aaron and his sons were given special garments for service, we, as priest of the Most High God, have been given His armor for service and warfare. It is our responsibility to use it. He gave us His *girdle* of truth and His *breastplate* of righteousness; our feet have been made ready to carry the gospel of peace to the world. We have His *shield* of faith to protect our front side from the attacks of the devil. Our head is covered with His impenetrable *helmet* of salvation. God has given us His *sword* of the Spirit, and His Word has defeated the enemy. He has not only clothed us for service; He also sends His angel before us and God Himself is our rear guard (Eph. 6:14-17, Is.52:12). God gave instructions as to how to use His armor. We are to pray always, to persevere in prayer for all the saints. The sight of God's armor causes the enemy to flee. Freed from the enemy's influence, we like the priest of the Tabernacle, are ready to serve one another. "Thou shalt love thy neighbor as thy self" (Gal. 6:2, Ja.2:8). Free from sin and filled with the power of the Spirit of God, we are able to, "Anoint with oil in the name of the Lord, and the prayer of faith shall save the sick, and the Lord shall raise him up; and if he has committed sins, they shall be forgiven him." (Ja. 5:15). We, the family of God, are admonished to stay in fervent prayer for one another (Ja. 5:16).

When Yeshua comes to reign for one thousand years in Jerusalem, those who have died, who are with Him in heaven, are going to come back with Him riding on white horses. They are called the armies which are in heaven. They are clothed in fine clean white linen, and the final article of the priestly garments, the golden plate, will be the adorning of the horses they are riding (Rev. 19:14). Zechariah wrote about this day when he said, "In that day shall there be upon the bells of the horses, **HOLINESS TO THE LORD"** (Zech. 14:20).

SUMMARY

THE GARMENTS:

1. **The coat**: ***symbolic of the righteousness of God that only He can give.***
2. **The blue robe of the ephod**: ***symbolic of the Holy Spirit, His gifts and fruit.***
3. **The ephod**: ***represents the righteousness of God that supports His love.***
4. **The breastplate**: ***symbolizes God's love for His children***
5. **The curious girdle**: ***is the belt of righteousness that held everything together.***
6. **The mitre**: ***the righteousness of God transforms the mind of man.***
7. **The golden plate**: ***is the crown that stands for holiness.***
8. **The linen breeches**: ***THE PICTURE OF SALVATION***

THE CONSECRATION OF AARON AND HIS SONS (Ex. 29:1-9, Lev. 8:1-13)

> And this is the thing that thou shalt do unto them to hallow them, to minister unto me in the priest's office: Take one young bullock, and two rams without blemish, and unleavened bread, and cakes unleavened tempered with oil, and wafers unleavened anointed with oil: of wheaten flour shalt thou make them. And thou shalt put them into one basket, and bring them in the basket, with the bullock and the two rams. And Aaron and his sons thou shalt bring unto the door of the tabernacle of the congregation, and shalt wash them with water. And thou shalt take the garments, and put upon Aaron the coat, and the robe of the ephod, and the ephod, and the breastplate, and gird him with the curious girdle of the ephod: And thou shalt put the mitre upon his head, and put the holy crown upon the mitre. Then shalt thou take the anointing oil, and pour it

> upon his head, and anoint him. And thou shalt bring his sons, and put coats upon them. And thou shalt gird them with girdles, Aaron and his sons, and put the bonnets on them: and the priest's office shall be theirs for a perpetual statute: and thou shalt consecrate Aaron and his sons" (Ex. 29:1-9).

The consecration of Aaron and his sons into the priesthood continued for seven days. Each day three animals were killed to comply with the various offerings required by God. That meant that *seven* bulls and *fourteen* rams died. Along with the animal sacrifices, three forms of unleavened bread were offered each day, making the total number of *bread* offerings twenty-one. The sum of all the elements used as offerings during the week of Aaron's consecration was 7+14+21 = 42. Number seven identifies God's perfection, and if we divide the total number of offerings by seven the answer is six, the number attributed to man. Or in other words, God required a perfect sacrifice for the sanctification of man. Yeshua is the perfect sacrifice; He was both the offering and the officiating High Priest over His sacrifice. He said, "For their sakes I sanctify myself that they also might be sanctified" (Jn. 17:19). Yeshua's consecration into the office of High Priest is forever. "For such a high priest became us who is holy, harmless, undefiled, separate from sinners, and made higher than the heavens; Who needeth not daily, as those high priests, to offer up sacrifice, first for his own sins, and then for the people's: for this he did once, when he offered up himself. For the law maketh men high priests which have infirmity; but the word of the oath, which was since the law, maketh the SON, who is consecrated for evermore" (Heb. 7:26-28; my emphasis). "How much more shall the blood of Messiah, who through the eternal Spirit offered himself without spot to God, purge your conscience from dead works to serve the living God. For Messiah is not entered into the holy places made with hands, which are the figures of the true; but into heaven itself, now to appear in the presence of God for us" (Heb. 9:14, 24).

Moses, as mentioned earlier, was the representative of God to Aaron and his sons providing a "Shadow" of the relationship between God the Father and His family. Moses did those things that only God can do for Aaron and his sons. He washed and clothed Aaron and his sons before they began performing the duties of the priesthood. They could not enter into the Tabernacle without being cleansed and properly dressed. God, in Messiah, is the One who sanctifies and justifies the believer. "Come now, let us reason together, saith the Lord: though your sins be as scarlet, they shall be as white as snow; though they be red like crimson, they shall be as wool" (Isa. 1:18). When the sacrifice was complete, man and God could once again have fellowship together.

THE ORDER OF SACRIFICES (Ex. 29:10-37)
Required before entering the service of the Lord

The order of the sacrifice offerings for the consecration of the priests provides two things, the "Shadow" of the new birth and the growing process of the believer. Each offering drew Aaron and his sons closer to the relationship God desires with His children, and finally to total surrender, which made them vessels through which God demonstrated His LOVE. Although the priests held one of the most respected and elevated positions, they were servants to God and to their brethren.

FIRST, THE SIN OFFERING

Have you ever been told that your sin killed Yeshua? I have, and for a long time I thought my sin was too bad to be forgiven. If this describes your situation, I want you to see that there is NO SIN greater than the price Yeshua paid for your forgiveness, but you must repent and accept what He has done. No one killed

Yeshua; He gave His life of His own free will (Jn. 10:17-18). The prerequisite for the remission of sin has remained the same since Adam; it is innocent blood. All blood belongs to God and He gives it to humanity to make an atonement for sin. "For the life of the flesh is in the blood: and I have given it to you upon the altar to make an atonement for your souls: for it is the blood that maketh an atonement for the soul" (Lev. 17:11). "Without the shedding of blood is no remission" (Heb. 9:22). God the Father required the death of His Son to satisfy the penalty for sin (Rom. 6:23). Yeshua said, "For this is my blood of the new testament, which is shed for many for the remission of sins" (Mt. 26:28). "Therefore doth my Father love me, because <u>I lay down my life,</u> that I might take it again. <u>No man taketh it from</u> me, but <u>I lay it down of myself</u>. I have power to lay it down, and I have power to take it again. This commandment have I received of my Father" (Jn. 10:17-18; my emphasis).

God required two offerings for sin--blood and bread. The same two things Yeshua said are necessary for life. He is the living bread that came down from heaven. The life giving bread acknowledged through His flesh (Jn. 6:51). Yeshua's death was necessary to provide the sin offering of bread and blood (Jn. 6:53). There is no alternative. To receive forgiveness and eternal life, you MUST acknowledge that He is the Son of God and that He willingly gave up His life for you. Yeshua is the SIN OFFERING for the world (Jn. 3:16).

The sin offering for Aaron and his sons was a young bull. The bull was brought to the outer court of the Tabernacle to be killed. Aaron and his sons placed their hands on the head of the animal signifying the transfer of their sin to the bull, but Moses, as God's representative, killed it. Aaron's consecration is the only time that someone other than the person bringing the sacrificial animal killed it.

Moses took four things from the Sin Offering--the blood, the fat, the caul over the liver, and the two kidneys. He put some of the blood on the horns of the brazen altar. Horns denote power. Putting the blood on the horns of the altar signified the power of the blood to pay the price for the sin of Aaron and his sons. Moses poured the remainder of the blood on the ground beneath the altar. Pouring the blood on the ground directs attention to the Cross of Calvary where the blood of Yeshua, our sin offering, was poured out.

The fat of the sacrificial animal, the caul over the liver, and the two kidneys were burned on the altar. The fat represents stored-up sin, the caul above the liver caught the impurities in the blood, and the two kidneys filtered the impurities. All three are symbolic of inward sin. Sin can sometimes be hidden from self and others but never from the eyes of God.

Science has proven that fat clogs the arteries; blood carries disease, and the liver and kidneys act as filters for the blood by expelling waste. God took every part of the sacrifice that is harmful to man and destroyed them with fire on the altar. What a beautiful "Shadow" of Yeshua becoming sin for us.

The flesh, skin and dung of the sacrifice are representative of death and decay. They represent outward sin that is visible to both God and men. The flesh, skin and the dung were burned outside the camp, signifying the place of Yeshua's death. He was crucified outside of the city, away from the temple, on the hill of Golgotha. Golgotha means the place of the skull (Mt. 27:33-35). The sin offering was mandatory for forgiveness just as accepting the blood of Yeshua is now. He is the ultimate Sin Sacrifice for all mankind.

SECOND, THE WHOLE BURNT OFFERING

Two Rams were offered for Aaron and his sons. **<u>The first Ram</u>** was the whole burnt offering. The entire animal was burned on the Altar. Aaron and his sons laid their hands on the head of the Ram, as with the sin offering, <u>and Moses killed it.</u> The whole burnt offering differed from the sin offering. When Aaron and his sons laid their hands on the head of the ram, it was not symbolic of transferring their sin, rather it meant that they were dying to self and surrendering to the will of God.

Moses did four things to this Ram. 1). He sprinkled the blood upon the altar. 2). He cut the ram in pieces. 3). He washed the Ram inside and out. 4). He rearranged the clean pieces in their proper order and burned them on the altar. The first step, sprinkling the blood on the altar symbolized dying to ones' own will (Rom.12:1). The second step, cutting the Ram into pieces symbolizes the cutting power of the Word of God (Hebrews 4:12). The third step, washing the Ram inside and out symbolizes two types of cleansing. Self-Cleansing, "Having therefore these promises, dearly beloved, let us cleanse ourselves from all filthiness of the flesh and spirit, perfecting holiness in the fear of God" (2 Cor. 7:1) God's Cleansing Power, "If we confess our sins, he is faithful and just to forgive us our sins, and to cleanse us from all unrighteousness" (1Jn. 1:9). The forth step, rearranging the Ram's parts in proper order is symbolic of the peace that comes from being in God's perfect will (Ps. 37:23. Moses, acting in God's stead, accepted Aaron's willing surrender and put the pieces of the sacrificed ram back in its original state. The ram represented Aaron and his sons. God does the same for those who are willing to surrender everything to Him. He bathes each yielded life with the pure water of His Word, and puts it back in perfect order. This is the point, in a believer's growth, where many fall short. Total surrender takes time and is usually done one step at a time. It's like learning to walk; if you fall, you get back up and try again.

The second Ram is Aaron's offering of consecration, his wave offering, and his peace offering. Moses also killed this Ram after Aaron and his sons laid their hands its head. The offering of consecration meant that Aaron and his sons are set apart from a worldly life to begin a new life with God. Moses put some of the blood from the ram on the right ear, the right thumb, and the right great toe of Aaron and his sons. He sprinkled some of the blood around the altar, mixed some of the blood with the Anointing Oil, and sprinkled the priest's garments. The blood is a "Shadow" of the cleansing needed to live a life set apart to the Holy God. The Anointing Oil represents the enabling power of the Holy Spirit to live holy in the world.

Putting the blood on the right ear shows that the priests are promising to hear only the voice of God. Blood on the right thumb meant they promise to hold tight to the things of God. Blood on the right great toe showed that they would follow God alone.

God does the same for believers as Moses did for Aaron and his sons. If you surrender your hearing, He will speak to you. If you surrender your desire to hold on to things, He will give you things to use to glorify Him. If you surrender your plans, He will direct your path, leading you to those He has prepared to hear the message of His great love (Pr. 3:5-6).

THIRD, THE WAVE OFFERING

The wave offering was taken from the second Ram. Aaron and his sons, after being cleansed and anointed with power to serve, took part in destroying the things that represented fleshly weaknesses. Moses took the fat and the rump, the fat on the inwards, the caul above the liver, the two kidneys and their fat, the right shoulder, one loaf of bread, one cake of oiled bread, and one wafer, and placed them in the hands of Aaron and his sons.

Moses put eight parts of this ram in the hands of Aaron and his sons. Eight is the number associated with a NEW BEGINNING and through this offering; Aaron and his sons begin a new relationship with the Lord. Aaron and his sons lifted the pieces of the sacrificed ram and waived them before the Lord. The up-lifted waving motion specified that they are giving up all that is corrupt as well as all that is good to serve a Holy God. Their hands held their substitute, symbolic of

Yeshua; the one who takes upon Himself those things that are harmful to man, and gives back those that represent His strength (the right shoulder) and His life (the Bread). The waive offering showed that Aaron and his sons accepted God's substituted sacrifice. It revealed the willingness of the priests to give up their lives to serve God. Lifting and waving the hands also revealed that Aaron and his sons have entered into a covenant relationship with God. Moses took the wave offering from the priests and burned it on the altar to signify Gods' acceptance of their offering. Next, Moses cooked the right shoulder of the ram and gave it to Aaron and his sons. Eating the right shoulder of the ram is symbolic of taking the strength of Yeshua into oneself. Eating the bread is symbolic of feeding on the life sustaining, sinless body of Messiah Yeshua. Yeshua said, "He that eateth my flesh, and drinketh my blood, dwelleth in me, and I in him" (Jn. 6:56). "I am the living bread which came down from heaven: if any man eat of this bread, he shall live forever: and the bread that I will give is my flesh, which I will give for the life of the world" (Jn. 6:51).

We, like Aaron and his sons, are to be active participants in achieving spiritual maturity. The book of Colossians tells the believer to mortify (prepare for burial) those things that once held them captive to sin. "Mortify therefore your members which are upon the earth; fornication, uncleanness, inordinate affection, evil concupiscence, and covetousness, which is idolatry: For which things' sake the wrath of God cometh on the children of disobedience: In the which ye also walked some time, when ye lived in them. But now ye also put off all these; anger, wrath, malice, blasphemy, filthy communication out of your mouth. Lie not one to another, seeing that ye have put off the old man with his deeds; And have put on the new man, which is renewed in knowledge after the image of him that created him: Where there is neither Greek nor Jew, circumcision nor uncircumcision, Barbarian, Scythian, bond nor free: but Christ is all, and in all" (Col. 3:5-11).

Consider this, if you refuse to obey, as this passage instructs, you are not fit to serve in the Royal priesthood of God. God cannot use you as He desires.

God, like Moses, will take all that you offer Him and mold you into the image of Yeshua.

FOURTH, THE PEACE OFFERING

The peace offering was also a part of the second Ram. The breast of the Ram represents the heart of Aaron and his sons. The breast was the portion of the offering that belonged to Moses, who is God's representative. Moses held the breast of the Ram in his hands and waved it to show that from that point forward the heart of Aaron and his sons belong to God. God received their offering and in return gave them His strength, represented by the shoulder of the Ram. The shoulder was the food of the high priest and his family. Eating the shoulder is figurative of feeding on Gods' strength.

Yeshua is humanity's peace offering. Yeshua said, "Peace (Shalom) I leave with you, my peace (Shalom) I give unto you: not as the world giveth, give I unto you. Let not your heart be troubled, neither let it be afraid" (Jn. 14:27). Shalom means so much more than peace. It means to be safe, to make amends, end, finish, make good, recompense, render, requite, make restitution, restore, reward, well, happy, friendly, health, prosperity, familiar, fare, favor, whole. When Yeshua gave His shalom, He gave all that His life represents. His shalom produces a change in character. The recipient begins to take on the attributes of Yeshua. The believer is admonished to, "Put on therefore, as the elect of God, holy and beloved, bowels of mercies, kindness, humbleness of mind, meekness, longsuffering; Forbearing one another, and forgiving one another, if any man have a quarrel against any: even as Christ forgave you, so also do ye. And above all these things put on charity, which is the bond of perfectness. And let the peace of

God rule in your hearts, to the which also ye are called in one body; and be ye thankful" (Col. 3:12-15.

The offerings had to be eaten the same day they were offered. For seven days Aaron and his sons fed on the strength of God and the Bread of Life. Moses prepared the meat in the holy place and gave it to the priests, along with the bread that was in a basket by the door of the Tabernacle. NOTE: Meat was in the holy place, but the bread was outside, symbolic of one accepting the Bread of Life and never entering into the place of fellowship. The LORD, like Moses, is preparing the Meat of His Word for us to eat daily. He is new every morning; Oh taste His goodness! (Ps. 34:8)

THE DAILY OFFERINGS (Ex. 29:38-44)

The consecration is complete, and now the priestly ministry can begin. Every day two lambs were offered, one in the morning and one in the evening, along with a meal offering of flour and oil and wine for the drink offering. The offerings were continually made at the door of the Tabernacle where God met with Aaron and his sons and spoke with them. "And the Tabernacle shall be sanctified by my Glory. And I will sanctify the Tabernacle of the congregation, and the Altar: I will sanctify also both Aaron and his sons, to minister to me in the priest office" (Ex. 29:42-43).

AT LAST FELLOWSHIP HAS BEEN RESTORED

The last two verses in the twenty-ninth chapter of Exodus contain the promise of God's presence with His people (Ex. 29: 45-46).

God established five different offerings. Two were required and three were voluntary. The Sin Offering and the Trespass Offering are required, but the Burnt, Meal and Peace Offerings are voluntary. The Sin Offering represents your position before

God, the Trespass Offering represents your walk with Him, the Burnt Offering represents your readiness to surrender to Him, the Meal Offering represents walking in communion with Him, and finally the Peace Offering represents celebrating the restoration of fellowship and relationship with Him.

Note <u>The Trespass offering was missing from Aaron's consecration. Since Aaron is a 'Shadow" of Yeshua, no trespass offering was required, because Yeshua never sinned!</u>

God's order for the offerings laid out His Master plan to be the perfect sacrifice, and Yeshua has fulfilled every requirement.

SUMMARY OF THE OFFERINGS

<u>The Sin Offering</u>--*He became sin for us.*

<u>The Trespass Offering</u>--*He is the perfect sacrifice, forgiving every sin past, present, and future.*

<u>The Burnt Offering</u>--*He willingly surrendered His life and was crucified on the north side of Jerusalem, just as the animal was killed on the north side of the altar.*

<u>The Meal Offering</u>--*He is the Bread of Life for all to feed on.*

<u>The Peace Offering</u>--*He is our peace; by accepting Him we are restored to a right relationship with God* (Lk. 2:14; Jn. 14:27, 16:33; Rom. 5:1; Eph. 2:11-19; Col. l: 16-23, 3:15).

The cleansing power of Yeshua's blood calls every believer into the priesthood of the kingdom of God. His love has given ALL. He fulfilled every sacrificial offering, making our duties light. In response to His love, we must be willing to give ALL to become workers with Him as members of His body. We, like the children of Israel, whose names proclaimed the message of the Messiah as they moved in one accord, must carry that message. They moved as one unit and we must operate as one body filled with the Spirit of God and anointed with the power to carry the good news of the gospel to the lost people of the world.

CHAPTER 15

The Golden Altar of Incense

"And thou shalt make an altar to burn incense upon: of shittim wood shalt thou make it. A cubit shall be the length thereof, and a cubit the breadth thereof; foursquare shall it be: and two cubits shall be the height thereof: the horns thereof shall be of the same. And thou shalt overlay it with pure gold, the top thereof, and the sides thereof round about, and the horns thereof; and thou shalt make unto it a crown of gold round bout. And two golden rings shall thou make to it under the crown of it, by the two corners thereof, upon the two sides of it shalt thou make it; and they shall be for places for the staves to bear it withal. And thou shalt make the staves of shittim wood, and overlay them with gold (Ex. 30:1-4).

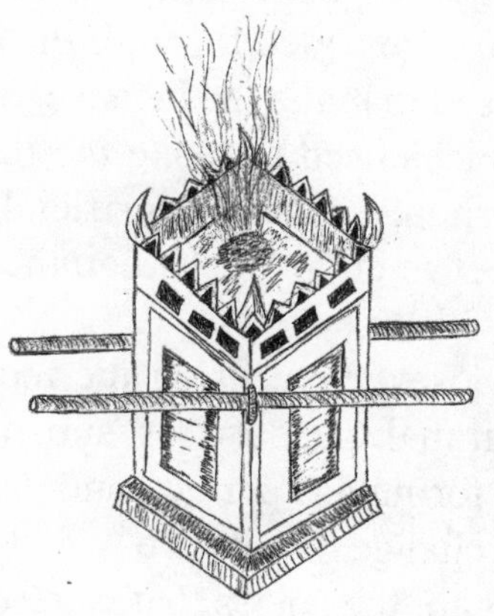

The Golden Altar of Incense

Moses waited to describe God's plans for the Golden Altar of Incense until after the concertation of Aaron and his sons into the priesthood. The Altar of Incense was the place of prayer. Aaron was not permitted to approach the Altar until God accepted his sin offering. As the high priest, Aaron was responsible for burning incense on the Altar every morning and every evening. Once each year, he applied the blood from the sin offering to its four horns. God called the blood and the incense *MOST HOLY* (Ex. 30:10, 36-38). The incense represents intercessory prayer, and the blood foreshadowed the new and living way into the presence of the Father through the blood of Yeshua.

The ingredients used to make the incense represent all of the elements found in the earth--animal, vegetable, and mineral.[17] Each of them foreshadows various benefits that come through Yeshua. The first four ingredients of the incense were tempered together with a fifth; *salt* (Ex. 30:34-38). Although the word salt is not used, the word translated *tempered (Malach in Hebrew)*, along with God's requirement concerning offerings made with fire, assures that salt was one of the elements of the incense (Lev. 2:13). Strong's Exhaustive Concordance defines *Malach*: to rub together, to pulverize, to salt, or rub together with salt, season with salt. Once again, God's Grace is revealed through the number five. Five ingredients were used to make the incense. Spices were valued possessions; the spices used to make the incense portray the fragrant life of Yeshua. Yeshua's sacrificial offering, like the incense, was a sweet smell to His Father, therefore, God called them SWEET SPICES.

God warned Moses about using the incense for anything other than its original purpose or substituting any of its ingredients. God's formula is perfect, and that is why He called it *MOST HOLY*; to change it or its use would mar the portrait of Yeshua. Following are the spices that were used along with an explanation of how they relate to the life of Yeshua.

STACTE is a spice that comes from a tree. The ancient Greek botanist Theophrastus described the manufacturing of stacte: "From the myrrh, when it is bruised flows an oil; it is in fact called "stacte" because it comes in drops slowly." http://www.making-incense.com/monographs/stacte.htm

The drops, referred to as tears, produce a gum-like substance with a sweet fragrant aroma. The method used to produce this spice foreshadowed the wounded body of Yeshua; "He was "wounded for our transgressions, He was bruised for our iniquities" (Isa. 53:5). A bruise is bleeding under the surface of the skin; Yeshua's blood is powerful enough to reach beyond the surface to the hidden sin that we might see it and repent.

ONYCHA comes from the shell of the Strombi (mussel). To produce the heavenly aromatic Onycha oil, the mussel shells are roasted. Their delightful fragrance comes from feeding on the spikenard plant.[18] Spikenard contains an agent used as medicine for the nerves. It took the heat of the fire to bring forth the strong fragrance. Yeshua suffered the fire of God's wrath, conquering death and hell to give us His peace. "Therefore being justified by faith, we have peace with God through our Lord Yeshua the Messiah" (Rom. 5:1). The peace we now have with God is the same peace that Yeshua had with His Father (Jn. 14:27a). We not only have peace with the Father, we have peace with each other. "But now in Yeshua the Messiah ye who sometimes were far off are made nigh by the blood of Messiah. For he is our peace, who hath made both one, and hath broken down the middle wall of partition between us" (Eph. 2:13, 14; my emphasis).

Today, science has discovered the medical secret of the spikenard plant in the use of aromatherapy. Aromatherapy is said to calm the nerves and produce a peaceful atmosphere. Yeshua's PEACE is the medicine all men need.

GALBANUM comes from a plant. It is a gummy substance that contains a unique quality which makes its fragrant aroma last. Galbanum was most likely the foundation for the incense, because it brought out the best from the other ingredients. Its unparalleled quality made it the base of the incense, and foreshadowed Yeshua, who is the solid base on which all things came to be (1 Cor. 3:11; Col. 1:16-17). He, by His powerful Word, holds all things together (Heb. 1:2-3). "And, Thou, Lord, in the beginning hast laid the foundation of the earth; and the heavens are the works of thine hands: They shall perish; but *Thou remainest*; and they all shall wax old as doth a garment; And as a vesture shalt thou fold them up, and they shall be changed: but *Thou are the same, and thy years shall not fail"* (Heb. 1:10-12; my emphasis). Galbanum is representative of the unchangeable sustaining power that is found only in Yeshua who is the same yesterday, today, and forever (Heb. 13:8).

FRANKINCENSE is an aromatic gum that comes from a tree found in Africa and Arabia. Yeshua, like the trees that produce the frankincense, is a root out of dry ground (Isa. 53:2, 11:10). The kings of the East presented Yeshua with a gift of frankincense pointing to His great worth. The Hebrew word translated frankincense is ***lebownah*** or ***lebonah***, which means the whiteness of smoke. The white smoke produced by the frankincense as it burned symbolizes the purity of Yeshua's name. Yeshua, our Mediator, applies the sweet incense of His name to our inadequate prayers and makes them perfect, a sweet smelling savor to the Father.

The fifth spice is SALT, a mineral. Salt is figurative of the eternal Covenant God made with His people (Nu. 18: 19). Salt preserves (*to keep something in spite of difficulties, opposition, or discouragement*) it adds flavor. Salt also acts as a purging agent (*to cleanse, to purify)* (Ezek. 16:4). Salt is the agent that fused the ingredients of the incense together making them inseparable foreshadowing Yeshua's love (Rom. 8:35-39). His love is the flavor of life, "Taste and see that the Lord is good" (Ps. 34:8). Yeshua, like the salt, purges our sins and fuses us to Himself as a part of His body (Heb. 1:3, 9:14: Eph. 5:30). As members of Yeshua's royal priesthood, we are called into

God's eternal Covenant of Salt. We, like the priests of the Tabernacle, receive a portion of God's Holy offerings. Yeshua is our portion. His indwelling presence is the flavor of every believer. (Mt. 5:13a).

We, the believers, are the bride of Messiah. It took all five spices to make the sweet aroma of the incense, and it takes the indwelling presence of Yeshua to maintain the sweetness of His bride through five Spiritual senses. He gives her F**aith**, the <u>eye of the Spirit</u> (Heb. 11:1), **Prayer,** the <u>taste of the Spirit</u> (Ps. 34:8, 81:10; Rom. 10:8), **Hope,** the <u>smell of the Spirit</u> (Col. 1:27, Heb. 6:18-20), **Reverence/obedience,** the <u>ear of the Spirit</u> (Ps. 111:10; Mt. 3:17, 17:5), and **Worship,** the <u>touch of the Spirit</u> (Jn. 14:20, 21, 23; 1 Cor. 6:17).

Solomon is considered to be a type of Yeshua. Solomon described his bride saying, "Who is this that cometh out of the wilderness like pillars of smoke, perfumed with myrrh and frankincense, with all powders of the merchant" (S of S 3:6). Faith, Prayer, Hope, Reverence/obedience, and Worship cause the sweet aroma of Yeshua to rise up like the smoke of the burning incense on the Golden Altar.

The Golden Altar had the second most prominent place in the Tabernacle, the first being the Ark of the Covenant. It was located directly in front of the Ark and the Mercy Seat. The only thing separating it from the presence of God was the Veil.

The arrangement of the Tabernacle furnishing forms the shape of a cross. Close your eyes and try to create a mental picture of Yeshua on the cross. Imagine where each piece of furniture would be located on Yeshua's body. His crown is the Ark of the Covenant and the Mercy Seat, His right hand holds the Golden Candlestick, **His heart is the Golden Altar of Incense**, in His left hand is the Table and the Showbread, the Brass Laver is at the bend of His knees, and He stands on the Brazen Altar. It is obvious why the Golden Altar had such a prominent place in the Tabernacle; it represents His heart.

The size and design of this Altar discloses many things about Yeshua. It was one cubit square; one speaks of unity. Yeshua was all God and all man. The use of the number one in the design of the Altar of Incense draws attention to the only *man* who was qualified to be the mediator between God and men, the man Messiah Yeshua (1 Tim. 2:5). As a man, He faced the same temptations as other men, but He did not sin. Therefore, as our High Priest, He is able to sympathize and show compassion (Heb. 4:15).

It was Aaron's responsibility, as the high priest, to keep the incense burning on the Altar. Burning incense represents the prayers of the saints intermingled with the prayers of the high priest (Rev. 8:3-4). The most beautiful intercessory prayer every recorded is the prayer of Yeshua found in John chapter 17. Please read it in its entirety, I promise you will be blessed.

Every morning and evening Aaron put fresh incense on the fire ensuring the sweet aroma never ended, providing a "Shadow" of how we are to pray. Paul said, "Praying always with all prayer and supplication in the Spirit, and watching thereunto with all perseverance and supplication for all saints" (Eph. 6:18).

The Altar was two cubits high, taller than the Ark and the Table. Number two draws attention to the fellowship we share with Yeshua when we pray. The added height of the Altar denotes the exalted name of Yeshua; His name is above every name that is named. Many names are used to describe the attributes of God and His relationship with man. He is called ***Elohim***--*Sovereign, Power, Creator*; ***Adonai***--*Master, Ruler, Owner*; ***Jehovah***--*The self-existing Lord, eternal, changeless*; ***Jehovah-Jireh***--*The Lord our provider*; ***Jehovah-Rophe***--*The Lord our healer;* ***Jehovah-Nissi***--*The Lord our Banner*; ***Jehovah-M'Kaddesh***--*The Lord who sanctifies;* ***Jehovah-Shalom***--*The Lord our Peace*; ***Jehovah-Rohi***--*The Lord our Shepherd*; ***Jehovah-Tisdkenu***--*The Lord our Righteousness*;

Jehovah-Shammah--The Lord who is there; and ***El-Shaddai***--God Almighty, powerful, just to name a few.

God called His Son ***Immanuel***, God who is with us, and exalted Him giving Him the name that is above every name, ***Yeshua/Jesus***--*Jehovah is Salvation* (Phil. 2:9-11). Yeshua said, "I am come in my Father's name" (Jn. 5:43a). His name is the realization of every description of God within the Hebrew names listed above.

Believers are to pray in the name of Yeshua. That doesn't mean to tag on His name at the end of each prayer; it means when we pray, it is Yeshua that the Father hears; therefore, our prayers should not be frivolous. Yeshua wants to grant whatever is asked in His name to bring glory to the Father (Jn. 14:13-14). Giving us His name is one of the steps of entering into His blood covenant and should not be taken lightly. His name gives every believer the privilege of entering into the presence of God with boldness; that doesn't mean arrogantly. We enter with a humble heart to find help and receive mercy (Heb. 4:16).

The Altar had four horns, one on each corner. Horns are symbols of power. Their presence on the Golden Altar reveals the power in the name Yeshua. All of heaven stands behind His name. The four horns of the Altar indicate that the power of His name is available to the whole earth (Mt. 28:18, Mk. 16:17-18).

The Altar also had a Golden Crown, revealing the divine royalty backing the power and authority of Yeshua's name. His authority and power reaches beyond the earthly realm, it goes into the depths of the earth and into the highest heavens. "Wherefore God also hath highly exalted him, and given him a name which is above every name: That at the name of Yeshua every knee should bow, of things in heaven, and things in earth, and things under the earth; And that every tongue should confess that Yeshua the Messiah is Lord, to the glory of God the Father" (Phil. 2:9-11).

The Golden Altar had two rings located on opposite corners. This feature is perhaps the most unique of all the other

Tabernacle furniture, which had four rings. The position of the rings on the Golden Altar kept it from becoming unbalanced and tipping over when the Levites carried it. It would right itself when going up or down an incline, therefore always remaining perfectly balanced. Yeshua's name keeps our relationship with the Father in perfect balance. The Father always honors the name of His Son. (Acts 4:12) Yeshua promised that the Father would honor His name when we pray. He said, "At that day ye shall ask in my name: and I say not unto you, that I will pray the Father for you: For the Father himself loveth you, because ye have loved me, and have believed that I came out from God. I came forth from the Father, and am come into the world: again, I leave the world, and go the Father (Jn. 26-28). Every believer has access to the name of Yeshua (Eph. 3:15). No matter what comes against you, it has a name. Therefore, you have the assurance that it can be overcome by the name of **YESHUA,** because His name is above every name. One day every knee will bow to that name. " That at the name of Jesus every knee should bow, of things in heaven, and things in earth, and things under the earth;" (Phil. 2:10).

SUMMARY

Only those who have been saved are authorized to use the name of Yeshua.

THE INCENSE: ***The sweet aroma of Yeshua's sinless life.***
THE HORNS: ***The power contained in His name.***
THE CROWN: ***The divine royalty backing the authority and power of His name.***
THE SIZE: ***His name is above every name.***
THE POSITION: ***Directly in front of the presence of God, the place of His heart. Yeshua has opened for us "a new and living way". The Veil is gone; we can now enter in.***

THE GOLD RINGS: ***Yeshua's name keeps our relationship with the Father in perfect balance.***

Yeshua has exchanged names with all believers, giving us a relationship with the Father that did not exist before He gave His name. *Relationship is a two-way affair*.

CHAPTER 16

The Brazen Laver

"Thou shalt also make a laver of brass and his foot also of brass, to wash withal and thou shalt put it between the Tabernacle of the congregation and the altar, and thou shalt put water therein. For Aaron and his sons shall wash their hands and their feet thereat: When they go into the Tabernacle of the congregation, they shall wash with water, <u>that they die not</u>; or when they come near to the altar to minister, to burn offering made by fire unto the Lord: So they shall wash their hands and their feet, <u>that they die not</u>: and it shall be a statute for ever to them, even to him and to his seed throughout their generations" (Ex. 30:17-21).

The Laver (by Christa Shore)

The Laver was solid brass; brass is a symbol of judgment. The absence of wood (the human element) is the key to understanding just how harsh that judgment will be. The Laver was made of a different type of brass than that found elsewhere in the Tabernacle. It was made from the polished looking glasses of the women (Ex. 38:8). Its polished surface glistened in the sunlight and reflected the image of anyone near it. The mirror finish of the brass is representative of two things; first, the brass is symbolic of judgment and second, the reflecting power of the Word of God. Yeshua is the judge of all men; He will judge both the living and the dead (Acts 10:42). "For the Father judgeth no man, but hath committed all judgment unto the Son" (Jn. 5:22). Judgment is inescapable; every human being will be judged, either at the great White Throne or at the judgment seat of Messiah. The Great White Throne judgment is for those who refuse to accept Yeshua as the Messiah. If you get to the Great White Throne, it will be too late, because all who appear there will be cast into the lake of fire where they will be tormented for all eternity (Rev. 20:11-15), but the redeemed stand at the Judgment Seat of Messiah where their works are tried before entering into eternal bliss with their Redeemer (Rom. 14:10, 1 Cor. 3:11-15).

The Lord withheld directions for the size of the Laver. That, like the Candlestick, was the decision of the ones in charge of its construction. There are two points represented by its unspecified measurement. First, it reveals the infinite power given to Yeshua to judge all men. Second, it shows the reflecting power of the Word of God to expose all sin. God's Word is the standard for self-judgment.

Yeshua is the Word of God (Jn. 1:1-2, Eph. 3:9, Col. 1:16); the Word is called judgments eighteen times in Psalm 119. Its power exposes ALL sin. James spoke of it as a *mirror* (Ja.1:22-25). Each time a priest approached the laver to wash his hands and his feet; his blood-splattered image was reflected in the polished brass. His clothes were soiled with the blood from the innocent animals killed for the sacrifices and offerings. The blood was a constant reminder that sin leads to death.

If the priest failed to wash at the Laver before entering into the Tabernacle, he would ***DIE*** (Ex. 30:19-21). Today, as the priesthood of the Messiah, we are told to judge ourselves and escape the judgment of man and God (1 Cor. 11:31). The Word of God is the standard for self-judgement. As we use the Bible as the standard for self-judgment, we will begin to see things about ourselves that conflicts with what it says. Then we are faced with a choice; we can repent and be changed, or refuse to repent and suffer the consequences. Yeshua said, "He that rejecteth me, and receiveth not my WORDS, hath one that judgeth him: The WORD that I have spoken, the same shall judge him in the last day" (Jn. 12:48; my emphasis).

The Word of God is also referred to as *Water;* the water in the Laver is a "Shadow" of the Word of God (Eph. 5:26). The first step of entering into the priesthood was a ceremonial cleansing. Moses washed Aaron and his sons, looking forward to the day that man would be washed clean by God Himself in the person of His Son, Yeshua, who sanctifies and cleanses all who will believe "Now ye are CLEAN through the WORD which I have spoken unto you" (Jn. 15:3).

During the evening of Yeshua's final Passover meal with the twelve disciples, He poured water into a basin and began to wash the disciples' feet and dry them with a towel. *"Foot washing was a courtesy shown to guest in a home, usually performed by a servant or the host's wife when the guest entered the house or while they were reclining at the table.*[19] *(Lk. 7:44, Mk. 1:7).* Yeshua demonstrated how the noblest of all men must be a servant (Mk. 10:43-44).

The Lord rebuked Peter for refusing to be washed when he said, "If I wash thee not, thou has no part with me" (Jn. 13:8). Peter did not understand that Yeshua was speaking of the Spiritual bath that is commanded before entering into the service of the Lord. His acceptance of Yeshua as the Messiah made him clean; it was not necessary to be washed again. The Hebrew word *Mikveh* means "immerse". It was the *ritual bath of purification* done by Moses for Aaron and his sons before they entered into the priesthood (Ex. 29:4). After Moses performed the initial cleansing, Aaron and his sons were responsible for keeping their own hands and feet clean (Ex. 30:19-21). When Yeshua washed the disciple's feet, He was demonstrating how to remain pure by becoming servants to one another. Yeshua (*THE LIVING WORD OF GOD*) took the position of a servant and washed the feet of His disciples, teaching them the importance of accountability. The disciples were being launched into the office of royal priests. They were to keep one another accountable to the ordinances of God. It is the *WORD OF GOD* that cleanses. To humble yourself and extend a bare foot to a brother or sister in Messiah symbolizes your willingness to surrender to the cleansing power of the *WORD OF GOD.* When you respond, you are promising to use *GOD'S WORD* to help your brother or sister walk as a believer. We are to hold each other accountable to follow *GOD'S WAYS* and **NOT OUR OWN**.

SUMMARY

THE WATER: The cleansing power of the *New birth*-"Not by works of righteousness which we have done, but according to his mercy he saved us, by the WASHING of regeneration, and renewing of the Holy Spirit. Which is shed on us abundantly through Yeshua the Messiah our Savior" (Titus 3:5-6; my emphasis).

THE POLISHED FINISH: The illuminating power of God's Word - "Thy WORD is a lamp unto my feet, and a light unto my path." The entrance of thy WORDS giveth light; it giveth understanding unto the simple" (Ps. 119:105 & 130; my emphasis).

THE PURPOSE: Self-examination – "But be ye doers of the word, and not hearers only, deceiving your own selves. For if any be a hearer of the word, and not a doer, he is like unto a man beholding his natural face in a glass: For he beholdeth himself, and goeth his way, and straightway forgetteth what manner of man he was. But whoso looketh into the perfect law of liberty, and continueth therein, he being not a forgetful hearer, but a doer of the work, this man shall be blessed in his deed" (Ja.1:22-25).

Continual cleansing - "So all of us, with faces unveiled, see as in a mirror the glory of the Lord; and we are being changed into his very image, from one degree of glory to the next, by the Spirit of the Lord" (2 Cor. 3:18). "Husbands, love your wives, even as Messiah also loved the church, and gave himself for it; that he might sanctify and cleanse it with the washing of water by the WORD" (Eph.5: 25-26; my emphasis).

My prayer is that we continue to learn from the example of the Brass Laver as we examine ourselves by the Word of God and let its cleansing power change us into vessels prepared for God's service. "Let us draw near with a true heart in full assurance of faith, having our hearts **sprinkled** from an evil conscience, and our bodies **washed** with pure water" (Heb. 10:22; my emphasis).

The Laver also issues a warning of judgment to all.

WARNING

"Behold therefore the GOODNESS and SEVERITY of God: on them which fell, {did not believe}, severity; but toward thee, goodness, if thou continue in his goodness; otherwise thou also shalt be cut off" (Rom. 11:22; my emphasis).

"For the time is come that judgment must begin at the house of God: and if it first begin at us, what shall the end be of them that obey not the gospel of God? And if the righteous scarcely be saved, where shall the ungodly and the sinner appear" (1 Pet. 4:17-18)?

CHAPTER 17

The Anointing Oil

> "Moreover the Lord spake unto Moses, saying, take thou also unto thee principal spices of pure myrrh five hundred shekels, and of sweet cinnamon half so much, even two hundred and fifty shekels, and of sweet calamus two hundred and fifty shekels, and of cassia five hundred shekels, after the shekel of the sanctuary, and of olive oil a hin: And thou shalt make it an oil of holy ointment, an ointment compound after the art of the apothecary: It shall be a holy anointing oil" (Ex. 30:22-25).

The anointing oil, like the incense, was made with _five_ ingredients and contained some of the same properties. Myrrh's soothing aromatic qualities acted as a calming agent and the pulp of the cassia plant was used as a purgative. The Cinnamon and the Calamus enriched the fragrance of the Myrrh. The purest quality olive oil was the base for the spices. The pure oil is what blended all of the fragrances together, enhancing the quality of its perfume.

Number five shows us that the Grace of God is about to be revealed again. The anointing oil was called *"the Crown of the Lord"*. It was Holy Oil because it represented the seal of God's approval (Lev. 21:12). The holiness of the Anointing Oil caused God to issue warnings concerning it. He said it was not to be used on man's flesh, it was forbidden to strangers, and it was not to be reproduced for personal use. If anyone failed to heed the warnings, he was cut off from the people of God (Ex. 30:31-33).

Anointing with the Holy Oil was the final step before entering into the service of the Lord. Moses, as God's elect representative, anointed the Tabernacle, its furnishings and the priest. Moses anointed Aaron, the high priest, providing a "Shadow" of the time when God would anoint Yeshua with the Holy Spirit and with power (Acts 10:38). When Moses poured the Anointing Oil on Aaron's sons, his actions foreshadowed the gift of the Holy Spirit being poured on the believers (Mt. 3:11, Jn. 1:32-34, Lk. 11:13, Acts 1:4-5). The Holy Spirit, like the Anointing Oil, is *"the Crown of the Lord"*. He fulfills the calming agent found in the ingredients used to make the anointing oil. The Holy Spirit is the ever-present Comforter who tabernacles inside every believer (Jn. 14:26, 1 Cor. 6:19). "For ye are the temple of the living God; as God hath said, **I will dwell in them, and walk in them; and I will be their God, and they shall be my people**" (2 Cor. 6:16b; my emphasis). When Paul wrote these words, he was quoting Exodus 29:45, which refers to the Tabernacle, God's original dwelling place in the midst of His people. Exodus chapter 29 is about the dedication of Aaron and His sons. Following the pattern found in Exodus we see the order of God's anointing. God first anointed Yeshua with the Holy Ghost and with power (Acts 10:38), then those who became His followers (Acts 2:8; 8: 14-17; 10:44-48). The Holy Spirit is the person of the Godhead that baptizes the believer into the body of Messiah and seals them until the day of redemption (1 Cor. 12:12-13; Eph. 4:30, 5:30). "Now he which stablisheth us with you in Messiah, and hath anointed us, is God; who hath also sealed us, and given the earnest of the Spirit in our hearts" (2 Cor. 1:22). He is the down payment or engagement ring ensuring Yeshua's' return for His bride. "That we should be to the praise of his glory, who first trusted in Messiah. In whom ye also trusted, after that ye heard the word of truth, the gospel of your salvation: in whom also after that ye believed, ye were sealed with the Holy Spirit of promise" (Eph. 1:12-13).

The Holy Spirit, like the Anointing Oil, is not available to strangers (those who have not accepted Yeshua as the Messiah). The apostle John called Him the Spirit of Truth and said the world cannot receive Him (Jn. 14:16-17). Only those who are the children of God are entitled to operate in the power of the Holy Spirit. Simon followed Philip witnessing the miracle-working power of the Holy Spirit. He watched the new believers receive the gift of the Holy Spirit when apostles touched them. Simon went through the motions of becoming a believer to get God's power for his own personal gain; he even offered to buy the power of God. Peter, realized what he was trying to do and said, "Thy money perish with thee because thou hast thought that the gift of God may be purchased with money. Thou hast neither part nor lot in this matter; for thy heart is not right in the sight of God" (Acts 8:20-21). Simon obviously did not know the written word, or its Author. If he had, he would have understood the consequences of his actions. The Lord said the Anointing Oil was not for personal use, and since the Holy Spirit is the fulfillment of the Anointing Oil, Simon was cut off from the people of God (Ex. 30:31-33). There are people today who go from one church to another seeking the miracles of the Lord. How sad, they need to be seeking the Lord of the miracles.

The gift of the Holy Spirit is available to every believer who asks. Yeshua gave the order in which the Holy Spirit was to be given. He said, "But ye shall receive power, after that the Holy Spirit is come upon you: and ye shall be witnesses unto me both in **Jerusalem**, and in all **Judea**, and in **Samaria**, and unto the **uttermost part of the earth**" (Acts 1:8; my emphasis). The gift of the Holy Spirit was first given to the **Hebrews**, which included the people of Judea, who lived in the rural areas outside of the city of Jerusalem. Those in the upper room with the disciples represented this group. They experienced similar happenings as those seen at Mt. Sinai when God first showed Himself to His people (Ex. 19:16-20; 20:1-21). He entered into the upper room with the sound of a rushing mighty wind and as fire (Acts. 2:1-4). God reveals himself in ways that are easy to recognize, because it is His desire for His children to KNOW Him. The Jewish believers knew the scriptures that contained God's promise to pour out His Spirit on all flesh (Joel 2:28-32). The next group to receive the gift of the Holy Spirit was the **Samaritans** (the half breeds), Jew and Gentile mixed. While Philip preached in Samaria, Peter and John came and laid their hands on the ones who had believed, and immediately they also received the gift of the Holy Spirit (Acts 8:14-17). The last group to receive the Holy Spirit was the **Gentiles**. It took about twenty-five years for the message of the gospel to be shared with the Gentiles. God chose Peter to be the first Messianic Jew to preach the good news to a Gentile family, the family of Cornelius. While he was still speaking, the Holy Spirit filled them in the same manner as He did at the beginning (Acts 10:44). He is still available to those who ask and believe.

We, like the priests of the Tabernacle who waited for the anointing of God before entering into His service, need to wait for the power of God's anointing that only comes from the Holy Spirit. Yeshua commands us to *WAIT*, because we are powerless without the anointing power of the Holy Spirit in our lives.

Please don't become discouraged if you are still waiting for the fulfillment of God's promise in your life. It took seven days of being anointed with the Holy Oil before the priests were ready to enter into the ministry of God, and it also took seven days for the Altar to be made ready for service. Aaron's position foreshadowed that of Yeshua as our High Priest, and the consecration of the Altar foreshadowed the cross and the sacrificial death of Yeshua. If it took seven days for Yeshua to be made ready, and forty-nine days for the first believers who waited in the upper room, why should you become discouraged if you are still waiting?

Stop seeking the gift and begin seeking the giver of the gift. He has not forgotten you; you are being made ready if you continue to trust Him and remain faithful. Please remember, Yeshua did not request that His followers wait; He commanded them to, and that commandment includes you. "Then Peter said unto them, repent, and be baptized every one of you in the name of Yeshua the Messiah for the remission of sins, and ye shall receive the gift of the Holy Spirit. For the promise is unto you, and to your children as many as the Lord our God shall call" (Acts 2:38-39). Like the sweet spices of the Anointing Oil, the Holy Spirit is the sweet anointing of God.

SUMMARY

THE ANOINTING OIL = *the Crown of the Lord* **(Lev. 21:12), THE HOLY SPIRIT**
THE INGREDIENTS = *five (the Grace of God)*

1. **Myrrh** = a calming agent, the Holy Spirit is the Comforter (Jn. 14:26).
2. **Cinnamon** = the gifts of the Holy Spirit operating through the believer's life draws men to the sweetness of the Lord (1 Cor. 12:8-10).
3. **Calamus** = the ministry gifts of the Holy Spirit. It takes both the ministry gifts and the Spiritual gifts working together to accomplish the will of God in the earth. That is why the weight of the Cinnamon and Calamus was half the amount of the Myrrh and the Cassia (1Cor. 12:28, Eph. 4:11-13).
4. **Cassia** = a purgative, the Holy Spirit convicts the world of sin and of righteousness, and of judgment, so that man can be purged from the sin that is within him (Jn. 16:8).
5. **Olive Oil** = the base for all the other ingredients; without the Holy Spirit's continual presence our lives

> are ineffective. He is the Power of God at work in the world (Acts 1:8).

Everything that was used in the service of the Lord HAD TO BE anointed with the Holy Anointing Oil. IT IS OBVIOUS THAT BEING ANOINTED WITH HIS POWER TO SERVE IS IMPORTANT TO GOD; therefore, it should be to us.

Epilogue

I began this book with the blood covenant because God is a covenant-making covenant- keeping God. He always speaks the end from the beginning. He began with one covenant and renewed it with every man that would accept Him and live by it. Some believe there are two separate covenants, however I believe the Bible teaches there is only one. God enlarged His covenant by adding more and better promises but His blood covenant has always been between the Father and the Son. I will show you why I believe this way. God makes a promise to his people concerning a new covenant in the book of Jeremiah. "Behold, the days come, saith the LORD, that I will make *a new covenant* with the house of Israel, and with the house of Judah: Not according to the covenant that I made with their fathers in the day that I took them by the hand to bring them out of the land of Egypt; which my covenant they brake, although I was an husband unto them, saith the LORD: But this shall be the covenant that I will make with the house of Israel; After those days, saith the LORD, I will put my law in their inward parts, and write it in their hearts; and will be their God, and they shall be my people. And they shall teach no more every man his neighbor, and every man his brother, saying, Know the LORD: for they shall all know me,from the least of them unto the greatest of them, saith the LORD: for I will forgive their iniquity, and I will remember their sin no more" (Jer. 31:31-34; my emphasis).

The Hebrew word translated NEW in this passage is *Ha Dash* (**הדש**).

The Hebrew letters that form *HaDash* are *hey* (ה), *daleth* (ד), and the *schin* (שׁ). Each letter of the Hebrew alphabet has a meaning associated with it.

<u>The ה represents the breath of God or the Holy Spirit.</u>

"And the LORD God formed man of the dust of the ground, and *breathed into his nostrils the breath of life*; and man became a living soul" (Gen. 2:7; my emphasis). "And when he had said this, he *breathed on them*, and saith unto them, *Receive ye the Holy Ghost"* (Jn.20:22; my emphasis)

<u>The ד represents the Door</u>.

"Verily, verily, I say unto you, He that entereth not by the door into the sheepfold,but climbeth up some other way, the same is a thief and a robber. But he that entereth in by the door is the shepherd of the sheep" (Jn. 10:1-2. "I am the door: by me if any man enter in, he shall be saved, and shall go in and out, and find pasture" (Jn. 10:9)

<u>The שׁ represents the eternal provision of God.</u>

"He shall cry unto me, Thou art my father, my God, and the rock of my salvation. Also I will make him my firstborn, higher than the kings of the earth. My mercy will I keep for him for evermore, and my covenant shall stand fast with him. His seed also will I make to endure for ever, and his throne as the days of heaven. If his children forsake my law, and walk not in my judgments; If they break my statutes, and keep not my commandments; Then will I visit their transgression with the rod, and their iniquity with stripes. Nevertheless my lovingkindness will I not utterly take from him, nor suffer my faithfulness to fail. *My covenant will I not break, nor alter the thing that is gone out of my lips"* (Ps. 89:26-34; my emphasis) "Let not your heart be troubled: ye believe in God, believe also in me. In my Father's house are many mansions: if it were not so, I would have told you.I go to prepare a place for you. And if I go and prepare a place for you, I will come again, and receive you unto myself; that where I am, there ye may be also" (Jn.14:1-3; my emphasis).

Now that we understand the precepts of this new covenant, here is how we enter into it.

The Holy Spirit ה *(the Breath of God)* baptizes us into the body of Messiah ד *(the Door)* through which is Everlasting life שׁ *(God's Eternal Provision).*

"There is one body, and one Spirit, even as ye are called in one hope of your calling; One Lord, one faith, one baptism, One God and Father of all, who is above all, and through all, and in you all" (Eph. 4:4-6). "For by one Spirit are we all baptized into one body, whether we be Jews or Gentiles, whether we be bond or free; and have been all made to drink into one Spirit" (1Cor.12:13). "Jesus saith unto him, I am the way, the truth, and the life: no man cometh unto the Father, but by me" (Jn.14:6). "For God so loved the world that he gave his only begotten Son, that whosoever believeth in him should not perish, but have everlasting life" (Jn. 3:16).

What changed in this covenant?

"But now hath he obtained a more excellent ministry, by how much also he is the mediator of a better covenant, which was established upon better promises" (Heb. 8:6).

There is no need for other sacrifices and the priesthood changed.

"By so much was Jesus made a surety of a better testament. And they truly were many priests, because they were not suffered to continue by reason of death: *But this man, because he continueth ever, hath an unchangeable priesthood.* Wherefore he is able also to save them to the uttermost that come unto God by him, seeing he ever liveth to make intercession for them. For such an high priest became us,who is holy, harmless, undefiled, separate from sinners, and made higher than the heavens; Who needeth not daily, as those high priests, to offer up sacrifice, first for his own sins, and then for the people's: *for this he did once, when he offered up himself"* (Heb. 7:22-27; my emphasis). *"But this man, after he had offered one sacrifice for sins for ever, sat down on the right hand of God;* For by one offering he hath perfected for ever them that are sanctified. This is the covenant that I will make with them after those days, saith the Lord, *I will put my laws into their hearts, and in their minds will I write them; And their sins and iniquities will I remember no more. Now where remission of these is, there is no more offering for sin.* Having therefore, brethren, boldness to enter into the holiest by the blood of Jesus, By a new and living way, which he hath consecrated for us, through the veil, that is to say, his flesh; And having an high priest over the house of God;" (Heb. 10:12,14,16-21; my emphasis).

The relationship between God and man changed forever.

We went from being the people of God to becoming the children of God. "Jesus saith unto her, Touch me not; for I am not yet ascended to my Father: but *go to my brethren,* and *say unto them, I ascend unto my Father, and your Father; and to my God, and your God* (Jn. 20:17; my emphasis).

Before starting our journey through the Tabernacle, I explained to you the hopelessness of man. Sin had separated him from his Creator, and there was nothing he could do that would be good enough to reestablish fellowship with the Holy God, the Great I AM. His only hope was for God to intervene and that is exactly what He did. God started revealing His infinite love for man with the Ark of the Covenant and continued with every piece of the furniture, every covering, through each color and measurement, down to the smallest detail.

We have seen the Tabernacle from God's perspective, now we are going to travel back through and examine it from mans' perspective. Man is standing outside the gate lost and helpless, waiting for his turn to present his offering to the Lord. There he finds Yeshua waiting, with His hands reaching out, bidding him to come to the Father through the sacrifice of His death. Once the man takes hold of Yeshua's hands and enters through the Gate, he is surrounded with the righteousness of God, protected, shielded, and concealed. Holding fast to Yeshua, the man approaches the brazen altar, where he is encouraged to present an offering to God. His offering is complete surrender to be a living sacrifice. The man continues and comes to the brazen laver, where he sees his reflection and washes himself in its pure water. Most people never get past this point in their relationship with Yeshua, but He continues to beckon. Yeshua has established relationship and desires the intimacy of that fellowship. Yeshua never ceases to plea with man to come through the door and feed on Him, the living Bread. Yeshua longs for man to understand the Father's love. He gestures for the man to come and pray with Him, as he teaches him the secret of prayer; Yeshua makes our prayers perfect. Yeshua wants to lead the man through the Veil into the presence of the Father. He has done all that He can do to make a way for man to be reunited with his heavenly Father.

If you are standing outside the Gate and don't know what to do, reach up and take Yeshua's hands and let Him lead you to the place of intimacy. Yeshua will not force you to come in, the choice is yours to make. Listen with your heart as he calls your name and bids you to come and let Him love you.

I pray that you were able to see how intensely God loves you in the revelations found in the Tabernacle. There will never be another that will go to such lengths to show his love. God loved you before the beginning of time, and there is nothing you have done or ever could do that is beyond His forgiveness. Won't you accept His love and forgiveness? I have presented you with the WAY to God--YESHUA. Now the choice is yours, choose life not death (Deut. 30:15-20).

Afterword

Many years ago I was given a book that changed my life entitled *Precious Gem in the Tabernacle* by B. R. Hicks. Her love for the Lord and her understanding of the Old Testament scriptures opened my eyes to the heart of God. She knew how to tie the Old and New together.

Although I was brought up in church and was taught what is considered the main Bible stories, i.e. Adam and Eve, Joseph and his coat of many colors, Daniel and the Lion's den, Noah and the Ark, etc., I was not taught that the revelation of Yeshua the Messiah (Jesus the Christ), the Son of God, began in the Old Scriptures. That is why reading *Precious Gem in the Tabernacle* had such a profound effect on my life. Note: From this point, I will be using the Hebrew name, Yeshua, in reference to Jesus.

I was thirteen years old when I accepted Yeshua as my Savior, but I was thirty- seven when He became the Lord of my life. I understood that God loved me and that He gave His Son (Yeshua) to die for me, but what I had never seen was that God started revealing Himself and His plan of redemption in Genesis.

The revelation of Yeshua found in the Tabernacle is what opened my eyes to the depth of God's love. It showed me His heart. From that time forward the Bible came alive. I saw God's heart on every page.

I began to read as many books about the Tabernacle that I could find. As the years went by, other people gave me books and videos about the Tabernacle. The more I learned, the more my heart was changed. I felt that I would explode unless I could share God's love with others. So I ordered a model kit of the Tabernacle to use as a teaching tool. As I assembled the model, I asked the Lord to teach me how to deliver its message. I asked Him to make a way for me to share the message of His love with those who are ready to be changed by it.

Soon, invitations to teach came from all directions. The Lord sent me to churches and home groups. He even allowed me to teach in the Messianic congregation where my husband and I attended. I shared the message of the Tabernacle first with the young children of the synagogue, then with the adult congregation. I have been so very blessed.

I am not a writer. It was never my intention to write a book about the Tabernacle. This book is the result of many requests from the people that have been taught the message of God's heart. It is impossible to remember every book that I read over twenty years. However, this book has been written in my own words based on all the books read and research done over a twenty year period. Therefore, I want to apologize to any author whose material might be included in some fashion without being acknowledged. It is without intent to plagiarize anyone's work.

I am now seventy years old; therefore, there are time limitations for me to continue teaching. My heart is to get the message of God's great love into as many hands as possible so that their lives will be changed as mine was changed. My prayer is that everyone who reads this book will fall in love with the Lord and that His love will draw them into the intimate relationship He desires.

Following is a list of the references that I remember. I would like to acknowledge their contributions to the information found in *The Secrete Place of the Most High.* ***B. R. Hicks, Dick Reuben, Kenneth Copeland, Bishop T.D. Jakes, Joseph Good, Ervin Hersberger, Dr. Joseph Hertz, David M. Levy, David H. Stern, Moshe Weissman, Larry Huck and Richard***

Booker. I gleaned many wonderful things from the teachings of these authors, but the one who deserves all credit is the God of Abraham, Isaac, and Jacob. It was He who preserved the written Word, which contains all of the mysteries of God.

The Apostle Paul wrote:

> "Let a man so account of us, as of the ministers of Christ, and stewards of the mysteries of God" (1 Cor. 4:1).
>
> "Even the mystery which hath been hid from ages and from generations, but now is made manifest to his saints: To whom God would make known what is the riches of the glory of this mystery among the Gentiles; which is Christ in you, the hope of glory: Whom we preach, warning every man, and teaching every man in all wisdom; that we may present every man perfect in Christ Jesus: Whereunto I also labour, striving according to his working, which worketh in me mightily" (Col. 1:26-29).

Bibliography

Booker, Richard, *Miracle of the Scarlet Thread,*(Destiny Image Publishers, Shippensburg, P.A. 1981)

Good, Joseph, *Rosh HaShanah and The Messianic Kingdom to Come, A Messianic Jewish Interpretation of the Feast of Trumpets*, (, Hatikva Ministries, Port Arthur, TX, 1989).

Hersberger, Ervin, *Seeing Christ in the Tabernacle*, (Vision Publishers, Harrisonburg, VA, 2007).

Hertz, Dr. Joseph, *The Authorized Daily Prayer Book*, (Block Publishing Co., New York, 1963).

Hicks, B. R., *Precious Gem in the Tabernacle*, (Jeffersonville, IN: Christ Gospel Press, 1985).

Jakes, T.D., *Rebuilding the Tabernacle* (Video Series)

Levy, David M., *The Tabernacle: Shadows of the Messiah: Its Sacrifices, Services, and Priesthood,* (Friends of Israel Gospel Ministry, Bellmawr, NJ, 1993).

Random House Webster's Dictionary, fourth edition, (The Ballantine Publishing Group, 2001).

Reuben, Dick, *five tape series recorded at Brownsville Assembly of God Church*, (Brownsville, Florida, 1993).

Stern, David H., *Jewish New Testament Commentary*, (Jewish New Testament Publications, Inc., Clarksville, MD, 1989).

Strong, James, LL.D, S.T.D., *Strong's Exhaustive Concordance of the Bible,* (Grand Rapids, MI: Zondervan, 2001)

The Open Bible, King James Translation, (Nashville, TN, Thomas Nelson, Inc., 1975)

Weissman, Moshe, *The Midrash Says on Sehmot*, (Brooklyn: Benei Yakov Publications, 1980).

Endnotes

1 Richard Booker, *The Miracle of the Scarlet Thread,* Destiny Image Publishers, Shippensburg, P.A., page 26.
2 *The Miracle of the Scarlet Thread*, ibidim, page 17.
3 Ervin N. Hershberger, *Seeing Christ in the Tabernacle,* Vision Publishers, Harrisonburg, VA, page 16.
4 *Seeing Christ in the Tabernacle,* ibidim, page 18
5 *Random House Webster's Dictionary*, fourth edition, The Ballantine Publishing Group, page 544.
6 *Random House Webster's Dictionary,* ibidim, page 835.
7 B. R. Hicks, *Precious Gem in the Tabernacle*, Christ Gospel Churches Int'l., Inc. Jeffersonville, IN, page 178.
8 *Precious Gem in the Tabernacle*, ibidim, page 186.
9 Joseph Good, *Rosh HaShanah and the Messianic Kingdom to Come,* Hatikva Ministries, Port Arthur, TX, page 37.
10 *Precious Gem in the Tabernacle,* ibidim, page 92.
11 *Seeing Christ in the Tabernacle,* ibidim, page 41.
12 The Open Bible, Authorized King James Version, Thomas Nelson, Publishers, Nashville – Camden – New York, page 20.
13 *Rosh HaShanah and the Messianic Kingdom to Come,* ibidim, page 37.
14 Dr. Joseph Hertz, *The authorized Daily Prayer Book,,* New York Block Publishing Co., page 791
15 Rabbi Moshe Weissman, *The Midrash Says on Sehmot,* Brooklyn Benie Yakov Publishers, page 182.
16 *Precious Gem in the Tabernacle,* ibidim, page 17.
17 *Precious Gem in the Tabernacle,* ibidim, page 142.
18 *Precious Gem in the Tabernacle*, ibidim, page 142.
19 David H. Stern, *Jewish New Testament Commentary,* Jewish New Testament Publications, Inc, Clarksville, MD, Luke 7:44; Mark 1:7.

Printed in the USA
CPSIA information can be obtained
at www.ICGtesting.com
LVHW040323211023
761730LV00002B/3